THE PEOPLE OF THE MOSQUES

THE PEOPLE OF THE MOSQUES

The Study of Islam

With Special Reference to India

L. BEVAN JONES

The People of The Mosques

ISBN: 978-81-8205-486-8

Published in 2009 in India by
ISHA Books
B-63, 1st Floor, New Gupta Colony,
Near DDA Market,
Delhi-110009
First Published October 1932

Lasser Type Setting by: Rudra Computer Graphics, Delhi
Printed at : Vishal Kaushik Printers, Delhi

IN GRATEFUL REMEMBRANCE

OF

THE REV. CANON EDWARD SELL

D.D., M.R.A.S.

OF MADRAS, A PIONEER IN ISLAMIC STUDIES,

WHOSE SCHOLARSHIP AND INDUSTRY HAVE

BEEN AN EXAMPLE AND INSPIRATION

TO TWO GENERATIONS OF

MISSIONARIES

PREFACE

THIS book, just an introductory study as the title shows, has been compiled to meet a special need in India. It was undertaken, in the first instance, in response to a request of a sub-committee of the National Christian Council. This will explain its appearance at a time when the general public in the West have it in their power to choose from a wide range of more scholarly books on this subject.* Nevertheless, it can be claimed that there are features in the present work which are not to be found in any of the existing manuals.

For some years past it has been felt that an up-to-date study book along these lines ought to be made available, *in the vernaculars*, for Indian clergy, pastors, evangelists, teachers and others, since most of these are shut up to a meagre supply of books, which, if not altogether obsolete, are inadequate for the present day. For others there is simply nothing at all.

The need is the more urgent because of the changing outlook among Indian Muslims. While it is true that the preponderating, orthodox party continues to make the old claims for Islām and entertains the same crude notions about Christianity, yet certain sections of the more educated class are conspicuous, as this book shows,

* The reader is referred for good bibliographies to the following works: *The Presentation of Christianity to Moslems*, by the Board of Preparation of Missionaries, New York; *Islām*, by Fr. Lammens, translated from the French by Sir E. Denison Ross, Methuen & Co.; and especially to *Indian Islām*, by Dr M. T. Titus, Oxford University Press.

for the way in which they attack not only the Christian missionary, but the antiquated *mulla* as well.

These more progressive leaders deal drastically with many of the cherished traditions of Islām and interpret the Qur'ān on a rationalistic basis. Meanwhile the orthodox, though professing to be shocked at their temerity, do not fail, when it suits their own purpose, to employ the arguments of these rationalists in their opposition to the preaching of Christianity.

The average Indian evangelist is ill-equipped and unprepared to meet such a situation, so that it is precisely with a view to helping him, and others like him, that the present volume is made to follow the line it does, more especially in the closing sections. A start has already been made on a translation of this book into Urdu, and it is expected that work on the Hindi and Bengali versions will soon follow.

This purpose—to make the book available for use in India—will explain the presence in it of a large number of Persian terms, as also the preference (shown in India) for the Persian rather than the Arabic form of many of the technical terms used.

Yet, notwithstanding what has been said, it is hoped that this manual will be found useful by students and others in the West, and by missionaries coming new to the field. Such have, in fact, been kept in view during its preparation, and it is gratifying to know that the Student Christian Movement Press have readily accepted the responsibility for its publication, because in their opinion it promises to meet a demand in their constituency.

I am indebted to so many scholars in this field of study and have drawn so freely on their published works, that I should feel ashamed to make the admission did I not know that these will be, as was the late Canon Sell himself, only too glad to find that their writings have been made use of for such a purpose. I gratefully acknowledge the help I have received, more especially from the late Canon Sell, Fr. Lammens, Vincent Smith (*History of India*), Stanley Lane-Poole (*Mediæval India*, a most readable book), and Dr M. T. Titus.

Moreover, Islām has been my special study for twenty years, and my chief interest as a missionary has been found among the Muslim people, several of whom it is my privilege to know as friends. During this period I have frequently lectured on the subject to the theological students of Serampore College, and, more recently, of Bishop's College, Calcutta. Extensive use has been made of my lecture notes for this volume.

For the convenience of the student the material gathered together here has been arranged in five sections, and these, in turn, have been divided into a number of short chapters, each with its own subdivisions. The Glossary, which is added as an appendix, is designed to serve the purpose of a working vocabulary of the more common Islamic terms in use in India. As such it is likely to prove useful when, after transliteration and translation, it is made available for Indian workers in their own vernaculars. All Islamic terms used are printed in italics. Occasionally these receive the English plural sign s, printed in Roman type; a hybrid form used commonly in speaking; thus *mullà*s.

I am under special obligation to my colleagues on the Staff of the Henry Martyn School for their valuable contributions in the form of chapters dealing with sections of the subject in which they are more especially interested; to the Rev. Laurence E. Browne for chapters

3 and 4 in Section I, and chapter 1 in Section IV; and to the Rev. J. A. Subhan for chapters 5 and 6 in Section III. Both of them read through the manuscript before it went to the press, thus making it possible for me to introduce several improvements into the book.

To my wife I owe more than I can very well set down here. Not only has she typed the entire manuscript for the printers, but by her wise counsel, sane criticism and unfailing sympathy, she has enabled me to make the volume a better thing than otherwise it would have been.

L. BEVAN JONES

LAHORE
Easter 1932

NOTE

The references in brackets, *e.g.* (ii. 100) appearing throughout the book are, unless otherwise stated, to the Qur'ān, chapter (*sūra*) and verse (*āyat*). The enumeration followed is that adopted by Rodwell in his translation, *The Koran* (Everyman's Library), the most handy edition for the student. since it attempts a rearrangement of the chapters in chronological order.

CONTENTS

SECTION II

THE FOUNDATIONS OF ISLĀM

SECTION III

THE FAITH AND PRACTICE OF ISLĀM

SECTION IV

ISLĀM IN THE MODERN WORLD

SECTION V

CHRISTIANITY AND ISLĀM

SECTION I

THE RISE AND EXPANSION OF ISLĀM

CHAPTER I

ARABIA AND ITS PEOPLE

IT is usual when approaching the study of Islām to begin with some account of Arabia and its people. There is good reason for doing so. That land was the cradle of Islām; it contains the birthplace and the tomb of the Prophet of Islām; it still jealously guards the central shrine towards which Muslims throughout the world direct their prayers, and to which they make the annual *hajj* or pilgrimage.

Ancient Legends

Nor is this all. It is believed by the orthodox that this sacred shrine, the Ka'ba at Mecca, the *Bait-Allāh*, or "House of God," had acquired peculiar sanctity long before the coming of their own Prophet. For instance, the crude fancy is commonly cherished and still taught to their children in school, that Adam laid the foundation of this shrine and placed in it the Black Stone which he had brought with him from Paradise, and that Gabriel taught him the ritual connected with the pilgrimage, including the circumambulation of this same shrine. It is also believed that it was to this very region that Abraham brought Hagar and Ishmael; that the water so fortunately found to slake the lad's thirst was drawn from the well *Zamzam*, situated in close proximity to the shrine; and that when the Ka'ba required to be repaired, after damage done by floods, God committed the work to Abraham and this son of his (cp. Qur'ān, ii. 119-22; xxii. 27).

Description of the Country

Arabia itself is an isolated and inhospitable country. Its very boundaries show how aptly the Arabs have called the peninsula which comprises their homeland, *Jazīratu'l-'Arab*, "the *island* of Arabia." On the east are the waters of the Persian Gulf and the Gulf of Oman, on the south the Indian Ocean, on the west the Red Sea, while to the north lies a desert which, like the sea, has often proved a formidable barrier.

Its least attractive part is that which first meets the eye, the coast. Immediately beyond this, and forming a kind of belt round the country, are low barren hills. Yet, contrary to expectation, Arabia contains surprises of fertility and climate. Two-thirds of the whole area, the greatest length of which is 1000 miles and the average breadth 600, is cultivated or cultivable land, the remaining portion being irreclaimable desert, chiefly to the south.

The general formation of the country is that of a central table-land of an average height of 3000 feet, surrounded by a desert ring, sandy to the south, west, and east, and stony to the north. Between this sandy ring and the sea are the above-mentioned low sterile mountains, but these in Yaman and Oman often rise to heights of 8000 and 10,000 feet, yielding a kindlier climate and more fertile soil.

Arabia has no rivers, and none of its mountain streams reach the coast. Even its *wadys*, channels cut by rain water, are dry for nine months of the year. The climate generally is rigorous; oppressively hot in summer and severe, at times, in winter. A further repellent feature are the black and barren volcanic tracts called *harra*, which cover a wide expanse, especially in the north-east.

This land is the home of about eight millions of people, whose physical appearance and general character reflect something of the harshness of the natural phenomena.

Our present concern with Arabia, however, is strictly

limited to the part it played in the emergence of Islām and to that section of it which can quite properly be called "the cradle of Islām," viz., the Hejāz. This province, comprising as it does the territories of Mecca and Madīna, is called *haramain*, or "the two sacred areas," enclosing the birthplace and the tomb of the Prophet, and as such is not to be defiled by the visits of infidels, i.e., non-Muslims (Qur'ān, ix. 28). Nevertheless several such bold adventurers have, at the risk of their lives, penetrated even to the sacred shrine itself and thus supplemented the information we gain from Muslim sources.

The People

The population is divided into two classes, the Beduins (*Badawīs*), or roaming shepherds, and the peoples who live a more settled life in villages and towns. These Beduins have always constituted the great majority and have succeeded in maintaining the original type of Arab character, whereas the townspeople have been affected by influences from without, and by marriages with non-Arabs. Nevertheless they are essentially one people, having the same language, customs, and religion.

Muslim historians, in their desire to enhance the glory of Islām, have been apt to give too dark a picture of pre-Islamic Arabia, leaving the impression that the Arabs were formerly a rude, ignorant, and superstitious people. Accordingly they speak of that period as "the days of ignorance." But the typical Arab surely refutes that assertion. Far from seeming to be one of a primitive and barbarous race, he is resolute in bearing and virile in appearance; a man who has developed the strength and sagacity to be expected in those who carry on a life-and-death struggle with a rigorous climate and the privations of the desert. Such, one feels, the Arab must always have been.

The qualities of the Arabic language and the well-known Arab love of poetry date from pre-Islamic times and serve to confirm this view. These illiterate people, even the womenfolk, have always loved and still love poetry, and cultivate it enthusiastically. Some rare fragments belonging to the century before the *Hijra* (the year of Muhammad's migration to Madīna, A.D. 622), are preserved to us. The Arabic language itself is a highly perfected language, and not such as would be found among a backward people.

Character of the Beduin

But it must not be supposed that the Arab character leaves nothing to be desired. Life in the desert, while developing certain admirable qualities, such as loyalty to the tribe, is responsible for less lovely features. For the Beduin is essentially an individualist, since the desert forces him to live in isolation. He wrangles and fights with his neighbour over the scanty water-supply and meagre pastures, without which existence would be impossible either for himself or his flocks. True to the Ishmael type, " his hand is against every man and every man's hand is against him." He is always on the lookout for loot, and will, without scruple, rob the passing traveller should he not happen to have the protection of a guide from a friendly tribe.

Consequently he is an expert in cunning and artifice, seeking to take his enemy by surprise. In such encounters deliberate flight is not thought to be an act of cowardice.

And yet he can be, and is, hospitable. Given a good year and plentiful harvests, he performs the part of the bountiful host, but more from self-aggrandisement than kindness or thought of others.

Such a hard and precarious existence has developed in him amazing tenacity, something other than patience, whereby he contrives to live on though Nature be unkind and his very neighbour a potential thief.

It is not, therefore, matter for surprise that he does not readily submit to being ruled. His *shaikh*, " senior " or chief, is chosen by the free election of the tribe, and is influential in so far as he treats all men as equals. But let such controlling force as even the *shaikh* exercises be removed and the latent anarchical spirit of the Beduin soon manifests itself.

Mecca and its People

In turning to consider the characteristics of the other class, the townspeople, it is necessary, just because they, unlike the Beduin, have always been subject to influences from without, that we should see them as they were in the days of Muhammad.

At that time Mecca was the religious and commercial centre of the Hejāz, consequently a brief account of its people and affairs may be taken as typical of this class.

The city in those days was prosperous because of its fortunate geographical position in close proximity to trading countries and the main route to India. The most influential tribe in Mecca was that of the Quraish, who through a kind of guild of merchants not only promoted commerce but maintained law and order also.

This guild was a gathering of chiefs of the tribal clans and included some from the richest and most powerful families. In Muhammad's time the most prominent of these chiefs, because the richest and most patriotic, was Abū Sufyān. Yet each member of the guild possessed the right and power of veto, so that they could unite to prevent any action being taken, say, by a man like Abū Sufyān, which they interpreted to be contrary to the public good.

They were suspicious especially of anything that threatened the trade of the city. For such traffic it was essential that the annual pilgrimage to the central shrine of all Arabia, and also the due observance of the months of truce, should be maintained against any interference. Should any offend in these respects he was first warned and then threatened. If that was of no avail he was outlawed and refused the protection of his own tribe. Such solidarity was, as we shall see, very characteristic of the Meccans in the time of Muhammad.

In any case, the absorbing passion of the Meccans was trade and growth in wealth. For this purpose the camel and the caravan occupied a foremost place in all their thoughts and plans. Sometimes the whole of the townspeople, women as well as men, would have financial interests, through investments, in the caravans that set out from the city with merchandise. When the caravan returned each one received his or her share of the profits, and in this way several among them became really wealthy.

It is the more surprising to find that the site of Mecca is very unhealthy. Situated between two steep and naked mountains, it lies in the hollow of a valley, into which flows and collects the water of the winter storms. These storms can be very destructive to property, and have at times demolished the Ka'ba itself. The place can be like a swamp in the rainy season, and a veritable furnace in the summer, when the scanty and not-too-palatable water of the well *Zamzam* is resorted to by the inhabitants for want of something better.

Religion and the Ka'ba

Repeated reference has been made to the central shrine of all Arabia, the Ka'ba at Mecca. What is it and what did it signify? This cube, for that is the meaning of *Ka'ba*, measures about 39 feet by 33 and is a little over 49 feet high. The chief object of veneration in it is the Black Stone, which is built into the south-eastern corner five feet above the ground. This stone is the oldest treasure of Mecca, and is probably an aerolite which therefore has been treated with awe from of old because it fell from the sky. But this was only one, though a very special one, of many stones looked upon as sacred by the Arabs in those days before the establishment of the new faith, Islām. These stones, of curious shapes, some long like human images and moulded by the action of wind and rain—these (and not man-made idols) were their objects of worship, representing to them gods and goddesses. Some of them were worshipped where they stood, others were surrounded by a circle of stones or, like the Black Stone, were built into a shrine. At one time there were over 300 of these stones inside the Ka'ba. Such a shrine usually had a well in the neighbourhood which was used for ceremonial ablutions, and perhaps a sacred tree on which the worshippers hung some votive offerings. The shrine and the surrounding area was *haram*, or sacred territory, and all living things, men or animals, could find safe refuge within it. The very trees were sacred and no one was allowed to pluck a branch from them. Such sites were deserted for most of the year, but on special occasions the tribes assembled at these shrines and offered sacrifices, chiefly camels, to the particular god or goddess of their tribe. At the time of those sacrifices all present had to perform certain purificatory rites. They poured the blood of the sacrificial animal on the sacred stones and, having shaved their heads, ate of its flesh.

Sometimes these sacred stones were carried in procession, as, for instance, when there was a prolonged drought or at the time of pilgrimages to the shrine, and then the procession concluded with a seven-fold circumambulation of the shrine itself. Divination was also practised at the shrines and in this the *kāhin*, or soothsayer, played his part.

There was no priestly class for the worship at the shrines. Their guardians and the soothsayers performed the necessary duties. The latter, especially the female ones, were believed to possess occult powers.

The Arabs were fatalists, with no clear idea of a future life or the immortality of the soul. They believed in and feared *jinn*, genii, beings half demon, half man, who had an alarming way of making themselves invisible. But in the century before Muhammad some Arabs were beginning to believe in Allāh, *the* God, of whom they said he was *Allāhu Akbar*, i.e., "Allāh greater than" other gods.

In the Qur'ān frequent reference is made to a people called *hanīf*, "sound in the faith" (cp. iii. 60, 89; x. 105; xxii. 32). It is usually supposed that these were a group of monotheists, neither Jews nor Christians.

Jews and Christians

It remains to speak briefly of the Jews and Christians who lived at that time in the Hejāz.

The Jews, who all belonged to the townspeople class, were settled in some of the oases and at Tā'īf, near Mecca, but their chief centre was Madīna where they had managed to get most of the commerce into their hands. The Arabs of Madīna, who were their customers, finally outnumbered them and aspired to the place of leadership themselves.

As compared with the Arabs the Jews were a superior people; certainly they considered themselves to be such. They had their *rabbis*, synagogues and schools, and above all, their *kitāb*, or (sacred) book. The Arabs, on the other hand, were Gentiles, and had no *kitāb*, so the Jews heartily despised them.

In comparison with the Jews the Christians were a small and inferior body; they were uninfluential also, partly because they were scattered. The most important were in Yaman; others were on the borders of Irāq, and there was a tribe on the Syrian border where Muhammad encountered friendly monks. In Mecca itself there dwelt a group of Christians from Abyssinia.

Like the Jews, the Christians of Arabia engaged in trade, travelling with their wares into towns and desert camps.

These Christians, many of whom had fled from their

own lands to escape persecution, were for the most part ignorant of their religion. Though it is probable that it was they who first reduced Arabic to writing, yet we know that in Muhammad's time they did not have the Bible in Arabic, and probably still used Syriac for their services. In the circumstances it is not surprising that Muhammad failed to understand what really constitutes the Christian faith.

CHAPTER II

MUHAMMAD

IT was in Mecca, the centre of so many interests in Arabia, that Muhammad was born, probably in the year A.D. 570.

The main sources for our information concerning him are the Qur'ān and the Traditions. But we need to be cautious in the use we make of the latter material since it is generally recognised that a great mass of it is spurious. This is particularly true of the Traditions dealing with the early years of Muhammad, so that, unfortunately, we have but little reliable information concerning that period of his life.

The Meccan Period

His parents though poor belonged to the Hāshimite clan of the influential tribe of the Quraish, the hereditary guardians of the Ka'ba, and this, as we shall see, meant much to Muhammad at the first. The child soon stood in need of staunch friends, for his father, 'Abdu'llāh, had died before he was born and he lost his mother, Āmina, when he was only about six years old. He was adopted by his paternal grandfather, 'Abdu'l Muttalib, a kind old man of eighty, who was held in high esteem as the head of the clan. Two years later he also died, having appointed his son Abū Tālib (father of the famous 'Alī) as the boy's guardian. It is said that Abū Tālib loved the lad so much that he would scarcely let him go out of his sight.

It is generally held that Muhammad was unable to read or write, although these arts were known in those days. Perhaps the fact that he was left an orphan early led to the neglect of his elementary education.

All authorities are agreed that Muhammad grew up to young manhood esteemed by his fellow-citizens. He won from them the name of *Al Amīn*, the Trusty, and became a prominent member of the guild in Mecca. An incident in those early days reveals in him a certain shrewdness of character. The walls of the Ka'ba were being repaired after damage by flood, when a dispute arose as to who should handle and replace the Black Stone. Each clan was claiming the right to do so when Muhammad unexpectedly entered the sacred enclosure. Being asked to decide the matter he spread his shawl on the ground and, having placed the sacred stone upon it, he called on four men, one from each of the contending clans, to lift it up and put it in its place.

Since his uncle was poor it became necessary for Muhammad to earn his livelihood, and so he joined himself to trading caravans. In this way he travelled a good deal, especially into Syria, and met with different classes of people—Jews, Christians, and others. Apparently he received kindness at the hands of Christian monks in Syria, for we read in the Qur'ān, "Thou shalt certainly find those to be nearest in affection to them (i.e., to Muslims) who say, 'We are Christians.' This, because some of them are priests and monks, and because they are free from pride." (v. 85.)

Khadījah, a wealthy Meccan lady who herself undertook commercial transactions, hearing of Muhammad's excellent qualities engaged him to take charge of one of her caravans of merchandise. He managed her business so satisfactorily and she was so attracted to him that she fell in love with him and later married him.

The alliance was a happy one notwithstanding the fact that Khadījah was forty years of age and Muhammad only twenty-five. Seven children were born to them, three sons (all of whom died in infancy) and four daughters. One of the latter, Fātima, survived

Muhammad and became the wife of 'Alī, Muhammad's cousin, the fourth Khalīfa.

Concerning Muhammad's personal qualities we gather that he was, as a rule, reserved in manner though he relaxed in the presence of friends. He was simple in his habits and in the matter of dress and food. It is said that he was fond of children. He was a man of high resolve and very strong will, as his opponents soon came to realise.

Al Ghazāli, in a well-known passage, thus extols Muhammad as a model of humility:

"Oh my son, eat unto God and drink unto God and dress unto God. But whatsoever thou doest of all these and there enters into them pride or hypocrisy, it is disobedience. Whatever you do in your house do it yourself as did the Apostle of God, for he used to milk the goats and patch his sandals and sew his cloak and eat with the servants and buy in the bāzār, nor did his pride forbid him from carrying his own packages home; and he was friendly to the rich and to the poor, and he gave greetings himself first to everyone whom he met."

Assumption of the Prophetic Office

Muhammad owed much to his marriage with Khadījah. She was a woman of noble character and her wise counsel and loyal support were an invaluable asset. Her wealth, too, set him free from anxieties that go with poverty and afforded him leisure for reflection. In her house he met the *hanīfs*, and among them Waraqa, her cousin. These appear to have been a small group of people who had given up idolatry and now worshipped the one true God. Their views, shared by Khadījah, considerably influenced Muhammad. This term *hanīf*, which Rodwell translates "sound in the faith," became the keynote of his early preaching. He even went so far as to claim that he had been sent to preach the religion of "Abraham the *hanīf*." (vi. 162.)

In order to meditate undisturbed Muhammad would retire to a cave in Mt. Hīra, three miles beyond the city. Others of the *hanīfs* joined him there. At such times he used to reflect on the ignorance, depravity, dissension and lawlessness of his countrymen, and would dream dreams of better times and of reforms in which he himself would have a share.

It was in this place, at the age of forty, that he passed through an experience comparable with conversion, in that it meant for him a definite break with the idolatrous practices of his own townspeople. He became aware of the presence of God, and afterwards declared that he had received a "call." He heard the voice of one saying: "Recite thou, in the name of thy Lord who created—created man from clots of blood—recite thou!" These words form the opening portion of the earliest Sūra, or chapter of the Qur'ān, viz. xcvi. 1-3 (cp. Isaiah xl. 6). He thus described his experience to others: "As I walked I heard a voice from heaven and raised my eyes, and behold! an angel came to me seated upon a throne between heaven and earth. At this I feared greatly and fell upon my knees upon the ground."

At home, in great perturbation, he said to Khadījah, "I have either become a *kāhin* or I am mad!" But she would not have it so. "You are truthful and good," she said. When she referred the matter to Waraqa he is reported to have declared that this was the *nāmūs* (message) which had come to Moses and Jesus, and added: "He will be the prophet of his people. Bid him be brave of heart."

This and subsequent similar experiences were proof to his adherents of his superior power of perception, and became for him, when his early fears had subsided, the ground of his unshaken confidence that he was the recipient of divine revelation, and, in fact, a prophet.

From now onwards, with one important break, Muhammad continued to recite, for some twenty-three years, communications on matters religious, social and political which, he said, came to him from God through the archangel Gabriel.

That confession of Muhammad to Khadījah that he feared he had become a soothsayer is interesting in view of the fact that his early utterances were in the style and spirit characteristic of the soothsayers of Arabia—a kind of rhymed prose pronounced when in an ecstatic condition. His opponents, indeed, taunted him with this: "You are a *kāhin*," they said (cp. lxxxi. 24; xxxvii. 35).

He himself was a victim to grave doubts more especially because, for a considerable period, no revelations came to him. Muslim writers call that period the *fatra*, and some say it lasted three years. Muhammad was at times so depressed that he even contemplated suicide.

It was his loyal wife Khadījah who roused him again and again to his task, and she gave practical proof of her faith in him by becoming his first convert. Thus encouraged, he acted upon the command to recite, and began to proclaim, though secretly, the one clear message of the Unity of God. Others of his immediate circle followed Khadījah's example. The earliest and most notable of his converts were 'Alī, son of his uncle Abū Tālib, a youth who became greatly attached to Muhammad; Zaid, son of Hāritha, a slave given to Muhammad by Khadījah and since set free; and Abū Bakr, a leading member of the Quraish clan. Muhammad and Islām gained immensely by this last accession, for Abū Bakr was intelligent, prosperous and influential. He won and retained to the end Muhammad's confidence, and eventually succeeded him as first Khalīfa.

Muhammad's teaching continued to bear fruit, and before three years were past about fifty Meccans, male and female, including 'Uthmān, who became third Khalīfa, embraced the new faith. So far Muhammad had worked in secret, but encouraged by these accessions, and notwithstanding the hostility of the influential Quraish, he now began to preach publicly. Believing that he had been told to "arise and warn," he appealed to them to abandon their idolatry, and warned them of the fate of peoples who refused to listen to the earlier prophets. But the Meccans only mocked him.

Muhammad then took a new line. He threatened them with hell fire and poured scorn and abuse on their gods. This infuriated them, the more so because they recognised in this new sect an enemy not only to their ancient superstitions, but to their vested interests also. Consequently they organised themselves to oppose him and began to persecute his followers.

The wife of Abū Lahab, an unfriendly uncle of Muhammad, treated the Muslims outrageously and drew down upon herself the hot wrath of Muhammad, for it is said that she scattered thorns over the place where the Muslims went for their prayers. She and her husband are accursed for ever in a chapter of the Qur'ān (111).

Amid such persecutions, insult and outrage, Muhammad maintained his way and was not a little comforted by the unfailing support of his uncle Abū Tālib, who, though not a Muslim, shielded Muhammad from his foes. An increasing number of the Meccans now threw in their lot with the Muslims, so that the Quraish became thoroughly alarmed. They awoke to the fact that this movement, unless checked, would develop into a serious revolution. The prestige of the guild was at stake.

The power of that guild is well illustrated by the tactics which the Quraish now adopted. They joined forces in a systematic persecution of the followers of Muhammad. He and his immediate friends were safe but on the rest the Meccans poured out their fury. Each household persecuted those of its members, clients, or slaves who were suspected of being Muslims. These were thrown into prison, starved and beaten with sticks. Some recanted, others feigned apostasy to escape torture; these Muhammad excused (see xvi. 108), but the majority stood firm. Prominent Meccans tried to seduce Muhammad with promises of position and wealth. It is thought that his dignified reply to such overtures is preserved in Sūra xli.

Moved by the sufferings of the faithful and being quite unable to protect them, Muhammad permitted those who wished to migrate to Abyssinia, where they enjoyed the kindly protection of the Christian king. Fifteen went at first but others joined them later so that, in all, about eighty men and twenty women were living in exile.

It is apparent from the study of the early chapters of the Qur'ān that under the stress of such circumstances Muhammad's tone changed. He had become embittered at the evil treatment meted out to his followers, and now enlarged on the future punishment of the idolatrous Meccans. He cites certain of these by name, e.g., Abū Lahab. With the doctrine of the unity of God he now joins the demand that he himself should be recognised as God's Apostle (cp. lxxii. 24). But when he reproduced stories from Jewish and Christian sources the Meccans said, "Surely a certain person teacheth him" (xvi. 105; cp. xxxv. 6).

The courage, patience, and tenacity of purpose exhibited by Muhammad at this time in the face of continued persecution afford striking proof of his own faith in his call and in the righteousness of his cause.

The Quraish next approached Muhammad's uncle, Abū Tālib, first appealing to him to prohibit his nephew from reviling their gods and then threatening that they would do away with Muhammad. In a memorable interview, moved by the resolute bearing and tears of Muhammad, Abū Tālib emphatically declared, "Speak what thou wilt, for by the Lord I will not in anywise give thee up" (Ibn Hishām).

It was at about this time, when the struggle seemed unending and the issue hopeless, that Muhammad was involved in a position which has embarrassed many a thoughtful Muslim. He appears to have stooped to compromise (but only for a brief while) with the idolaters whom he had hitherto ceaselessly denounced.

Muhammad was reciting in the Ka'ba a passage that forms part of Sūra liii. When he came to the words, " Do you see Al Lāt and Al 'Uzza and Manāt the third idol besides ? " (vv. 19, 20), it is said that someone added audibly, " They are exalted damsels, and their intercession with God may be hoped for." The Quraish were both astonished and delighted, and when the words, " Prostrate yourself then to God " (ver. 62) were uttered they readily complied. But who had spoken those arresting words ? The late Sayyid Amīr 'Alī, following certain early writers, says it was an idolater who was present at the time and whom tradition has turned into the devil. There are other writers who deny that the incident ever occurred, but Amīr 'Alī seems to think that under the prolonged strain Muhammad did on this occasion compromise, but he stresses the fact that it only happened once and that the lapse was more than compensated for by " his magnificent recantation " (cp. *The Spirit of Islām*, Amīr 'Alī, p. 35 f.). Sūra xxii. 51 (" God shall bring to nought that which Satan hath suggested ") is considered by some to be a later echo of this incident, pronouncing exoneration.

It was now the sixth year of Muhammad's mission, a year made notable for two remarkable accessions to the ranks of his followers. One was the fiery warrior Hamza, who smote the hostile Abū Jahl a blow for abusing the Prophet, and in the excitement of the moment abruptly declared, " I follow his religion." Later came 'Umar binu'l-Khāttab, destined to be second Khalīfa. Himself a bitter opponent of the new sect he became incensed at his sister embracing Islām. One day he surprised her and her husband while they were reading verses of the Qur'ān and in wrath he wounded her in the face. Regretting his cruelty he asked to be allowed to see what she was reading, but she calmly answered, " Let none touch it but the purified." Complying with the conditions, he read, was charmed and became a convert. Muhammad and his friends were thrilled, for the event very considerably altered the outlook for the Muslims. They went in a body to the Ka'ba, 'Alī leading the way with a drawn sword. The Meccans were aghast and exclaimed, " We sent 'Umar to kill Muhammad and lo, now he follows him ! "

But they met Muhammad's increasing boldness with a change of tactics. They resolved to boycott the Muslims so as to compel them to leave the place. Up till now practically all the Quraish who had sided with Muhammad belonged to his own, the Hāshimite, clan. It was a struggle, therefore, between the rest of the Quraish and the Hāshimites. A solemn league and covenant was drawn up whereby the larger body promised to have no dealings whatsoever with the Hāshimites. The latter were thus compelled to retire to a confined quarter in Mecca, where they existed in great distress for two or three years until the ban was lifted.

This was at last removed by the intervention of some of the Quraish, and a period of liberty followed. Muhammad was now fifty-one and had entered upon the tenth year of his mission. Before its close he suffered heavy bereavement through the death of Khadījah. As has been said he owed much to her and his loss was correspondingly great.

Muhammad was persuaded to marry again, and shortly afterwards took to himself two wives. One was 'Āyesha, the daughter of his great friend Abū Bakr, then but a young girl ; the other was Sauda, the widow of a Muslim who had died in Abyssinia. In course of time he added to their number until he had at one time as many as nine, besides concubines. A large part of Sūra xxxiii. is devoted to his domestic affairs.

In that same year his influential uncle Abū Tālib also died, and in consequence Muhammad's position in Mecca became precarious. He resolved to move to

Tā'if, seventy miles east of the city, but the idolatrous residents would not suffer either his presence or his preaching and drove him away, stoning him. He therefore returned to Mecca after extracting a promise of protection from a leading citizen.

Though Muhammad had failed at Mecca he did not lose faith in his mission. As a matter of fact at this juncture a new prospect of success began to open up before him.

Amongst those who came to the annual pilgrimage were men of the Khazraj tribe in Yathrib, later called Madīna. These listened to Muhammad's message with keen interest. In their own city there was constant strife between Jews and Arabs, and the idea now occurred to them that Muhammad might prove a strong deliverer. It was not until the following year, however, that they committed themselves to his cause by taking, secretly, an oath of obedience. Muhammad sent them back with Mus'ab, an earnest disciple who was to be their teacher. A year later, such had been Mus'ab's success in the interval, seventy-five persons, two of them women, secretly allied themselves to Muhammad. They pledged their very lives in his cause.

But a Meccan spy soon spread the news of this confederacy and Muhammad's life was no longer safe. The Quraish plotted against him; his bitter foe, Abū Jahl, proposed that, in order to avoid a vendetta, various leaders should stab him simultaneously. Muhammad and Abū Bakr hid in a cave while the Meccans scoured the country for them. It is said that once when the pursuers were close at hand, Abū Bakr in alarm exclaimed, "We are but two"; whereat Muhammad rejoined, "Nay, we are three, for God is with us." After further adventure they eventually reached Madīna in safety.

The selection of the site for the first *masjid*, or mosque, in Madīna was made in a dramatic manner at the time of their arrival. Receiving many invitations to alight and accept hospitality, Muhammad discreetly replied, "The decision rests with the camel, make way for her." On the spot on which she sat down, a mosque was afterwards erected.

'Alī was not so fortunate. At the suggestion of Muhammad he had, on the first night of the flight, wrapped himself in Muhammad's well-known green mantle and lain in Muhammad's bed. It was a most courageous thing to do. When discovered he managed to escape through the window and, though roughly handled on the way, he rejoined the others, having taken care to travel only by night.

Such was the *Hijra*, or migration from Mecca to Madīna, the event which forms the starting-point of the Muslim era. Some make the date to have been the 16th July, A.D. 622.

The Madīna Period

This incident also marks a great turning-point in Muhammad's career, and the interesting and insistent question arises as to whether Muhammad's ideals changed with the changed outlook. Did he see, at last, an open road to triumphs on which his heart had long been set? That is possible, for we have seen that a political element entered into the recent pledge he had exacted. A view commonly held, however, is that in Mecca Muhammad was the prophet or religious reformer, pure and simple, but that in Madīna he exchanged this rôle for that of a secular ruler, or prophet-king.

It seems more probable that the patriotic sentiment was in his mind from the first and that, in consequence, the ardent preacher and zealous reformer of Mecca unfolded, in the more favourable conditions of Madīna, into the military commander and autocrat.

Certain it is that the conditions at Madīna offered Muhammad much promise of success. A strong Jewish element in the city ensured greater interest in religious matters than had been shown in Mecca; the ravages of civil strife plainly indicated the need of a strong ruler, and there was already keen rivalry between Madīna and Mecca should he care to take advantage of it. Indeed, in estimating the causes of Islām's early success, we need to take these factors into account. It was here that Islām first began to thrive. Madīna was the real birthplace of the new faith.

Various Groups at Madīna

Muhammad quickly took in the situation at Madīna and accustomed himself to think and speak of its inhabitants as belonging to one or other of several distinct groups.

1. First in order of importance to the mind of Muhammad were the *Muhājirīn* or Emigrants, i.e., those Muslims who had come from Mecca, either before Muhammad or with him, or shortly after his arrival.

2. The *Ansār*, or Helpers. These were people of Madīna who had accepted Islām either before or after the *Hijra*. They did not rank as highly in the thought of Muhammad as those of the first group because they had not endured so much for Islām, nevertheless these two groups provided the main strength of Islām, and Muhammad bound them together in a compact of fraternity so that the loneliness and poverty of the *Muhājirīn* were dispelled by the generosity of the *Ansār*.

3. The *Munāfiqīn*, or Hypocrites. These were a group of influential residents of Madīna who had ostensibly embraced Islām, but had no intention of surrendering their position to the intruders from Mecca. For this reason Muhammad called them "hypocrites."

4. Finally there were the Jews who, as has been stated, constituted a large and influential community. Muhammad, realising both their power and importance, sought to win them over to his cause. His foresight and genius for organisation are seen in the way in which

he bound them, along with the first two groups, in a treaty of obligation. This treaty (1) provided against sedition, (2) proclaimed the Quraish to be outlaws, and (3) while granting religious toleration to the Jews, demanded their support whenever the Muslims should require it. Sayyid Amīr 'Alī, commenting on the terms of this treaty, says, "It constituted Muhammad the chief magistrate of the nation" (*The Spirit of Islām*, rev. ed. 1923, p. 59). Elsewhere he quotes from Carlyle's *The Hero as Prophet*: "No emperor with his tiaras was obeyed as this man in a cloak of his own clouting" (*op. cit.*, p. 52).

The Jews

Muhammad indeed must be given the credit for introducing order into Madīna, but he soon discovered that the Jews were a peculiarly obstinate people, a veritable thorn in his side. Amīr 'Alī remarks that they had business relations with the outlawed Quraish, that they were half-hearted in their allegiance to Muhammad, and that within a month they broke out into open sedition. Why, then, had Muhammad bound them to himself in that treaty? Was it because he coveted their support or because he suspected them? Or was it a combination of both these reasons? Amīr 'Alī makes the astonishing suggestion that it was the Jews who were eager for the alliance, and that they thought to use Muhammad for the conversion of Arabia to Judaism! (*op. cit.*, p. 59 f.)

Muhammad did much to conciliate the Jews. He related Islām to Abraham and, as we have seen, associated the patriarch and his son Ishmael with the Ka'ba; but though a handful of them became Muslims the Jews as a body held proudly aloof. Gradually Muhammad was forced to the conclusion that the Jews were profoundly hostile towards him. It was plain that they resented his suggestion that he, an *ummī*, an unlearned fellow, could be in the line of the prophets. Thus Muhammad came to realise that he had escaped from the controversy in Mecca only to become embroiled in another in Madīna. The former, however, had been with debased idolaters; this was with a keenly intellectual people, withal possessors of a Book, their Scriptures. Thus arose a bitter altercation. The Jews criticised and poured scorn on Muhammad's claims, while he sought to bring them into discredit. For instance, he charged them with having concealed and misrepresented the contents of their Scriptures, and then tried to intimidate them by uttering terrible threats (cp. iv. 50).

The breach with the Jews had now become complete, and Muhammad introduced changes in the religious ceremonial of the Muslims that served to emphasise it. For instance, Jerusalem had been the *qibla* (the direction to be faced in prayer) but Mecca now took its place (ii. 136-139).

Economic Distress of the Muslims

Meanwhile the economic condition of Muhammad and his followers was causing anxiety and resentment. The Emigrants considerably outnumbered the Helpers, so that the former had little food and clothing. The wrath of the Muslims was kindled against the Jews, who now proved themselves indifferent and niggardly. The situation was getting desperate and something had to be done. We need to remind ourselves that in such circumstances it was the normal thing for Arabs of one tribe to attack and loot the caravans of another tribe. This, in fact, was the course which Muhammad now proceeded to adopt against the Meccans, and by so doing he virtually declared war.

Modern apologists for Islām seek to exonerate Muhammad from all blame by urging two reasons in extenuation. Much is made, on the one hand, of the traitors within the Muslim ranks, in particular the Jews, who, it is alleged, were intriguing with the Meccans. On the other hand, it is stated that the Quraish army was in the field before Muhammad was prepared to do battle. And, we are told, Muhammad "was not simply a preacher of Islām; he was also the guardian of the lives and liberties of his people. As a Prophet, he could afford to ignore the revilings and the gibes of his enemies; but as the head of the State, 'the general in a time of almost continuous warfare,' . . . he could not overlook treachery" (*op. cit.*, p. 60 f.).

The facts, however, appear to have been these. The Quraish were returning to Mecca from Syria with a caravan of merchandise; in this sense only they might be said to have been "first in the field." But why should they risk loss by an unprovoked assault upon the Muslims? Ibn Hishām says that before the first big battle (i.e., Badr) Muhammad had sent out a force to capture a caravan of the Meccans, who subsequently despatched an army to protect it. (Ibn Hishām in the chapter *Ghazwa Badr-ul-Kubra.*)

The next raid was ordered to take place, much to the amazement of the Muslims and the genuine alarm of the Meccans, in a sacred month, during which, according to an ancient custom, there should be a truce between hostile tribes. The attack, being unexpected, was successful and brought in much booty. But it required a special pronouncement from Muhammad to silence the objections of his followers (ii. 214).

Sometime later a rich caravan was returning from Syria to Mecca in charge of Abū Sufyān, one of Muhammad's inveterate foes. Muhammad determined to intercept it, but Abū Sufyān managed to give the alarm to his townspeople. Subsequently Abū Sufyān out-distanced the Muslims and saved the caravan, but he failed to stop the disorderly crowd that had issued forth from Mecca to do battle with the Muslims at Badr (A.D. 624). Though possessing great numerical superiority, the Meccans were hopelessly defeated. The victory was another turning-point in the career of Muhammad, and it produced a very marked change in the minds of his followers (cp. iii. 119). But the victory rankled in the minds of the Jews, and their poets lampooned Muhammad. It is recorded that he had one of the latter, a woman, removed. She was stabbed in her sleep by a blind Jew (cp. Wāqidī).

From this time Muhammad turned his unwelcome attention to these people. He began by expelling, for some reason, the Banī Qainuqā from their homes, at the same time confiscating their property. Singular to relate, the various Jewish tribes, apparently blind to their fate, failed, as here, to go to the help of one another, with the result that Muhammad was able to deal with each group separately, and so finally disposed of them. The next tribe to suffer were the Banī Nadīr, three miles out of Madīna, who had broken a treaty with Muhammad. They were banished from their homes and Muslims were installed in their place. Sūra lix. makes direct reference to this occasion.

In the meantime the Meccans, far from taking the defeat at Badr with equanimity, were making great preparations for revenge, and to this end they devoted the whole of the profits realised from the caravan which the skill of Abū Sufyān had rescued from the Muslims. Thus in the following year at the battle of Uhud, 3000 men under the command of Abū Sufyān completely defeated the Muslims. Muhammad himself was wounded, and a report was spread that he was slain. It was on this occasion, says Baidhāwī, that he uttered the words: "Muhammad is no more than an apostle; other apostles have already passed away before him; if he die, therefore, or be slain, will ye turn upon your heels?" (iii. 138). But, through failing to follow up their initial success, the Meccans won a hollow victory. Muhammad had proclaimed the victory of Badr as a mark of Allāh's favour; he now explained this defeat as a test of the constancy of his followers and as a rebuke to those who in the fight had disobeyed his orders. He, however, refused to be discouraged and soon re-established confidence among his followers.

It was well he did so, for the Meccans resolved to make a last desperate effort to rid themselves of this man who threatened their very existence. They called up their Beduin allies and their mercenary troops. There is reason to believe that they had an understanding with the Jewish tribe called Banī Quraiza in Madīna that help would be forthcoming from that quarter. In 627 this new Meccan army, about 10,000 strong, appeared before Madīna. Muhammad defended the exposed part of the city and his numerically inferior force by means of a trench, which effectively prevented the enemy from storming his position. Put to the test the Beduin proved untrustworthy; in any case Muhammad succeeded in dividing the enemy's forces and so the siege was raised with very little loss on either side.

The Banī Quraiza took no part in the fight but Muhammad suspected treachery, and this, following their habitual scorn and sarcasm, now drove him to exasperation. He has left it on record that in his opinion the Jews, of all men, were the worst enemies of the Muslims (v. 85). He took desperate measures with the offending tribe. 'Alī, with 3000 men, set out against them. After a siege of fifteen days the Jews sent a request to be allowed to depart as the Banī Nadīr had done, but the petition was refused. The whole tribe capitulated. Muhammad agreed that a third party should decide their fate. The decision of this man, no friend of the Banī Quraiza, was that all the males should be slain, and that the women and children should be sold into slavery. Men, to the number of about 600, say some authorities, were beheaded. Muhammad meanwhile stood by consenting to their death. It is perhaps fair to add that Sayyid Amīr 'Alī says, "The number of the men executed could not have been more than 200 or 250" (*op. cit.*, p. 82).

Secure at his base and with the Meccans disheartened by failure and defeat, Muhammad now had the road to Mecca lying open before him. He displayed great insight and sound judgment in now claiming the Ka'ba for Islām. He declared the *hajj* ceremonies to be "the sacred ordinances of God" (cp. xxii. 31). As a policy it was a master-stroke for gaining influence at this time. Here was a means for uniting the scattered and mutually hostile Arab tribes. But the leadership still lay with the Quraish, and his cause could not prosper until they were dispossessed or won over.

When sometime later he attempted the *'Umra*, or lesser pilgrimage, with 1400 of his followers, he was opposed by the Quraish, who refused to let him enter the city. The parties fell to debating the matter, and Muhammad secured terms from the Meccans by the Treaty of Hudaibīyya (628). Islām gained in prestige by this treaty, inasmuch as Muhammad as head of a state had dealt with the proud Meccans on equal terms. Some of the Quraish even came over to his side as the result of it. This "victory" is referred to in the Qur'ān (xlviii. 1). There was to be no fighting for ten years, and though Muhammad and his followers were refused admission into Mecca on that occasion it was agreed that they should come the following year.

Muhammad made memorable his return to Madīna by issuing letters to rulers of neighbouring states demanding their submission to Islām. Each letter bore the impress of a seal with the words, "Muhammad the Apostle of God." Heraclius the Byzantine (Roman) Emperor, the King of Persia, and the Maqauqis of Egypt were among those so addressed. But his orders were either flouted or evaded.

In 629, at the time of the lesser pilgrimage, Muhammad and his adherents were permitted to enter Mecca. It was a time of great enthusiasm, since some of them had not been in the city for seven years. Muhammad led the way in performing the customary ritual. The fervour of the Muslims made a deep impression on the townspeople and there were considerable accessions to their ranks from among the Quraish, the most notable being Khālid ibn Wālid, known in after years, because of his prowess in battle, as "the Sword of God."

Though Muhammad, after this, returned to Madīna stronger than ever, he had not yet achieved that success through which Islām would become the one politico-religious force in all Arabia. Mecca must become the centre of Islām even as it was the centre of the affections of the Arabs.

The truce of Hudaibīyya would have proved irksome long before it had run its course. As it was, through the defection of an obscure Arab tribe, Muhammad found a pretext for proceeding against Mecca when only two years had passed. He assembled an army of 10,000 men and appeared before the city. And now Abū Sufyān, Muhammad's old foe, seeing the folly of resistance, came forward to Muhammad, repeated the *Kalima* ("There is no god but God; Muhammad is the apostle of God"), and embraced Islām. His desertion disheartened the Meccans and they calmly submitted to the inevitable.

Thus Muhammad entered Mecca at last as victor; more than that, he came also as an ardent reformer. Proceeding to the Ka'ba and having kissed the Black Stone, he ordered all the idols within the shrine to be broken to pieces. Moreover, in his hour of triumph he showed mercy towards his old foes. He proclaimed a general amnesty to all in the city. There were a few exceptions, it is true, but they probably deserved their fate.

What a dramatic change was this in Muhammad's fortunes! Eight years before he had left Mecca a fugitive, despised, outcast, barely escaping with his life. Now he is master, and his word is law. Witness the manner in which idolatry was promptly banished.

There was an immediate response from the side of

the Arabs. Tribe after tribe came in to give Muhammad their allegiance. His ideal was being realised. Arabia would yet be a nation united and free, a match for all invaders. But all who entered Islām were obliged to accept its teaching, perform the necessary ritual, give alms, and in everything render implicit obedience to "God and His Apostle."

Rumours now began to reach Muhammad that the Byzantine Emperor Heraclius was collecting a large army on the Syrian border with a view to attacking Madīna. Though Muhammad went out himself at the head of a large army he failed to find the enemy, so he contented himself with making a demonstration against the Jews and Christians over the border. Several Christians from this time became *dhimmīs* (non-Muslim subjects in a Muslim state) and paid the *jizya*, or poll tax. The very late date of the passage Sūra ix., ver. 29, "Make war upon such of those to whom the Scriptures have been given as believe not in God," etc., would seem to indicate that a certain amount of intolerance, if not of compulsion, against both Jews and Christians was encouraged in Muhammad's closing years.

While Muhammad continued to receive embassies from all parts of Arabia, he began in his last year to plan a great expedition into Syria against the Byzantines. In the midst of these preparations he was seized with his last illness. There is reason to believe that there lingered in his system the effects of poison in meat he had eaten some months before. Fever intervened and great pain, from which he was released by death on 8th July, 632, at the age of sixty-three. His followers were quite unprepared for this catastrophe.

Chapter III

THE FIRST FOUR KHALĪFAS (CALIPHS)

Abū Bakr	. .	A.D. 632–634
'Umar	. . .	A.D. 634–644
'Uthmān	. .	A.D. 644–656
'Alī	. . .	A.D. 656–661

The death of Muhammad in 632 was unexpected, and neither he nor his followers had made any plans for the furtherance of the movement of Islām after his death. The men of Madīna naturally wished to appoint one of their own number as their leader, for the success of Islām had been almost entirely due to the people of Madīna. If they had done so, the tribe of the Quraish would have fallen away from them ; for although Muhammad had done his best to break down the old tribal system of Arabia, it was still very strong, and the Quraish at that time certainly would not have followed a leader of another tribe. The Companions of Muhammad, as those of his immediate circle were called, agreed to have Abū Bakr as their leader, and after much argument the men of Madīna also agreed to accept him. Abū Bakr therefore became the first Khalīfa.

One of Muhammad's last acts before his final illness was to order an expedition to go against Syria. The expedition was all ready to go, but was delayed on account of his illness. The moment that Abū Bakr assumed power he had the difficult question to decide whether the expedition should go forward or not. There were immediate signs of revolt against Islām all over Arabia, and the expeditionary force included nearly all the men on whose loyalty Abū Bakr could count. He took the bold course of saying that the expedition must go forward because Muhammad had ordered it. It was the decision of a strong and fearless man. Until the return of the expedition he was in a precarious condition as he had only a handful of men with which to repel attacks of Arab insurgents against the city. Abū Bakr's fearlessness impressed the Arabs, and, as soon as the expedition returned after a successful raid in southern Palestine, he sent forces into all parts of Arabia, and within one year had compelled all the Arab tribes to return to Islām. Although at that time compulsion was needed to make them adhere to Islām, within a very short time they were heart and soul in the new movement; for as the Arab armies marched out of Arabia and won their first spoils of more civilised lands, the Arabs came to believe in the truth of the new religion which was giving them such unexpected success.

Some scholars believe that several thousands of years before this there had been a great emigration from Arabia which had peopled the lands of Syria and Irāq. Whether that was so or not, there is no doubt that for many centuries the Arabs had been hemmed in within their vast barren land, and had been unable to make any progress outside it. On one occasion, it is true, not many years before, perhaps in the lifetime of Muhammad, an Arab tribe had completely defeated a Persian army at the battle of Dhū Qār, near Kūfa, but the disunity of the Arab tribes had prevented the Arabs from following up their victory.

There is a good deal of evidence that Arabia was at one time a more fertile land, but owing to decreasing rainfall it was becoming less able to support its Arab population. This is indicated by Arab traditions, and also by the evidence of geology and signs still existing of old caravan routes in parts which are now entirely deserted. It is believed by some scholars that the gradual drying up of Arabia was the cause that compelled the Arabs to seek new lands, and that the unification of Arabia by

Muhammad made it possible for them to burst the bonds by which they had been held in for centuries.

As soon as Abū Bakr had recalled the scattered Arab tribes to their loyalty to Islām, the great Arab expansion began. Armies went forth and met Roman and Persian troops in battle, and before Abū Bakr's short reign of just over two years closed the Arabs had already gained a firm footing in Syria and Irāq, Irāq being at that time a part of the Persian empire.

Abū Bakr, mindful of the chaos that had followed the death of Muhammad, had been careful to nominate a successor; so that as soon as he died 'Umar took over the control and pushed forward the Muslim conquests.

On the north-west of Arabia there was a Christian tribe known as the Banī Ghassān, and on the north-east a tribe, partly Christian, known as Banī Hīra. For many years these two tribes had been subsidised by the Roman and Persian governments respectively, to act as bulwarks against Arab raids. The misfortunes of the Roman empire had compelled them to withhold the usual subsidy from the Banī Ghassān, so that they were less inclined than heretofore to play the part of frontier police. On the Persian side the Banī Hīra were divided in their allegiance; for some of them, Christians though they were, threw in their lot with the Muslim invaders of Irāq. We read, too, of a Nestorian patriarch who gained special privileges for the Christians because he had helped the Muslims in the days of 'Alī in the attack on Mosul by providing them with corn. Such indications show that in the early days the Muslims were out for conquest rather than for converting men to Islām. Many of the Christians must have regarded Islām merely as a war of Arab conquest, and not as a religion, and in a certain sense they were right.

The Persians fought bravely to defend their homeland, and the Muslims did not win the victory without many hardly contested battles. The Persian forces had been weakened by the long-continued wars between Persia and the Roman empire. Not only so, there was division among the Persians themselves over the question of the succession to the Persian throne; whilst over against them were the united forces of the Arabs fighting with desperate bravery, and not caring if they died because they had been imbued by Muhammad with the idea that if they died fighting "in the way of the Lord" they would enter at once into the delights of Paradise—a Paradise conceived as more luxurious than the abundant wealth of Persia. A Christian writer, two hundred years later, describes the Arabs as "a needy and barbarous race, feeding on lizards and such like, with no shelter from the hot blast of summer, nor covering from the cold winds of winter; hungry and naked." This description may have been written in hate, but it contains much truth, and we can well understand the desperation with which they fought for the luxuries of Persia.

In Syria the Muslims had an easier task. Syria at that time was an outlying province of the Roman empire. The capital of the empire in those days was not Rome, but Constantinople, and the people were mostly Greeks, but they still called it the Roman empire, and the Arabs called it Rūm. Another name for Constantinople was Byzantium, and soon afterwards the empire came to be known as the Byzantine empire. The Emperor in the days of the Muslim conquest of Syria was called Heraclius. When he first came to the throne he was very lazy and the empire suffered much at the hands of the Persians. Then he suddenly bestirred himself and fought against the Persians, and won great victories. But again he became lazy, and after being once beaten in battle by the Muslims, he went back to Constantinople and did not trouble much about losing Syria. The Syrians themselves did not mind very much whether they were ruled by the Greeks or the Arabs. They hated Heraclius because they mostly belonged to a Christian Church called the Jacobites, and Heraclius had persecuted them very severely to try to make them join his Church, which was called the Melkites. The result was that the Muslims had very little difficulty in taking possession of Syria.

In Egypt the Muslims met with much more resistance, for the Egyptians fought bravely to defend their country. But Egypt, too, at that time was a province of the Roman empire, and the chief officers over the Egyptian army were Romans, who were either lazy or very incompetent. Even so, the Egyptians would have been able to conquer the Muslims if it had not been for the treachery of a man called the Maqauqis, who made a shameful treaty to hand over Egypt to the Muslims. It is a curious thing that although the historians tell us much about the Maqauqis, they do not explain who he was. Some think he was the Governor of Egypt, and others that he was the same as Cyrus, whom the Emperor had appointed as Patriarch or chief bishop of the Egyptians. The Egyptian Christians belonged to a Church similar to the Jacobites and were known as Copts. Under the orders of Heraclius, Cyrus had persecuted them terribly in order to make them Melkites, and many of them had been killed or had gone into exile. After the Muslim conquest many of the Christians in Egypt became Muslims. One reason for this was that they had been so bitterly persecuted by their fellow-Christians that they were sick of Christianity; but another reason undoubtedly was that many of their ancestors had been converted to Christianity in a great mass movement, and had never been properly taught about Christianity.

When Islām began to be established a rule was made that none except Muslims might remain in Arabia. So the Jews and Christians who would not accept Islām had to leave the country, with the exception of Yaman, where we find a Christian community still existing two centuries later. Arabia was to be the home for Muslims. In the days of 'Umar the Arabs rarely held any land in the conquered territory, and when they were not fighting they returned to their homes in Arabia. Practically all the land in the conquered territory was held in those early days by non-Muslims, and they had to pay heavy taxes to the Muslims.

Later on, when Muslims also were allowed to possess lands, the taxes were divided into two kinds, *kharāj*, or land tax, and *jizya*, which was a tax levied on non-Muslims only. As the non-Muslims did not have to fight in the army, the *jizya* may be regarded as a tax paid instead of doing military service. Thus, theoretically, it was quite fair that non-Muslims should pay this extra tax; but in actual practice the *jizya* may have been made an excuse for much unfair extortion. As the Muslims returned to Arabia with much booty and many captive women as their wives, the numbers of the Muslims increased enormously, and that explains how they were able to put such large armies in the field.

'Umar died after a reign of ten and a half years, being stabbed by a Persian slave. In his time Egypt was taken by his general 'Amr ibnu'l 'As, and the conquest of Syria and Persia was completed. 'Umar appointed a small committee to choose his successor, and after much dissension and wrangling 'Uthmān was accepted as the third Khalīfa.

During the days of Abū Bakr and 'Umar, when Arab armies were winning great victories, the different tribes of Arabia held together. But with the change from conquest to settlement in the conquered lands the old rivalries began to reappear. The Quraish thought themselves very superior to all the other Arabs, and the other Arabs hated the Quraish because of their claims. 'Uthmān was a weak and foolish man. Instead of trying to make peace between the Quraish and the other Arabs, he favoured the Quraish. There were two sections of the Quraish, the house of Hāshim, to which Muhammad and 'Alī belonged, and the house of Umayya, to which 'Uthmān and Mu'āwiya, the Governor of Syria, belonged. 'Uthmān showed favouritism to the members of his own family, and put Umayyads in all the chief positions. If he had been a strong man he might have subdued his enemies, but he was too weak to do that, and so he was hated both by the Banī Hāshim and also by the Arabs who were not of the Quraish. They hated both him and the Umayyad Governors, whom he had appointed in all the towns. Finally, rebel forces set out from the towns of Kūfa and Basra in Irāq and from Egypt and attacked 'Uthmān in Madīna and slew him. During his reign the Muslim forces had invaded Asia Minor, and also pushed along the north coast of Africa.

The people of Madīna elected 'Alī as Khalīfa. He was at Madīna at the time, and though he had not joined the rebels he had not helped to defend 'Uthmān. If he had been wise he would have either killed the rebels, or have sided with them and said that 'Uthmān had been justly killed for his misgovernment. But he condemned the rebels for their deed, and yet was afraid to punish them. The discontent against 'Uthmān's rule had been chiefly in Irāq and Egypt. In Syria the discontent was less because Syria was governed by Mu'āwiya, who was a strong man. One of the chief reasons for the discontent was that 'Uthmān had appointed Umayyads to all governorships. 'Alī's first action was to recall these governors and replace them by men of the house of Hāshim, to which he belonged. This was equally displeasing to those Arabs who were not of the Quraish, and to the non-Arabs. Mu'āwiya refused to give up the governorship of Syria, and immediately raised an army to defend himself.

To understand the struggle of non-Arabs against Arabs, and of other Arab tribes against the Quraish, we have to go back to Muhammad. Muhammad was obliged to fight against his own tribe of the Quraish. According to old Arab custom this was the vilest perfidy. But Muhammad announced a new principle that all Muslims were equal, and that tribes were nothing. In Sūra xlix. 13, he said, "O men! we have created you of a male and a female; and we have divided you into peoples and tribes that ye might have knowledge one of another. Truly, the most worthy of honour in the sight of God is he who feareth Him most." The effect of this new principle in Islām is illustrated by a tradition concerning 'Umar, that one day he heard two people striving with one another and saying, " I am the son of so-and-so, who did such and such noble deeds." 'Umar said, " If you have understanding you also have ancestors. If you have good characteristics you also have honour. If you have the fear of God you also have worth. But if you have none of these things, any ass is of more worth than you."

If 'Alī had understood the new principle of the equality of Muslims he might have held all the Muslims together. But he trusted too much in the fact that he belonged to the Quraish and was son-in-law of the Prophet. The first to rebel against him was 'Āyesha, who raised an army against him and charged him with the murder of 'Uthmān. 'Alī gathered together an army from Irāq, including the men who had killed 'Uthmān, and fought against 'Āyesha and her army at the battle of the Camel. 'Alī won the battle, but by accepting the help of the rebels he showed that he approved of the murder of 'Uthmān.

From Kūfa, which he made his capital, 'Alī set out with his army to fight against Mu'āwiya. A fierce battle was fought, and many were killed on both sides. At last 'Alī was winning the victory. But some of Mu'āwiya's men thought of a clever ruse; they placed leaves of the Qur'ān on the tips of their lances, and holding them aloft shouted out that the Qur'ān should decide between them. 'Alī wanted to go on fighting to victory, but his troops refused to follow. It was decided that there should be a truce of six months, and that a decision between 'Alī and Mu'āwiya should be made by two umpires. As 'Alī's army was returning, many of the men changed their minds, and wished they had fought the battle to a finish. They accused 'Alī of weakness, and deserted him, and formed a sect known as the Khawārij. In due course the umpires gave their decision, and by a trick Mu'āwiya was declared Khalīfa.

'Alī tried to raise an army again to fight against Mu'āwiya, but the Khawārij were raiding in Irāq and causing much trouble, and 'Alī's army had to turn aside to fight them. 'Alī's army then refused to go out to Syria to fight against Mu'āwiya. So Mu'āwiya was left in charge of Syria, while 'Alī ruled in Persia, Arabia and Egypt. But 'Alī did not even maintain his hold on those lands, for Mu'āwiya sent an army into Egypt and took possession of it and appointed as Governor the original conqueror of Egypt, 'Amr ibnu'l 'As. He also made the men of Mecca and Madīna swear allegiance to him. As time went on the Khawārij became more and more discontented. They said that they were the only true Muslims, and that all the other Muslims would go to hell. They saw that the Khalīfas were only ruling for temporal power, and so they would not make a Khalīfa of their own. Finally they decided to assassinate, on one day, 'Alī, Mu'āwiya and 'Amr. Of the three 'Amr escaped, Mu'āwiya was badly wounded but recovered, but 'Alī died.

In the days of Muhammad, 'Alī had fought bravely, but as Khalīfa he was a complete failure and became more and more unpopular. The reverence of the Shī'as for 'Alī did not begin till long after his death, and was apparently based rather on his relationship to Muhammad than on anything in his own character. In somewhat the same way the unpopularity of 'Uthmān during his lifetime was forgotten by later generations. With a complete disregard of history, 'Uthmān and 'Alī, whose weakness and favouritism wrought untold harm to Islām, are classed side by side with 'Abū Bakr and 'Umar who had served Islām truly and well, as the Four Rightly Guided Khalīfas.

'Alī's son Hasan was made Khalīfa in Irāq. But he never exercised any power, for he surrendered to Mu'āwiya after a few months and retired to Madīna, where he lived for eight years till his death.

Chapter IV

THE SUBSEQUENT EXPANSION OF ISLĀM

The Umayyad Khalīfas

The dynasty of the Umayyad Khalīfas began with Mu'āwiya in 661, and lasted till 750. It is noteworthy for the change that was coming over Islām that Mu'āwiya's two chief Governors were not of the Quraish but of another Arab tribe called Thaqīf. During the reign of Mu'āwiya Herāt was captured and the Muslim rule extended as far as the river Indus. Later in the same dynasty, in the year 711, a Muslim army crossed the Indus and captured Multān with much booty, but the victory was not converted into a permanent occupation.

As Mu'āwiya had been Governor of Syria before becoming Khalīfa, the capital of all the Umayyad Khalīfas was at Damascus. Damascus was also the best centre because Syria was at peace, the Muslims and the Christians living peaceably side by side; whereas in Irāq the two chief towns, Kūfa and Basra, were held as military strongholds, but the mass of the people were unfriendly to the Muslims. It is to be noticed that Arabia was no longer the centre of Islām.

After Mu'āwiya's death he was succeeded by his son Yazīd. Nearly all the Muslim leaders had already sworn allegiance to him before Mu'āwiya's death. But a few refused, and the people of Kūfa encouraged Husain, the son of 'Alī, to rebel. Husain marched from Mecca towards Kūfa, but as he approached the city he found that the people of Kūfa had changed their minds and would not fight for him. Most of his followers deserted him, and with a mere handful of supporters he was attacked by the Governor of Kūfa at Karbalā and slain on the 10th day of Muharram, 680. The manner of his death, which was practically a murder in cold blood, stirred the people's feelings. They felt for the first time the shame of the death of the two grandsons of Muhammad. Among the Arabs before Islām there had been no idea of an hereditary succession of tribal chieftains. But hereditary succession was the rule in all the surrounding kingdoms, and this idea was accepted in Islām by the Shī'a sect, which rested its hopes in the line of 'Alī, that is, the descendants of Muhammad through his daughter Fātima.

During the Umayyad period the Muslims gradually pushed along the north coast of Africa. From there they passed over to Spain, and from Spain into southern France. In the year 732 the Muslims were defeated at Tours, in southern France, by Charles "the Hammer." That date marks the end of the western advance of Islām, not merely because of the defeat in battle, but because the Muslims had exhausted their strength and numbers. In the east they held Armenia, but could not conquer Asia Minor although several times they attacked Constantinople. The most serious of these attacks was a siege of Constantinople from 714 to 716 which ended in the complete failure of the Muslims. The use of "Greek fire" by the Greeks added to the difficulties which the Muslims suffered through hunger, frost and pestilence. This defeat of the Muslims before Constantinople, and their overthrow by Charles "the Hammer" in France, saved Europe from Muslim invasion. It is not too much to say that if the Muslims had been successful in these two encounters, the whole history of European civilisation might have been entirely different.

It has already been mentioned that many of the Christians of Egypt very soon became Muslims. The same thing happened amongst the Christians of Syria and Irāq, though exact information is lacking. In the earliest days of the conquest Christians were not encouraged to become Muslims, because on becoming Muslims they no longer paid the *jizya*. The Khalīfa 'Umar seems to have been favourably inclined towards Christians, and when he conquered Jerusalem he treated the Christians very fairly. The Christians, along with the other inhabitants of the conquered lands, must have suffered much from the ravages of the troops; but more than one Christian historian says that Christians in Syria preferred the Muslim rule to that of the Romans, under whom they had suffered such persecutions for the Jacobite form of their Christian faith. Under the Umayyads the Christians undoubtedly suffered a certain amount of persecution, but we must confess that some at least of these persecutions were stirred up by complaints made to the Muslim authorities by one Christian leader against another. The early Muslim rulers did not distinguish between the different sects of Christians, so that in addition to the Nestorians we now hear of Jacobite and Melkite bishops in Persia. Under the previous Sassānid kings only the Nestorian form of Christianity was allowed. From what little information we have it appears that in the early days of the Khilāfat those Christians who adopted Islām did so of their own accord. Probably many nominal Christians became Muslims in order to avoid paying *jizya*. At a later time, from about the ninth century A.D. onwards, the economic position of the Christians may have led some of them to embrace Islām; but during the Umayyad period this can hardly have been the case, as many of the important positions in the state were practically reserved for Christians on account of their better educational standard. It is probable that from the time of the first Muslim conquests many Christians were convinced by the success of the Muslim armies that Islām was approved of by God; and this argument appears to have had increasing weight as time went on and the number and influence of the Christians decreased.

During all the Umayyad period there was discontentment, and frequently civil war. The Khawārij still caused trouble. There was also the Shī'a sect who supported 'Alī's family, and a party which supported the house of 'Abbās. The rebellion which destroyed the house of Umayya started in Khurāsān. A man named Abū Muslim became leader, and proclaimed that he was fighting for the house of Hāshim. Hāshim was the ancestor of both 'Alī and 'Abbās, so Abū Muslim was joined by people of both parties. The great mass of the people joined the rebellion, for they were tired of the Umayyads, and regarded them as merely political rulers who cared nothing for Islām. But it must have been a disappointment for the Shī'as when they found that the result of the rebellion was the elevation to the throne not of a man of 'Alī's line, but of the family of 'Abbās.

The 'Abbāsid Khalīfas, 750-1258

Arab power practically fell with the Umayyads. We have seen how the Persians had been gradually asserting themselves against the pretensions of the Arabs. The Shī'a movement in the beginning was mainly not that of a religious sect so much as of a political party in Irāq. An indication of the new claims is to be seen in a tradition, dating no doubt from this period, which said, "Despise not a Persian, for no one despises a Persian without God taking vengeance on him in this world and in the world to come." It was the Persians who gave the Khilāfat to the house of 'Abbās, and although the Khalīfas themselves were Arabs the real power rested with the Persians. For this reason the capital was moved from Damascus to Irāq. At first the capital was at Kūfa, but it was soon transferred to Baghdād, which retained the dignity until the downfall of the Khilāfat.

Many who considered the godless reigns of the Umayyads must have been filled with new hopes for Islām when the 'Abbāsid era dawned. So we find a tradition which says, "The Khilāfat shall abide among the children of my paternal uncle ('Abbās) and of the race of my father until they deliver it unto the Messiah." Yet from the moment that the 'Abbāsids came into power the empire of the Khalīfas began to break up.

The first country to declare itself independent was Spain. Spain never acknowledged the 'Abbāsid Khalīfas. A certain 'Abdu'r-Rahmān, of the house of Umayya, escaped from the slaughter which befel his family after their downfall, and fled to Africa. There he learnt of the state of affairs in Spain, and eventually was welcomed by the Spanish Muslims as their Amīr. The Umayyad dynasty of Spain that he founded lasted for two and a half centuries. As we shall not be returning to the subject of Spain, it may be mentioned here that, at a later time, the Muslims and Jews of Spain brought from the East the Greek philosophy which Europe had forgotten, but which had been preserved in Asia, first by Syriac-speaking Christians and then by Muslims. Schools of philosophy were founded in Spain from which the torch of knowledge was handed on in turn to the rest of Europe, thus bringing about what is known as the Revival of Learning in Europe.

Spain being farthest away from Baghdād was the first of the Khalīfa's dominions to secede. North Africa followed soon after; first an independent dynasty called the Idrīsids was set up in the farther West which we now call Morocco, in 788. Twelve years later a dynasty called the Aghlabids gained control of the whole of the rest of North Africa. Nominally they were governors appointed by the Khalīfa of Baghdād, but actually ruled as independent sovereigns. They were chiefly noted as pirates of the Mediterranean Sea, and they took possession of several islands including the important island of Sicily.

Turning our attention now to Persia, we find that one general after another proclaimed himself independent, thus raising up a number of states which paid only a nominal allegiance to the 'Abbāsid Khalīfa of Baghdād. The first of these new dynasties was one which began in

Khurāsān in 820. Most of these independent rulers were Persian by race and of the Shī'a sect. Although the Shī'as did not accept any Khalīfa after 'Alī, these Shī'ite rulers often found it convenient to recognise the Khalīfa, who was of course a Sunnī. The name of the Khalīfa might be mentioned in the Friday prayers, and the independent rulers sometimes received from him a formal recognition of their accession to the throne. Before the middle of the tenth century A.D. the Khalīfa's authority scarcely extended beyond Baghdād itself, and all his power was usurped by a Persian Shī'ite dynasty called the Buwayhids.

In the early days of the Khilāfat, governors of Yaman and of Mecca or Madīna had been appointed by the Khalīfas, while the rest of Arabia sank back into the divided state in which it was in the days before Muhammad, each tribe or district being under its own *shaikh*, or chief. At the very time when the first dynasty independent of Baghdād was springing up in Khurāsān, the same thing was happening in Arabia, and an independent kingdom arose in Yaman and continued for two centuries.

The Shī'as, who had originally started as a political party, began to develop peculiar religious views. Instead of recognising any Khalīfas after 'Alī, they looked to a series of *Imāms*, or spiritual guides, of the line of 'Alī. They broke up into many sects which pinned their hopes in one or other of these Imāms, believing that he had not died but was hiding and would some day return as the *Mahdī*, or divinely directed leader. This belief may have arisen from the Christian hope of the second coming of Christ. Another thing about the Imāms was that they were treated as divine, a notion probably borrowed from the old Persian belief in the divinity of their kings. Some of the minor Shī'a sects believed in reincarnation, but even liberal-minded Muslim theologians could not regard such sects as being within the pale of Islām. Numerically the most important group of the Shī'as was the sect that believed in *twelve* Imāms; this group is still the most important in the present day. One of the most peculiar of the Shī'a sects was the Sab'iya or Ismā'īlians who placed their hopes in Ismā'īl, the seventh Imām, who had died in 760. It is not quite clear whether the sect started immediately on the death of Ismā'īl. Anyhow it was greatly furthered a century later by a certain 'Abdu'llāh ibn Maimun, who developed it into a vast secret society, whose ulterior object (known probably to but few of the initiates) was simply atheism. One of this sect, who called himself 'Ubaidu'llāh al-Mahdī, was hailed as Amīru'l-Mu'minīn in North Africa in 909. This man, claiming descent from Ismā'īl, and so from 'Alī and Fātima, founded the Fātimid dynasty which first ruled in North Africa, and then conquered Egypt and Syria. Egypt and Syria had previously been, at times, independent or semi-independent of the Khalīfas of Baghdād, but under the Fātimids attained permanent independence. At the height of their power the Fātimids ruled over the whole of North Africa east of Morocco, and the islands of Sicily and Malta, as well as Egypt and Syria.

It appears, though it is not absolutely certain, that a century before the rise of the Fātimid dynasty the European Emperor Charlemagne entered into friendly relations with the Muslims of Syria, and was able to establish a Frankish protectorate over the Christians in Syria. At any rate the Christians in Syria for some time were allowed a great deal of liberty, so that a writer in the year 869 could say of the Muslims, "They are just, and do us no wrong or violence of any kind." This tranquillity of the Christians was rudely broken a century later by a Fātimid Khalīfa named al-Hākim, who apparently went mad, and as part of his madness initiated a terrible persecution of Christians and Jews in Syria and Egypt, which lasted from 1009-1020. The Church of the Holy Sepulchre in Jerusalem and other churches and monasteries were destroyed. In 1020 his disposition towards Christians changed and the persecution stopped, but his madness took a new form, for he declared himself to be God. For this blasphemy he had to flee from Egypt to Syria, where he died or disappeared in 1021. The sect of the Druses, who live in the Lebanon, still worship him as God. His son and successor in the Fātimid Khilāfat made a treaty with the Byzantine Emperor containing the most unusual concession, not only that the church of the Holy Sepulchre might be rebuilt, but also that the Christians who had been forcibly converted to Islām might return to Christianity.

Under the 'Abbāsid Khalīfas the position of the Christians was at first very favourable, for as they were more educated than other people they obtained many of the important positions in the state. As the Muslims became more educated themselves they found this preference for Christians rather galling, and Muslim protests begin to be heard in the ninth century A.D. It is difficult to generalise about the amount of liberty accorded to ordinary Christians. *Dhimmīs*, i.e., non-Muslim subjects, were under restrictions as to dress, were not allowed to ride on horseback, might repair churches but not build new ones, and suffered certain disabilities in the law-courts. But, on the one hand, these restrictions were not always enforced, so that, for instance, from time to time new churches were built; while, on the other hand, more severe restrictions were occasionally imposed. One restriction was apparently always observed, that the conversion of a Muslim to Christianity was absolutely prohibited. To make up for this, the Christians carried on vigorous missionary work outside the Khalīfa's dominions. Converts had been won among the Turks in Central Asia a century or more before Muhammad, and missionary work was successfully continued amongst them right up to the middle of the ninth century A.D. when the Muslims conquered the lands north of the river Oxus and began to establish Islām there. A Christian monument in China, dated 779 A.D., is evidence of a well-established church there at that time as a result of the labours of Persian missionaries.

The Turks

Gradually the Turks began to play an important part in Persian politics. Harūn-ur-Rashīd (786-809) was the first Khalīfa to employ Turks as officers in the army, and one of his sons, Mu'tasim, employed a bodyguard of 3000 Turks. As forming the bodyguards of the Khalīfas the Turks often wielded great power. The first Turkish Muslim state was that of the Ghaznavids, which arose in the second half of the tenth century A.D. Sabaktagīn, a slave of a Turk named Alptagīn who had made himself an independent ruler in the mountain fastness of Ghaznī, was the real founder of the dynasty, and extended its territory from Peshawār to Khurāsān. His son Mahmūd still further extended his dominions, the limits of which were Isfahān, Samarqand, and Lahore.

Hitherto the political changes in Persia which we have described were scarcely more than changes in the ruling princes. But in the eleventh century A.D. one of the Turkish nomadic tribes called the Ghuzz began to migrate into Persia, and a defeat by the Ghaznavid sultān only resulted in scattering them more widely throughout Persia. One section of the Ghuzz, descendants of a Turkomān chieftain named Saljūq, set up a new dynasty in Khurāsān, and in 1055 under Tughril Beg took possession of Baghdād. The original Saljūq may have been a Christian, for he had a son with a Christian name, but at the time of the invasion of Persia the Saljūqs were Muslims. With the assistance of other Turkish tribes the power of the Saljūq sultāns increased until they had conquered all the independent princes and ruled a great empire stretching from the borders of Afghānistān to the borders of Syria (the Fātimid Khilāfat) and Asia Minor (the Byzantine empire). This united empire of the Great Saljūqs lasted from 1037-1092, when it split up into a number of distinct Saljūq dynasties.

Five years after the split in the Saljūq empire a new power appeared upon the scene. In the year 1097 the first contingent of European Crusaders landed in Syria. We have already seen that, except for a few years in the reign of Hākim, Christians were well treated in Syria, in consequence of which large numbers of European Christians made the pilgrimage to Jerusalem. Two incidents occurred to make the pilgrimage more difficult. The first was the great schism of European Christianity in A.D. 1054 between the Western Church of Rome and the Eastern Church of Constantinople. From that time pilgrims passing through the Byzantine empire were not accorded the same facilities as heretofore. The second incident was the conquest of Syria and Asia Minor by the Saljūqs, 1067-1070, which made the pilgrimage more difficult, and also made men fear an invasion of Europe by the Turks. From mixed motives, of which undoubtedly the most potent was the desire to free Jerusalem from the Turks, enthusiasm was stirred up in France and in other parts of Europe for the first Crusade. The Crusaders arrived at an opportune moment when the forces of the Saljūqs were divided, and thus were able to establish themselves. Four Latin kingdoms were founded, with their capitals at Antioch, Tripolis, Edessa and Jerusalem, and their strength was maintained with varying fortunes by the continual arrival of fresh contingents of Crusaders at frequent intervals throughout the twelfth and thirteenth centuries. There can be little doubt that the spectacle of Christians taking up arms in the name of Christ did more than anything else to misrepresent Christianity in the eyes of the Muslims, and to intensify their hatred of the Christians. As the thirteenth century advanced the Muslim power was being strengthened, and the Latin states were weakening owing to waning interest in Europe in the eastern enterprise. Finally, in 1291, the last Christian town of Syria was captured and the episode of the Crusades was closed.

The Mongols

Meanwhile a new menace to civilisation had arisen in the Far East. The first of the Mongols was Chingiz Khān, one of the most remarkable, and also one of the most ruthless, conquerors in history. Starting as the ruler of a tribe of only 40,000 tents, Chingiz Khān conquered an enormous stretch of territory from North China right across Central Asia as far as eastern Russia. At that time the Mongols were heathen, and their practice was to lay waste cities and lands, and as far as possible to destroy all the inhabitants of the conquered lands. The grandson of Chingiz Khān was Hūlāgū, who pushed the Mongol conquests into Persia and captured and sacked Baghdād in 1258. The inhabitants of Baghdād, including the last of the 'Abbāsid Khalīfas, were massacred; but the Christians were spared, for Hūlāgū professed himself a Christian. At that time a number of the leading Mongols were Christian, and several embassies passed between the Mongols and the European sovereigns with the object of forming an alliance against the Turks. Nothing, however, came of all these embassies, and the final overthrow of the Christian states in Syria seems to have convinced the Mongols of the falsity of Christianity. For some time they had been wavering between the acceptance of Christianity or Islām. But the defeat of the Crusaders in 1291 decided them. Their persecution of the Christians began in 1296 and was of unexampled severity. Many of the Christians became Muslims, and the rest were slain, so that by the end of the fourteenth century Christianity had practically ceased to exist in Persia and Central Asia. The great kingdom founded by Hūlāgū, which extended from India to the borders of Egypt and the Mediterranean Sea, only lasted eighty years, and then split up into rival kingdoms as its predecessors, the 'Abbāsid and the Saljūq kingdoms, had done.

The Ottoman Turks

In the year A.D. 1258, in which Hūlāgū sacked Baghdād, there was born a man named 'Uthmān of a Turkish tribe related to the Saljūqs. He and his successors came into prominence in Asia Minor, and just a century after the birth of 'Uthmān, that is, in 1358, they crossed over into Europe and took possession of the Balkan Peninsula. Nothing remained of the Byzantine empire except the city of Constantinople itself and the surrounding district, which was saved for the moment by the appearance on the scene of Tīmūr (Tamerlane), who defeated the Ottoman Sultān, Bāyazīd, at Angora in 1402. The Ottoman empire, however, recovered from the defeat, and Constantinople itself was taken in 1453. Tīmūr during his lifetime ruled at Samarqand over all the lands from Delhi to Damascus, and as far north as the Sea of Aral, but his kingdom broke up immediately after his death. Salīm I. enlarged the borders of the Ottoman empire by the annexation of Egypt, Syria and Arabia. Up till that time a member of the 'Abbāsid family had resided at the court of the Mamlūk sultāns of Egypt and held the title of Khalīfa without any power. With the conquest of Egypt by Salīm I., in 1517, even the nominal Khilāfat ceased to exist, and did not reappear till late in the eighteenth century, when the Ottoman Sultān, 'Abdul Hamīd I., used the title to support his claims to supervise the Muslims in Russia.

The Shāhs of Persia

We have seen how one foreign power after another founded great empires in Persia—the Arabian Khalīfas, the Turkish Saljūqs, the Mongols, and, lastly, Tīmūr, himself of Mongolian stock. At length the Persians came into their own and became rulers of their own land. The greatest dynasty was that of the Safavids which lasted from 1502-1736. It was early in that period that the Shī'ite belief, essentially the Persian form of Islām, became the official creed of Persia, as it remains to the present day.

SECTION II

THE FOUNDATIONS OF ISLĀM

CHAPTER I

THE FOUR FOUNDATIONS

IT is a complaint frequently made by educated Muslims that the Islām of to-day is not the simple Islām of the Prophet Muhammad. That there is much truth in their contention will appear obvious in this and the next section of this book.

In Muhammad's time the Qur'ān with its meagre legal provisions was the only foundation of Islām, and it was demanded of all Muslims that they should comply with its directions. The term *Islām* (cp. Qur'ān iii. 17), a verbal noun, itself seems to imply this, viz., " the act of submitting one's self " to the will of God as involving the performance of specified duties, i.e., *compliance*. The word has in it the further idea of *resignation* to the will of God (cp. Qur'ān ii. 106, 125). The one who so submits is designated by the term *Muslim*, a participial form of the same root.

But even in the lifetime of Muhammad another standard of conduct was emerging, that of his own example in everything. After his death, his Companions recalled all such things in detail and handed them down orally to succeeding generations. This *sunna*, or "custom" of the Prophet formed the second foundation of Islām. We shall refer to it in our next chapter.

From the Qur'ān and the *sunna* there was evolved in course of time an immense and very complicated legal system called *fiqh*. For the present we need only indicate briefly the methods by which this development took place.

As might be expected, situations continually arose in

which no precise rule on a given question could be found in either the Qur'ān or the *sunna*. In such circumstances Muslim lawyers were compelled to exercise their own reason and thus deduce, by analogy, a new and suitable ruling, which they were nevertheless careful to see did not contravene the spirit and purpose of the first two foundations. This procedure, called *qiyās*, or reasoning by analogy, forms the third foundation of Islamic law.

The method, however, gave rise to a considerable diversity of interpretation. The attempts to reconcile these differences resulted in the formation of a fourth principle or foundation, called *ijmā'*, i.e., agreement. According to this principle, guidance was to be found through the "unanimous consent" of the *'ulamā*, or learned doctors of Muslim law.

Unfortunately, however, the *'ulamā* did not always agree, and so, as we shall have occasion to observe later, there came to be recognised four distinct legal schools.

We will now proceed to deal with each of these "foundations" in turn. They are often spoken of as *usūl*, or roots.

The Qur'ān—orthodox opinion

The Qur'ān, the sacred book of the Muslims, is held in extraordinary esteem by the followers of Muhammad, notwithstanding the fact that multitudes of them are illiterate and that many others, who do read it, find its language, Arabic, difficult to understand.

The simple are impressed by the text usually inscribed on the covers, a quotation from within, which utters the warning, "Let none touch it but the purified" (lvi. 78). It is not surprising, therefore, that many of the orthodox resent its coming into the possession of one of another faith. Yet the covers of the ornate Ahmadīyya edition, printed and published in England, retain this caution, although many must be handling it who do not perform the customary ablutions.

Muslims, the world over, love to chant its periods in a low monotone that is not without its peculiar charm even for the uninitiated; while to be a *hāfiz*—to achieve the feat of committing to memory the whole book—is still the highest ambition of countless Muslim children and an accomplishment bringing much merit. Selected verses also are brought together in an abbreviated edition called *Hamā'il.* It is a very common practice to chant these as a means of warding off evil and sickness. Similarly, charms containing such verses are hung round the neck.

The Traditions ascribe to Muhammad a variety of statements regarding the value and reward attached to the repetition of certain portions of the book; e.g., "The chapter entitled 'The Earthquake' (xcix.) is equal to half the Qur'ān; the declaration of 'The Unity' (cxii.) is equal to a third of the Qur'ān, and that commencing, 'Say, O ye unbelievers' (cix.) is equal to a fourth of the Qur'ān." Again, "The person who repeats two hundred times every day, the declaration of God's Unity (cxii.), his faults of fifty years shall be blotted out, unless he shall have debt upon him" (*Mishkātu'l-Masābih*, Book 8, chap. i., PART II.).

A view prevalent among strictly orthodox Muslims concerning the origin of the Qur'ān enables us to understand how it is that this high regard for the book becomes at times scarcely distinguishable from superstition.

According to this view the Qur'ān is eternal; the very words now found between its covers were inscribed from eternity on the *lauhu'l mahfūz*, or Preserved Table (lxxxv. 22). The whole collection of these writings was brought down from its place near God's throne, long ago in *lailatu'l qadr* ("the night of power"), in the sacred month of Ramdhān, to the lowest heaven, and there stored up until it was revealed, "piecemeal," as occasion required, to Muhammad (xcvii. 1).

And these believe that the Qur'ān is God's uncreated Word, something inherent in God's essence. It follows that in their view we have here the very words of God Himself, albeit in Arabic. Not the ideas alone but the very words, in their spelling, their grammar, their pronunciation, all are God's own and God's alone.

Other books, including the Old and New Testaments, were revelations delivered to men in the form of ideas which inspired prophets gave forth after clothing them in human language. Not so with the Qur'ān. Its actual text was pronounced by Gabriel in the ear of Muhammad (lxxv. 16-19). For this reason orthodox Muslims include every word of the Qur'ān in the category of *Qāl Allāhu*, "Allāh has said," and consequently, they rate the Christian Scriptures much lower because they are not cast entirely in this mould.

The unique origin of the Qur'ān is, in their eyes, further enhanced by the consequent claim that it is alike incomparable and incorruptible. Much is made in this connection of the fact that Muhammad was illiterate, and though the term *nabī ummī*, applied to him in the Qur'ān (vii. 156, 158), may mean the *Gentile* prophet, it probably signifies the unlettered one (see Rodwell's note, *loc. cit.*).

In any case the Qur'ān has come to be looked upon as the standing miracle of Islâm and as occupying a unique place among all scriptures. Muhammad declared it to be the one sufficient "sign" granted to men through him (xxix. 49-50). Arabs were challenged to produce something like it (lii. 34-5; xvii. 90; ii. 21).

Another Point of View

But there is another side to all this. Muhammad seems to have been very sensitive to any criticism of the high claims he himself made for the Qur'ān, claims out of which still more extravagant ones developed. In a short Sūra (lxxvii.) of fifty verses the phrase is repeated ten times, "Woe, on that day, to those who are charged with imposture."

His enemies found one reason for this charge in the way he made disjointed pronouncements from time to time, claiming each to have been revealed to him by God. The charge and his reply are preserved in the Qur'ān: "And the infidels say 'unless the Qur'ān be sent down to him all at once. . . .' But in this way would we stablish thy heart by it, in parcels have we parcelled it out to thee" (xxv. 34; cp. xvii. 107). And it is unquestionably the fact that numerous passages in the book are of an "occasional" nature, i.e., relating to particular events and emergencies.

Sale, writing about 150 years ago, aptly described this manner of revelation in the introduction to his translation of the Qur'ān: "Whenever anything happened which perplexed and gravelled Muhammad, and which he could not otherwise get over, he had recourse to a new revelation, as an infallible expedient in all nice cases." (The Koran, The Preliminary Discourse, Sect. iii.).

The methods used by Muhammad for recording these utterances varied. At times he would employ a scribe, in particular, Zaid ibn Thābit, who wrote out the portions "upon palm leaves, leather, stones, or the broad shoulder-blades of some animal." Much, however, was not transcribed but stored in the minds of the Companions. Special value attached to this method because at an early date the recital of a passage of the Qur'ān formed an essential part of public worship. But though the Arab mind was remarkably retentive it was not infallible. Even Muhammad's memory seems to have failed him at times (cp. 2, 100).

A situation arose in the eleventh year of the *Hijra*, within two years of Muhammad's death, which caused both Abū Bakr and 'Umar to fear for the safety of the Qur'ān. In that year at the battle of Yamāma many Muslim warriors, who were also *qārīs*, or reciters of the Qur'ān, lost their lives. The fear lest the book of God should be lost led these two Companions of the Prophet to employ Zaid ibn Thābit to collect all the material. What a task he took in hand! Tradition records that he gathered it "from palm-leaves, skins, blade-bones and the hearts of men."

But who shall say that Zaid managed to secure all that Muhammad had ever uttered and all that had been committed to memory?—that no portion was irretrievably lost in the death of some *qārī* or other? As a matter of fact a tradition according to 'Umar asserts that "the verse of stoning" (*re* the penalty for adulterers) was extant as a revelation in Muhammad's time though it is not to be found in the Qur'ān to-day. (See *The Verse of Stoning*, 31 pages, by W. H. T. Gairdner *et al.*, C.L.S. Madras.)

Its Compilation and Preservation

Judging by the command given to Muhammad the meaning of the word *Qur'ān* is 'recital' ("Recite thou, in the name of thy Lord," xcvi. 1), and it can apply not only to the whole book but to any portion of it (xii. 3). There are in use among Muslims other names for the book, e.g., Furqān, Al Kitāb. These are found in the book itself, but it is customary in speaking of it to add some such attribute as *sharīf* (noble), or *majīd* (glorious); thus, *Qur'ān sharīf*.

In length the Qur'ān is slightly longer than the New Testament, but it has a certain unity which cannot be claimed for either the O.T. or the N.T., inasmuch as it comes from one source and exhibits the working of a single mind.

The book is divided into 114 sections, or *sūras*, of very unequal length. These are named, not numbered, the name of a particular *sūra* being supplied either by the opening words of that *sūra* or by some subject or person mentioned therein. In twenty-nine *sūras*, however, certain mysterious letters serve as a title. At the head of each *sūra* is a note indicating whether it was "revealed" at Mecca or Madīna. Then, as a kind of preface to the contents of the *sūras* we find an invocation, the *bismillāh* (i.e., *bismi 'llāhi'r-rahmāni 'r-rahīm*, "In the Name of God, the Compassionate, the Merciful"). This appears in all but the ninth *sūra*. Each *sūra* is divided into *āyāt*, "signs," or, as we might say, "verses."

Muslims are accustomed to divide the Qur'ān into thirty parts to facilitate the reading of the whole book in one month, viz., in Ramdhān. These parts are called *juz* in Arabic, and *sipāra* in Persian. Again the *sipāras* are subdivided into several *rukū'*, "acts of bowing," these being sections of the sacred text used by Muslims in prayer.

The nature of the Arabic language is such that it is comparatively easy to make use of rhymes. This was a style frequently used by Arabs and it abounds in the Qur'ān. Its verses are made to close with words having similar sounds for their last syllables. An expert reader makes the most of this kind of rhythmical prose.

Unfortunately there is, in the form in which it is usually available, no recognised order or arrangement in the chapters of the Qur'ān. What is noticeable is that after the opening section, called *Fātiha*, the longest chapters come first and the shorter ones, some of them with less than a dozen verses, at the end. This is clearly intentional, but it means that as they stand the chapters are neither in chronological order, nor arranged according to their subject-matter.

It amounts to this really that when Zaid was commanded to collect the Qur'ān he put his materials together as they came to hand, often without regard to continuity of subject. Accordingly, we have late Madīna *sūras* placed before early Meccan ones; indeed the short *sūras* at the end are admittedly some of the earliest portions. Not only so, verses of undoubted Meccan origin are found embedded in Madīna *sūras*, and vice versa. All this makes it peculiarly difficult to read the Qur'ān intelligibly.

There is, however, another side to this. If we regret that Zaid did not exercise more freedom and judgment in his task, we must acknowledge that he was scrupulously honest and that as a result we have a volume which, taken as a whole, is in a high degree authentic.

Before long, however, Zaid's services were again required. His compilation had more or less fixed the text of the Qur'ān, but not the reading of it. 'Uthmān, the third Khalīfa, had to deal drastically in his time with a widespread scandal whereby different persons claimed the right to read certain passages of the Qur'ān in different ways. Some of these differences were due to the peculiar use made in tribal dialects of certain words. Thus arose differences of interpretation and consequent wrangling. Besides which it would appear that Muhammad himself on occasion dictated the same passage to different persons with different readings; cp. the tradition, "the Qur'ān was revealed according to seven modes of reading" (*Mishkātu'l-Masābih*, Book 8, ch. iii. 1).

Alarmed at the bitter feelings roused by these disputes 'Uthmān was persuaded to intervene by Hodzaifa, who is reported to have said: "Stop the people before they differ regarding their scriptures as do the Jews and the Christians" (quoted by Muir, *Life of Mahomet*, Vol. I., p. xiii.). Accordingly he appointed a commission, consisting of Zaid with three men of the Quraish, to decide finally upon the text and to fix the reading according to the pure Quraish idiom. When this edition was completed 'Uthmān sent copies to all the principal cities of the empire and ordered all the previous copies to be burnt. 'Uthmān's recension, made in 660, has remained the authorised text down to the present time. But while it may be true that no other work has remained for twelve centuries with so pure a text, it is probably equally true that no other has suffered so drastic a purging.

Rearrangement of the Chapters

In consequence of the lack of order in the compilation of the Qur'ān, scholars, both Muslim and Christian, have attempted a rearrangement of the chapters in their chronological order. A most natural division is that whereby the contents fall into two main groups, viz., the passages which are said to have been revealed at Mecca, and those revealed at Madīna. In other words, the principle has come to be accepted that the Qur'ān is only properly explained by continual reference to the life of Muhammad. As a modern writer has put it, "the book of Allāh is the diary of Muhammad's life." *Note.*—In English the most handy edition showing this rearrangement of the *sūras* is Rodwell's translation, "Everyman's Library."

Such a rearrangement not only makes the book more readable, it enables one to trace the career of Muhammad and the development of Islām. We can see, too, how this professedly "piecemeal" revelation fitted new situations as they arose.

Read in this order the earliest *sūras* are found to be marked by a certain grandeur of expression rarely found in the later Madīna ones. God's omnipotence, omniscience and unity are favourite themes. These chapters also reveal in Muhammad an exalted state of mind and a conviction that his call was from God (cp. lxxiv. and xciv.). The following is a striking passage:

> By the Sun and his noonday brightness!
> By the Moon when she followeth him!
> By the Day when it revealeth his glory!
> By the Night when it enshroudeth him!
> By the Heaven and Him who built it!
> By the Earth and Him who spread it forth!
> By a Soul and Him who balanced it,
> And breathed into it its wickedness and its piety,
> Blessed now is he who hath kept it pure,
> And undone is he who hath corrupted it!
>
> (xci. 1-10.)

We can see Muhammad in those early days denouncing the idolatry of his fellow-townsmen and threatening them with the tortures of hell if they will not hearken (cp. lxxvii.; cxi.; civ.; xcvi.). Over against such passages we have others which are intended to reassure and encourage his persecuted followers; e.g., the graphic accounts of the Paradise that awaits them (lxxviii. and lvi.).

Muhammad also rebuts charges of imposture and utters threats against those who doubt the divine inspiration of the Qur'ān (lxxvii. and xxv. 5-6). References to former prophets now begin to appear and are meant to show that they, too, were treated with scorn and accused of imposture (cp. *Sūra* xxvi.). The closing portion of the Meccan period, made difficult by the boycott of the Quraish, is reflected in a passage like vi. 106: "Follow thou that which hath been revealed to thee by the Lord: there is no God but He! and *withdraw* from those who join other gods with Him."

The Madīna *sūras*, constituting rather more than one-third of the whole collection, bear, as we should expect, a different character. In them there is less stress than formerly on dogma and more on the precepts and laws which are to guide the daily lives of Muslims. The dictates of the practical administrator of the affairs of the new state replace the burning eloquence of the preacher. Muhammad is obliged now to deal with questions of social life, domestic details, peace and war. This part of the book may not inaptly be termed the legal section of the Qur'ān.

Muhammad's conflict with the Jews is as marked in this section of the Qur'ān as is his controversy with the Meccans in the earlier one. In Mecca his tone towards the Jews had been friendly. "Dispute not with the people of the Book except in kindly manner" (xxix. 45). In Madīna, being vexed that they cannot find, or refuse to admit, references to himself in their scriptures, he indignantly charges them with concealing the truth (cp. ii. 73; iii. 72; iii. 64; vii. 161). And when things had reached an extreme pass he utters the most terrible predictions concerning them: "O ye to whom the Scriptures have been given! believe . . . ere we efface your features, and twist your head round backward, or curse you. . . ." "Those who disbelieve our signs we will in the end cast into the fire: so oft as their skins shall be well-burnt we will change them for fresh skins, that they may taste the torment" (iv. 50 and 59).

Strained relations with the Meccans and doubts regarding the attitude of Arab tribes soon led to the sanction of fighting. Thus: "War is prescribed for you: but from this ye are averse"; and "Fight for the cause of God" (ii. 212, 245).

One chapter (xxxiii.) is concerned for the most part with the domestic affairs of Muhammad, overmuch of it indeed with his wives (see ver. 49). In this same chapter we find the phrase commonly used, "God and His Apostle." In Mecca he had stressed that he was a plain-spoken "warner" (cp. lxvii. 26); but in Madīna he demands that special deference be shown to him; "address not the Apostle as ye address one another" (xxiv. 63). Disobedience is not only an offence against God, but against "His Apostle" also (xxxiii. 36).

Contents and their Sources

The general design of the Qur'ān seems to be to unite the adherents of the three different religions then followed in Arabia, most of whom were idolaters, the rest Jews and Christians, in the knowledge and worship of the One Living God. For this purpose certain laws and ceremonies were sanctioned, some of them ancient, some quite new. At the head of this community stands Muhammad, combining in himself the double office of pope and prince, to whom all are obliged to render obedience since he has been sent of God to establish true religion, but not a new religion, on earth.

The above statement is fully borne out by a consideration of the contents of the Qur'ān; in particular, it can be shown how Muhammad incorporated into his system not only articles of faith but customs and ceremonies that had for long been associated with the religions of the peoples mentioned.

The Qur'ān, indeed, testifies to the fact that his critics observed this tendency and charged him with borrowing; The infidels say, "This Qur'ān is a mere fraud of his own devising, and others have helped him with it. . . ." And they say, "Tales of the ancients that he hath put in writing: and they were dictated to him morn and even" (xxv. 5, 6; cp. xvi. 103, 105; lii. 33; xxi. 5). Muhammad, however, rebuts the charges, declaring that the statements referred to have been "sent down" or "brought down," that is, by Gabriel.

1. There are elements in the Qur'ān from *pagan* sources.

(*a*) From the heathen Arabs Muhammad took over most of the ceremonies connected with the *hajj* (cp. xxii. 27 ff). The perplexity felt by some at such incorporation is illustrated by a remark attributed to 'Umar, the second Khalīfa who, in the act of kissing the Black Stone, ejaculated, "Verily I know that thou art a stone; thou dost no good or harm in the world; and if it were not that I saw the Prophet kiss thee, I would not kiss thee!" (*Mishkātu'l-Masābih*, Book 11, ch. iv., Pt. 3).

(*b*) From the Zoroastrians of Persia Muhammad incorporated, in somewhat modified form, conceptions of heaven and hell, judgment and reward. From this source come the *hūrīs*, or virgins of Paradise, and fables about the *jinn*.

2. A considerable amount of material comes from *Jewish* sources.

In a number of passages in the Qur'ān we find a curious likeness, and unlikeness, to narratives in the Old Testament. This is due to the fact that Muhammad had to do with Jews who had accustomed themselves to use not so much the Old Testament as the Talmud, which had been completed in the century before Muhammad. The apocryphal stories of this Talmud formed the basis of instruction in the Jewish schools of his day. Muhammad would have heard these stories rather than the Biblical narratives. There is more than one curious illustration of this fact in the Qur'ān; e.g., the story of Cain and Abel (v. 30-35), where a raven is sent which "scratched upon the ground" to show Cain how to dispose of his brother's body. There is nothing of this in Genesis, but in the Pirke Rabbi Eliezer, c. 21, it is to *Adam* that the raven shows the method of burial.

Whole chapters are devoted to Abraham (xiv.) and Joseph (xii.). With regard to the former it is repeatedly stated in the Qur'ān that he was cast into a *fire* because of his refusal to worship idols (see xxxvii. 95; xxi. 68-70; xxix. 23). Now this curious idea is found in a Jewish book called the Targum of Jonathan in reference to Gen. xi. 28, and xv. 7. The Jewish author took *Ur* (of the Chaldees), the name of a district, to be literally "fire," which is what the word itself means. The rest of the story in the Targum about Abraham being thrown into the fire for refusing to worship idols is a pure invention on the part of the Jewish writer, yet the Qur'ān has incorporated the whole thing!

Finally, words of undoubted Hebrew origin occur in the Qur'ān, e.g., *taurāt*, *jahannam*, *sabt*, *sakinat*.

Modern educated Muslims like the late Sayyid Amīr Alī of London, and the late Prof. S. Khuda Bakhsh of Calcutta, have themselves admitted that Muhammad drew some of his materials from these sources.

3. There is, on the other hand, surprisingly little in the Qur'ān from Christian sources, and most of that can be traced to apocryphal literature. This is most evident in the narratives concerning Mary, the mother of Jesus. The story that "they cast lots" as to who should be her guardian when she was a child (iii. 32-39) is recorded at length in the *Protevangelium of James the Less*, and in the Coptic work, *The History of the Virgin.*

That the pains of childbirth came upon her "by the trunk of a palm" (xix. 22-25) is part of a story recorded in an apocryphal work called *The History of the Nativity of Mary and the Infancy of the Saviour.*

The influence of the gnostic teaching of heretical sects is perhaps to be found in references made in the Qur'ān to the doctrine of the Trinity and the Crucifixion.

Some Special Features

1. *The Previous Scriptures.*—Muhammad's acquaintance with, and early respect for, the Jews and the Christians, to whom he gave the distinctive title *Ahl-i-kitāb*, or "the People of the Book," ensures a prominent place for their Scriptures in the pages of the Qur'ān. It declares that they were "given by God" (xxxii. 23; xvii. 56; v. 50); to be "a light and direction to men" (vi. 91) and calls them "the book of God" (v. 48) and "the Word of God" (ii. 70). But, as has already been indicated, there is little to show that Muhammad had any acquaintance with these Scriptures. The fact that he proclaimed that they contained predictions concerning himself (vii. 156; lxi. 6) rather goes to prove this. The Jews' unyielding repudiation of his claim led to a whole series of charges that they were in the habit of manipulating their Scriptures (ii. 56; ii. 72; ii. 73; iii. 64; iv. 48); by which he meant that they so furnished him with information from their book as to convey a different sense from that which its words intended.

2. *Former Prophets.*—The Qur'ān has much to say concerning the prophets; mention is made of some who would be unknown to "the People of the Book." These prophets and others, thousands in number, are also mentioned in the Traditions. Muhammad's idea was that men need guidance in the matter of faith, and that these prophets are sent from time to time with divine revelations. But this guidance is essentially the same

from the time of Adam to Muhammad. In other words, Muhammad does not claim to bring a new revelation. With wearisome repetition legends concerning the earlier prophets are told in the Qur'ān (xix. 50-64; xxxviii. 45 ff; xxxvii. 77 *et passim*; vi. 83-86). They form a long line, from Adam through Noah, Abraham, Lot, Ishmael, Moses, on to Jesus, and ending in Muhammad, who is declared to be " the Apostle of God, and the *seal* of the prophets " (xxxiii. 40).

3. *The Christology* of the Qur'ān is significant. A number of passages can be cited to show that the Qur'ān gives a place to Jesus the like of which is not accorded to any other prophet, not even to Muhammad himself. He is Mary's " holy son " (xix. 19; cp. iii. 31). He is " illustrious in this world and in the next " (iii. 40). He is " his (God's) word . . ." " and a spirit proceeding from Himself " (iv. 169). Adam is known among Muslims as *Safī-ullāh* (the chosen of God); Noah as *Nabī-ullāh* (the prophet of God); Abraham as *Khalīlu 'llāh* (the friend of God); Moses as *Kalimu'llāh* (one who speaks with God); Muhammad as *Rasūlu'llāh* (the messenger of God), but Jesus is here called *Kalimatu 'llāh*, the word of God (vii. 158).

And yet the most common title given to Christ in the Qur'ān is *'Isā ibn Maryam*, " Jesus, the son of Mary " (cp. v. 116; lxi. 6; iv. 157); as though Muhammad would popularise *this* name by way of protest against all that is implied in the phrase familiar to Christians, " Jesus, Son of God " (cp. also xliii. 59; v. 76-79).

The Qur'ān denies, too, that Jesus died upon the cross. It was only an " illusion," another was mistaken for Him (iv. 157). The fact is that Muhammad either could not understand or would not admit the wondrous love displayed on Calvary. A French poet of insight puts these words into the mouth of Muhammad:

> " In death I shall surpass Thee! Thy death was too sublime,
> O Jesus! for Thou gavest the victory to crime! "

Muhammad's anxiety to be considered "the seal of the prophets" led him to recast Christ's promise of the Paraclete so as to make it a prediction concerning himself: "Jesus, the Son of Mary said, O children of Israel! of a truth I am God's apostle to you to confirm the law that was given before me, and to announce an apostle that shall come after me whose name shall be Ahmad." (61, 6.) *Ahmad* and *Muhammad* are variant forms from the same root.

Chapter II

THE TRADITIONS—*SUNNA*

For the Arabs among whom Islām took its rise the Qur'ān provided simple legislation in regard to their social, political and religious needs, though even this was not systematised.

But as the Muslims extended their conquests and imposed the rule of Islām on peoples of other nations and other civilisations the limitations of this Quranic legislation became apparent.

The immediate successors of Muhammad were thus faced with a serious problem. On the one hand there was this clear demand for some enlargement and adaptation of the scanty dogmas of the Qur'ān to meet the needs of new peoples coming under their sway; while, on the other, they did not feel free to act in contravention of the recognised principle that in all matters of law and politics, as well as faith, the Qur'ān was to be the sole guide. Muhammad himself had been ruled by it, how could it be otherwise with his less divinely-guided successors, the Khalīfas? It was clear, however, that something had to be done, because the Qur'ān did not suffice; how, then, were its deficiencies to be supplied?

The solution they found has already been indicated above. Shortly after the Prophet's death an *oral* law came to be recognised, called the *sunna*, i.e., the "custom," or "usage," of the Prophet, according to which the sayings and practices of the "noble pattern" (33, 21) were made to do duty as a supplement to the Qur'ān. There is ground, however, for believing that Muhammad did not, in his lifetime, think of himself as infallible, nor look upon his utterances (other than those for which he claimed divine inspiration) as a sure and certain guide. A story concerning him confirms this view. It is recorded that he once ruined a date-crop by forbidding the owners to continue a long-established custom of artificial fertilisation of the palm trees. On seeing the disastrous result of his prohibitory order he is said to have confessed that he had spoken in ignorance. He was not, he explained, on that occasion delivering a revelation, hence his error. (*Mishkātu'l-Masābih*, Book 1, ch. vi., Part I.) Notwithstanding this, the requisite authority for his *sunna* was found in those injunctions in the Qur'ān where the believers are told to obey the Prophet as they would God Himself (e.g., xxxiii. 36; xlviii. 17; cp. xlvii. 2). Thus a new doctrine came to be formulated, according to which it was believed that the words and actions of Muhammad were under the control and inspiration of God and therefore authoritative. He was to be, in fact, the "noble pattern" in everything.

In the present chapter we shall consider the outstanding features of that body of literature called *Ahādīth* (plur. of *hadīth*), i.e., the Traditions of Islām. *Hadīth*, literally "communication" or "narrative," is an act or saying attributed to the Prophet (or to his Companions) to be used as evidence in justification and support of the *sunna*.

More precisely the Traditions are the records of,

1. What Muhammad did; what he declared; and that which was done in his presence and which he did not forbid.

2. They also include records of the conduct and sayings of the *Ashāb*, or "Companions" of Muhammad. Thousands of believers enjoyed the privilege of consulting the Prophet and thus earned the exclusive title of the "Companions." When no other guidance was forthcoming the agreement of these Companions came to be looked upon as infallible, since they too were the object of God's pleasure (xlviii. 18).

It goes without saying, then, that these Traditions are held in great respect throughout the Muslim world. Certain statements, preserved in the Traditions and alleged to have been made by Muhammad himself concerning such matters, ensure for them this high regard. We quote from the popular collection known as *Mishkātu 'l-Masābih*, Book I., ch. vi.:

"Verily the best word is the word of God, and the best rule of conduct is that delivered to Muhammad."

"That which the Prophet of God has made unlawful is like that which God Himself has made so."

"I have left you two things and you will not stray so long as you hold them fast. The one is the word of God, and the other is the *sunna* of His Prophet."

It will be as well to say here a word about the contents and scope of these Traditions.

A very large portion of them deals with legal provisions, religious obligations, such as the prescribed prayers and the rules appertaining thereto; fasting, alms, pilgrimage, and *jihād* (holy war); details concerning *farz* and *wājib* duties; things *halāl* (allowable) and *harām* (forbidden); ritual purity and laws regarding food; criminal and civil law, and concerning courtesy and manners. There are also sections on dogma—retribution at the day of judgment; Hell and Paradise; angels; the creation and revelation.

Interspersed among these are edifying sayings and moral teachings attributed to the Prophet. These have been separately edited in recent times and called the Table Talk of Muhammad.

But the Traditions served the further purpose of supplying a much-needed commentary on the Qur'ān, seeking amongst other things to reconcile its conflicting passages.

How the Traditions grew up

The manner in which these traditions came into existence can be readily imagined.

After the death of Muhammad, in the intervals of leisure on military campaigns, the thought and conversation of the Companions would naturally turn to recalling the acts and sayings of their remarkable leader who had put them in the way of becoming a conquering nation. As time passed the wonder of his achievement grew upon them until he himself came to be thought of as endowed with supernatural power.

But such an attitude of awe regarding Muhammad was still more marked in Muslims of a later generation who had never seen the Prophet and for whom his Companions themselves were objects of veneration. There are stories on record which clearly indicate this. Here is one.

"Is it possible, father of 'Abdu'llāh, that thou hast been with Muhammad?" asked a certain pious Muslim in the mosque at Kūfa; "didst thou really see the Prophet, and wert thou on familiar terms with him?" "Son of my uncle," came the reply, "it is as thou sayest." "Well, by the Lord!" exclaimed the ardent listener, "had I been alive in his time, I would not have allowed him to put his blessed foot upon the earth, but would have borne him on my shoulder wherever he listed."

It seems reasonable to suppose that the luxuriant growth of material embodied in the traditions took its rise under conditions similar to those we have described.

Fabrication

When we consider all the circumstances—this passionate demand for detail, the need for a more elaborate code of law, and the authority claimed for such sayings—it is not surprising to find that traditions were fabricated. The requirements of those early, exciting days brought into existence not only hundreds but thousands of hitherto unknown sayings and practices alleged to have originated from the Prophet. Every kind of story about Muhammad, false or true, was put into circulation until the thousands grew to hundreds of thousands. So notorious was the practice that Muslims themselves, as we shall see, do not deny, and never have denied, that gross fabrication went on.

Essential Features of Ahādīth

Strictly speaking a *hadīth* has two parts:

(1) The *isnād* (or *sanad*), i.e., the "support" for the trustworthiness of the statement. This *isnād* consists of the *names of persons* who have handed on the substance of a tradition to one another. Thus there is a chain of transmitters ending with the original authority.

(2) The *matn*, or "text" of the *sunna*.

The following may be taken as a specimen of a perfect *hadīth*:

'Abū Kuraib said to us that Ibrahīm ibn Yusuf ibn Abi Ishāq said to us from his father, from Abū Ishāq, from Tulata ibn Musarif, that he said, I have heard from 'Abdu'r-Rahmān ibn Ausajah, that he said, I have heard from Bara ibn Azib that he said I have heard that the Prophet said: "Whoever shall give in charity a milch cow, or silver, or a leathern bottle of water, it shall be equal to the freeing of a slave."

According to Muslim doctors a genuine tradition must possess a number of characteristics, the chief of which we shall proceed to quote. The narrator must have distinctly stated that such and such a thing had been said or done by the Prophet; the chain of narrators from the last link up to the Prophet must be complete; every one of the narrators must have been persons conspicuous for their piety, virtue and honesty, and every one of them must be well known for his learning; the import of the tradition must not be contrary to the injunctions of the Qur'ān, or to the doctrines deduced from it, or to such other traditions as are proved to be "sound."

The need for observing great caution in regard to

circulating traditions seems to have been felt by the older Companions of Muhammad. It is, for instance, recorded that 'Uthmān, when Khalīfa, issued orders as follows: "It is not permitted to anyone to relate a tradition as from the Prophet, which he has not already heard in the time of Abū Bakr and 'Umar. And, verily, nothing hinders me from repeating traditions of the Prophet's sayings (although I be one of those endowed with the most retentive memory among all his Companions) but that I have heard him say, "Whoever shall repeat of me that which I have not said, his resting-place shall be Hell" (*Wāqidī*, p. 168).

This mass of material, constituting a supplementary code of law, was for a long time oral in form. No attempt was made to preserve it in writing; it was committed to memory and transmitted orally. A teacher who had memorised a mass of traditions would recount them to a student, and in this way they were passed on to others.

It has been suggested in explanation of this method that the superstition prevailed that the Qur'ān would not tolerate any literature besides itself. Possibly, too, men were afraid lest such documents should become incorporated into the text of the Qur'ān.

Collection and Classification

We have already observed to what extravagant lengths the traditions grew. The next task was to collect them and finally scrutinise and classify them.

We are told that towards the close of the first century of the *Hijra* men developed a positive passion for searching out these traditions. They travelled from city to city and from tribe to tribe from one end of the Muslim world to the other, personally interviewing any surviving Companion of the Prophet, or their successors, in the hope of securing some fragment concerning his life.

But the business was too serious to be thus left to

private enterprise, and so we learn that the Khalīfa 'Umar II., about a hundred years after the death of Muhammad, issued orders for a more formal collection of all extant traditions.

The earliest compilation of which we have knowledge belongs to a date towards the end of the second century of the *Hijra*. The material thus amassed has been handed down both in the form of biographies of the Prophet, and in collections of traditions which bear upon every conceivable aspect of his life.

In compiling these collections the question of evidence assumed great importance.

Two main classes of Companions, or successors of the Prophet, took precedence in the transmission of the traditions.

1. The *Ashāb*, i.e., the actual Companions of the Prophet. The evidence of their own eyes and ears was considered sufficient.

2. The *Tābi'ūn*, or "successors," i.e., the people of the first generation after Muhammad, who are supposed to have got their information from the *Ashāb*.

There were other, less important, classes also.

Just as there are classes of the narrators of the traditions, so too there are well-known classifications of the traditions. Only the main groups need be mentioned here, viz., those that are:

1. *sahīh*, i.e., *sound*; traditions containing no weakness and no contradiction of current belief.

2. *hasan*, i.e., *fair*; a mediocre tradition, and not faultless since the narrators are not of the first class.

3. *za'īf*, i.e., *weak*, either because the contents are suspicious or because the authority is unreliable.

Some Famous Collections

It is significant that no official codification of these traditions has ever been made, though certain collections mentioned below are treated as of very high authority.

The method adopted in the earliest collections was to arrange the various traditions according to their *isnād*, from which fact they came to be called *Musnad*. In this compilation each *hadīth* was placed under the name of the person last named in the chain of attestors. Thus under the names of 'Āyesha, Fātima and Abū Huraira we have traditions that are ultimately traced back to these notable persons. One of the oldest and most typical *Musnad* is the six-volume work of Ahmad ibn Hanbal, the founder of one of the four orthodox "schools" of Muslim jurisprudence. This collection is said to contain about 30,000 *hadīth*, selected from 750,000, and traceable to 700 Companions.

The later collections, on the other hand, were for the most part arranged according to the subject-matter of the traditions, e.g., prayer, pilgrimage, war, food, the use of omens, the resurrection, hell, etc., and so were called *Musannaf*, or *digest*.

Six of these *Musannaf* collections, all dating from the third century of the *Hijra*, gained wide recognition and are to this day highly esteemed. These belong to: Al Bukhārī, d. 870; Muslim, d. 875; Abū Dāūd, d. 888; Al Tirmīdhi, d. 892; Al Nasāī, d. 915; Ibn Māja, d. 886. These go by the name of the *Sihābu's-sitta*, "the six sound" books, but the first two are held in very special esteem, for the reason that they only include traditions of the *sahīh* class.

Other collections appeared in course of time, but these are only compilations based on the works we have mentioned. The best known of these are the *Mishkātu 'l-Masābih* and that of *As-Suyūti*.

How far are the Traditions reliable?

We have it on the authority of some of the early collectors that in the second century of the *Hijra* tens of thousands of these traditions had not a vestige of truth in them. Some idea of the scandalous way in which the name of Muhammad was abused to give support to fabrications may be gathered from the fact that Bukhārī finally came to these conclusions; that,

(1) Out of 40,000 persons whose names had been used as "transmitters" only 2000 could be considered reliable.

(2) Out of 600,000 *hadīth* which he found to be current, only 4000 could be retained as authentic.

It is recorded that Bukhārī set himself this task of compiling an authentic collection as the result of a vision. He dreamed that he was "driving flies" off the person of Muhammad. An interpreter of dreams explained to him that he was destined to "drive lies" far from the Prophet!

Quite obviously the work of men like Bukhārī and others was not just another way of collecting the traditions, but an attempt to submit the accumulated mass to certain standards of criticism. Yet the moment we enquire into what those standards were it becomes equally evident that their efforts were inadequate and futile.

In the first place they never applied the principles of internal criticism to the *matn*, or text, of a tradition. If they could satisfy themselves that the *isnād*, or chain of narrators, was *sahīh* they passed the rest, even though the narrative was in itself improbable, impossible or absurd.

More precisely, their methods of criticism were wholly external; they confined themselves to scrutinising the genuineness of the *isnād*. But even here it can be shown that they failed to carry out their task, for although they sometimes did reject a tradition on the ground that the "chain" revealed chronological or other impossibilities, yet their courage seems to have largely failed them when it came to passing adverse criticisms on the transmitters themselves. While they might, and did, deal drastically with narrators nearer their own time, it was not a task to their liking to find fault with those wonderful men of an earlier age, the Companions of the Prophet and their immediate successors. It resulted in this, therefore, that for all practical purposes these Companions were exempt from criticism. But in a matter of this kind it is the upper end of the chain, the source, that requires the more rigid scrutiny, for defects there affect all that follows; but it was just at this point that they least applied their criticisms.

The significance of these remarks becomes apparent when we turn to enquire who the Companions were whose names stand at the upper end of the "chains." As a matter of fact nearly all the best of this select class died off between twenty and thirty years of the death of Muhammad, and we seldom find their names mentioned among the narrators. Instead, we find that the greater number of the traditions are attributed to the younger companions of the Prophet. We will mention those most frequently appearing.

Abū Huraira is made accountable for thousands of traditions, although he embraced Islām only four years before Muhammad's death, and during those years was an unknown youth.

Ibn 'Abbās, to whom also thousands of traditions are attributed, was only a lad of fourteen when Muhammad died, and was in contact with him for the last four years only.

Anas bin Malik, a man of no education, was only nineteen years old when Muhammad died.

Yet it has been estimated that more than half of even Bukhārī's selected traditions are attributed to these "lads." In the famous history of *Ṭabarī* (d. A.D. 923) Ibn 'Abbās is quoted 286 times, Abū Huraira 52 times, Anas bin Malik 47 times, whereas the first four Khalīfas are not quoted once!

There remains the name of 'Āyesha, Muhammad's favourite wife. Naturally no objection can be brought against her name on the ground of the brevity of her association with the Prophet, but she is notoriously partisan.

The conclusion to be drawn from these facts is that a seemingly correct *isnād* may possess very little objective value; least of all can we be sure that such Muslim narrators of the first generation are reliable. Notwithstanding these defects it needs to be said that all parts of these traditions are not equally liable to suspicion.

1. Those that deal with the more prosaic incidents of the life of Muhammad and the Companions are those which can be most readily credited. It would have served no one's interest to garble them. For this reason the Madīna period is much better vouched for than the Meccan, not merely because it was less romantic, but because it was witnessed by many more people. The traditions of the Meccan period and of Muhammad's early years are full of details of very uncertain validity.

2. The romantic incidents are much more open to doubt, while those telling of miracles are suspect if only because of the plain statement of the Qur'ān (xxix. 49). It is enough to know that this type of tradition is attributed to the group of four mentioned above. Not only was there a demand for such tales about the Prophet, but it seems to have been an accepted principle that, to quote the words of Ash-Shāfi'ī, "in glorifying the Prophet it is allowable somewhat to exaggerate."

3. The class of traditions attributing pious sayings to Muhammad is open to similar objection. Goldziher, the late eminent scholar, has shown, for instance, that a tendency prevailed in early times (it may have been an unconscious one) to draw a picture of Muhammad that should not be inferior to the Christian Church's picture of Jesus. So not his deeds only, but his words, also, must be brought into line with that standard. In this way sayings borrowed from the Old Testament and from the Gospels found their way, sometimes slightly altered in form, into the traditions. We may quote here a few examples of the last class which illustrate the general tendency.

"Verily God does not look on your outward appearance

or your possessions, but He looks at your heart and your actions."

"O God, place a distance between me and my sins as Thou hast placed a distance between East and West."

"Our Lord God, which art in heaven, hallowed be Thy name: Thy kingdom is in heaven and on earth. As Thy mercy is in heaven so show Thy mercy on earth. Forgive us our debts and sins."

Here is one from a rare variety of traditions, called *Hadīth Qudsī*, i.e., a holy tradition, in which, it is alleged, Muhammad received the substance of God's truth either by inspiration or in a dream and then clothed the idea in his own words.

"God said: I have prepared for my servants who are pious that which eye hath not seen nor ear heard, nor that which has entered into the heart of man."

There is a saying quoted in the introduction to Ibn Māja's collection and attributed to Muhammad, which fully justifies one's grave suspicion concerning this type of tradition, viz., "Whatever good word has been said, I said it."

4. There is a further class of traditions that deal with the domestic details of Muhammad's life. 'Āyesha is alleged to have furnished many of these. Scholars are averse to translating much of these as being unfit for publication. We are left to wonder how they ever came to be recorded.

5. There is a last class of traditions which we need to consider, those which supply the material for canon law. It is very noteworthy that the earliest school of systematic legists very largely dispensed with the traditions they found on *fiqh*, or canon law, for the reason that it was known that the most unblushing forgery had been practised in their production. Al Baghawī (d. about 1120), who was honoured as "a reviver of the *sunna*," confesses in the introduction to his *Masābih as-sunna* that the majority of traditions normative for *fiqh* depend on *hasan isnāds*, i.e., those of second-class authority.

Specimen Traditions

The compiler of the famous collection of traditions called the *Mishkātu'l-Masābih*, belonging to the fourteenth century, arranged his material under twenty-five main heads. We shall conclude our study by quoting a few at random from this collection. It is to be remembered that in each case the statement or custom is attributed to Muhammad.

" I am ordered to make war on men until they bear witness that there is no God but Allāh and that Muhammad is the Apostle of Allāh " (Bukhārī and Muslim *from* 'Umar).

" When anyone of you awakes from sleep and performs his ablutions, let him cleanse his nose three times, because verily Satan takes up his abode in the nose " (Bukhārī and Muslim *from* Abū Huraira).

" He who builds a mosque for God, God will build a house for him in Paradise " (Bukhārī and Muslim *from* 'Uthmān).

" The Black Stone came down from Paradise. It was whiter than milk, but the sins of the children of Adam have made it black " (Tirmīdhi *from* Ibn 'Abbās).

" When the Apostle of God, said 'Āyesha, wished to go on a journey, he used to cast lots amongst his wives, and would depart taking her with him whose name came out " (Bukhārī and Muslim).

" God has cursed the thief who steals an egg and his hand shall be cut off. And the hand of a thief who steals a rope shall be cut off " (Bukhārī and Muslim *from* Abū Huraira).

" Do not cut meat with a knife, for that is done by foreigners; but tear it with the teeth, for that is pleasanter and healthier " (Abū Dāūd *from* 'Āyesha).

" The Prophet, said Anas, forbade a man to drink in a standing position " (Muslim).

Chapter III

MUSLIM CANON LAW

We have previously remarked that the legislation of the Qur'ān is imperfect and that it failed to deal with numerous subjects on which early Muslims required rulings. Conversely, it may be said that of the elaborate system occupying many pages in Muslim books of law only the beginnings are to be found in the Qur'ān.

The Prophet's *sunna* was the first resort in seeking to supplement the Qur'ān, so that the course which the early Khalīfas decided to adopt was comparatively simple. All they had to do was to administer the law according to the opinions which they knew he had held. " In forming their (earliest) judgments they had no recourse either to speculation, to private opinion, or to arguments founded upon analogy. . . . When Islām was firmly established and its foundations strengthened, the more distant people received it by means of their adherents; but after a while that teaching suffered modification, and they had to *deduce* from the sacred writings maxims to apply to numerous cases which constantly came before the tribunals " (Ibn Khaldūn, *Muqaddama*). In other words, with the expansion of the empire and under new conditions of life questions arose about which Muhammad had given no explicit direction. In these circumstances recourse was had to the principle known as *qiyās*, or analogical reasoning.

The Principle of Qiyās

Justification for such a procedure might have been found in an incident recorded in the life of the Prophet.

Muhammad wished to send a man named Mu'adh to Yaman to receive some money collected for alms, which he was then to distribute to the poor. On appointing him, he said, "O Mu'adh, by what rule will you act?" He replied, "By the law of the Qur'ān." "But if you find no direction therein?" "Then I will act according to the *sunna* of the Prophet." "But what if that fail?" "Then I will make a logical deduction and act on that." Muhammad is reported to have raised his hand and said, "Praise be to God Who guides the messenger of His Prophet in what He pleases!"

Some illustrations of the application of this principle of *qiyās* may be given here. The Qur'ān says, "Thy Lord hath ordained . . . kindness to your parents. . . . Say not to them, 'Fie!' neither reproach them, etc." (xvii. 24 f). It is concluded from this that disobedience to parents is prohibited, and prohibition implies punishment if the order is disobeyed. Again, it is said in the Qur'ān that the maintenance of a woman who suckles an infant rests upon him to whom the child is born. From this the opinion is deduced that the maintenance of the infant also falls upon the father. The Qur'ān forbids the use of *khamr*, an intoxicating substance, and so it is argued that wine and opium are unlawful, even though not forbidden by name. The Wahhābis extend the prohibition to the use of tobacco also. Finally, there is a tradition which shows that Muhammad himself made use of this method of reasoning. "One day a woman came to the Prophet and said, 'My father died without making the pilgrimage.' The Prophet said, 'If thy father had left a debt what wouldst thou have done?' 'I would pay the debt.' 'Good, then pay this debt also.'"

Now this principle embodies the idea, held tenaciously by the orthodox, that in Islām a perfect law has been given, even to the details of religious, social and political life. In other words, it is believed that the teaching of Muhammad contains the solution of every difficulty likely to arise; that is to say, every law not provided can be, and must be, deduced analogically, and since all first principles are contained in the Qur'ān and the *sunna*, what does not coincide with them must be wrong.

From all of which it will have become clear that Islām is essentially a *legal* religion and that nothing is left to the believer's free will or initiative. The *sharī'at*, or Quranic law, supplies the Muslim with a family code, with penal and public law, and with guidance for his relations with non-Muslims. In fact, it aims at regulating all departments of his life. True, by this means there is produced and preserved a certain type of uniformity, but it is at the cost of intellectual liberty.

At this point another feature claims our attention. There was nothing to prevent the learned lawyers of those early days, when exercising this privilege of reasoning by analogy, from drawing conflicting conclusions from the available material.

Two sayings attributed to Muhammad indicate the way out of this dilemma. The first is: "My people will never agree in an error"; and the other, that "Disagreement is a mercy from God." These statements are manifestly contradictory, but they help us to understand further developments in the formulation of canon law in Islām.

The Principle of Ijmā'

When ambiguity arose, or in cases where the aforementioned three sources led to no solution, then the further principle of *ijmā'*, or unanimous consent, was made use of.

An interesting example of the exercise of this principle in its simplest form can be seen in the election of Abū Bakr to the Khilāfat. This act came to be spoken of as the *ijmā'-ul-ummat*, or the unanimous consent of the Muslim community. The "six books" of *hadīth* and the four schools of law also owe their official recognition to the *ijmā'* of the Muslim people. In general it meant that the *agreements* of leading theologians came to be recognised as a further "source" for law.

At first it seemed natural to conclude that such agreement should be found only in the opinions of the Companions of the Prophet and their successors, because, as the first disciples, they were supposed to have been directly trained by Muḥammad, and because all of them had lived in what came to be thought of as the golden age of Islâm. Some there were who restricted the principle to the *ijmā'* of the *Ashāb*, i.e., the Companions, including the four first Khalīfas. But in practice it was found impossible to limit its use to these.

Finally, in the absence of any text in the Qur'ān or the *sunna* or any ruling according to *ijmā'*, the compilers of the canon law sometimes made use of *ra'i*, or individual opinion, but this was considered an exceptional course to take and lacked the authority of the four foundations.

The Four Schools

It is not surprising that, with such sources to draw upon, and in view of the preference shown in the use of this rather than that "foundation," there should have sprung up different juridical "schools." Such a school was called *madhhab*, rite or guidance. In the beginning a variety of opinions prevailed because each man sought his own path. Thus some followed not so much the Qur'ān or *sunna*, but their own *ra'i*.

These different "schools" struggled to gain recognition, but disappeared one by one until, in the seventh century of the *Hijra*, it was agreed to recognise only *four*, viz., those founded by the famous *Imāms*, or leaders, Abū Hanīfa, Ibn Mālik, Ash-Shāfi'ī, and Ibn Hanbal. These *Imāms*, though manifesting certain individual peculiarities were all considered to be equally orthodox. They were reckoned to be *mujtahids* of the first class. The highest rank that a Muslim theologian could reach was that of a *mujtahid*, the conventional term for a learned Muslim who makes an *ijtihād*, or exertion; that is, one who *exerts* the faculties of his mind to the utmost for the purpose of forming an opinion in questions of law respecting a doubtful case.

The interest and importance attaching to these four men and their legal opinions will be apparent from the fact that it is the orthodox view, at any rate, that after them there has been no *mujtahid*. For instance, in a standard theological work current in India it is stated: "*Ijmā'* is this, that it is not lawful to follow any other than the four *Imāms*. . . ." "In these days the *qāzī* must make no order, the *muftī* give no *fatwa* (i.e., a legal decision) contrary to the opinion of the four *Imāms*. . . . To follow any other is not lawful" (*Dawabitu'l Furqān*, p. 17).

1. Imām Abū Hanīfa, who enjoys the greatest popularity, was born at Basra in 699, but spent the greater part of his life at Kūfa, dying at Baghdād in 776. Unlike Mālik, who lived at Madīna with its memories of Muhammad, Abū Hanīfa made little use of the traditions as the basis of his judgments. At Kūfa Islām came into contact with peoples of other races, and for them the one law was the Qur'ān revealed to Muhammad. Passages from the book could be quoted to prove the correctness of this assumption; e.g., "For to thee have we sent down the Book *which cleareth up everything*" (xvi. 91), and, "Nothing have we passed over in the Book" (vi. 38). If, then, a verse could not be found bearing on any given question, analogical deduction was resorted to, and this was done to such an extent that Abū Hanīfa came to be known as a master in the art of *qiyās*.

An example of the reasoning of the Hanafī jurists may be given. The Qur'ān says, "He it is who created for you all that is on earth" (ii. 27). This is taken to be a deed of gift which annuls all other rights of property. The "you" refers to Muslims. The "earth" is classified under three heads: (1) land which never had an owner; (2) land which had an owner and has been abandoned; (3) the person and property of the infidels. Arising out of the last interpretation these jurists deduce the lawfulness of slavery, piracy, and constant war against the unbelievers.

Abū Hanīfa admitted very few traditions as authoritative for his system, though his followers, the chief among them being his pupils Muhammad and Abū Yusuf, used them much more freely, and in consequence greatly modified his system.

2. Imām Ibn Mālik was born at Madīna in 711, and died there at the age of eighty-two. He so imbibed the spirit of the place that his system is founded on the "customs of Madīna." That city, indeed, was known as *dāru's-sunnu*, the abode of the customs, i.e., of Muhammad. Mālik made it his business to arrange and systematise such traditions as were current in the city of the Prophet, and to form out of them and the *sunna* a system of jurisprudence embracing the whole range of life. He called his treatise *Muwatta*, or the Beaten Path. It draws largely on the legal maxims and opinions delivered by the Companions. The traditions were his delight. It is said that his one fear, as death approached, was lest he should have exercised at any time his private judgment, *ra'i*, in delivering a legal opinion.

3. Imām Ash-Shāfi'ī, related to the founder of the 'Abbāsid dynasty, was born in Palestine in 776. He was unrivalled for his knowledge of the Qur'ān, the *sunna*, and the sayings of the Companions. He carefully studied the systems of Abū Hanīfa and Ibn Mālik, and subsequently developed an eclectic system of his own. It was an attempt to reconcile the acute differences between the followers of those two systems. He and his followers at least succeeded in determining with greater exactitude the respective value of the four foundations, and in particular prescribed rules for the use of *qiyās*, which had been open to abuse.

4. Imām Ibn Hanbal was born at Baghdād in 780. His name has already been mentioned as the author of the *Musnad*, a collection of traditions. For a long time men only thought of him as a traditionist, so that when his followers sought recognition for his method as a separate juridical school they encountered opposition, and it was only after many a bitter struggle that this fourth "school" was accorded a place. The system as such was a deliberate and uncompromising return to traditionalism, and manifested a combative tendency. It adhered to the letter of the Qur'ān and the *hadīth*. Of the four schools it manifests the most hostility to *Sūfism*.

Such an attitude is to be explained by the fact that during Ibn Hanbal's day, under the Khalīfa Al Ma'mun, the followers of Abū Hanīfa were in favour. He thought these were carrying the principle of analogical deduction to dangerous lengths in their endeavour to please the Khalīfa. Consequently, fearing that the Faith would be undermined, he entirely discarded the principle of *qiyās*. On the other hand, he saw that the system set up by Mālik, founded on the *sunna* of Madīna, was inadequate to meet the needs of a rapidly expanding empire; but in seeking to establish his system on what he held to be the surer ground of the traditions he did not succeed in improving matters.

Characteristic Features of the Schools

The general tendencies of these schools can now be illustrated by a few examples of their rulings. There was the question, much discussed at the present time, as to whether it is permissible to translate the Qur'ān. All four schools are in agreement on the ritual and liturgical use of the Qur'ān, while Ash-Shāfi'ī expressly lays it down that the words used in prayer must be recited in Arabic. Abū Hanīfa, on the other hand, allows an exception to be made in the case of the foreigner who is incapable of pronouncing the Arabic. Then there is the allied question: "Is it lawful to *teach* the Qur'ān to non-Muslims?" an occupation that inevitably entails the translation of the text. The more liberal Abū Hanīfa sees no difficulty in the proposition. He relies on the *hadīth*, and here finds himself in apparent agreement with the ruling of the Hanbali school. Ash-Shāfi'ī contents himself with setting forth the arguments for and against, but Mālik is entirely opposed to the idea. He is just as uncompromising over the question of a complete translation of the Qur'ān. Ash-Shāfi'ī, as before, hesitates to make a definite pronouncement. The Hanafīs and Hanbalīs approve of interlinear versions, such as at present exist in Persian, Urdu, English, etc., or of a version in which the Quranic text in Arabic faces the translation, as is the case with the English translation made by Maulana Muhammad Ali, printed in England.

Their judgments in other matters reveal the fact that they are by no means always in agreement. For instance, in regard to the important question as to what should be done to prisoners taken in a time of *jihād*, we find that Abū Hanīfa rules that they should be condemned to death or slavery. Ash-Shāfi'ī, on the other hand, allows them to be freed on payment of ransom, or even without it. They differ, too, in their attitude to a Muslim heretic. Abū Hanīfa holds that before being condemned such must be invited to repent. But the Māliki school do not require this; both this school and the Shāfi'ī condemn the apostate, irrespective of sex, to death. Abū Hanīfa rules that the punishment for a woman heretic shall be, not death, but solitary confinement. Their disagreement shows itself also in matters where we should least expect it; e.g., in what was considered the legal duration of gestation. Compared with the other three *Imāms*, Mālik held the most extreme views, allowing the period to last as long as four years, thus permitting the absurd conclusion that a child born three years after its father's death can claim its inheritance in law. Such reasoning inevitably led to casuistry, encouraging the *'ulamā* to exercise their subtlety in the most fantastic fashion. All sorts of imaginary cases are discussed by them with the utmost seriousness; as, for instance, whether marriages with the *jinn*, genii, involve consequences affecting the law of inheritance. In this way a whole tradition of hypocritical laxity regarding the *sunni* law has been introduced, permitting believers to respect the letter in order the more easily to act contrary to its spirit.

However, these four *Imāms* are recognised to be of one mind on all the fundamental doctrines of Islām, and their "agreement" is enough to establish a general law which is binding on all *Sunnis*, that vast body of the orthodox to which the majority of the Muslims belong. It is the belief of the Sunnis, though in this the Shī'as differ, that there has been no first rank *mujtahid* since the time of the four *Imāms*. Such phrases as the following occur in the works of Muslim authors: "We are shut up to following the four *Imāms*." "It is of the grace of God that we are shut up to these four *Imāms*. God approves of this, and into this matter proofs and explanations do not enter."

Every Muslim is expected to belong to one of the four orthodox *madhāhib*, or schools, and to conduct himself in accordance with the *fiqh*, law, of that school. He is not necessarily bound to it for life; should he desire he may pass to another school. In the same family, for instance, father and son may belong to different schools.

The Position To-day

It has been agreed among the orthodox that, from the fourth century A.D., "the door of *ijtihād* is closed." All that the *'ulamā* may do is to attempt to interpret the *ijmā'* of the four *Imāms*. To them the faithful turn, when in doubt, for a solution of their perplexities and for a ruling on controversial points of doctrine. The written answers which they obtain are founded on (1) Quranic texts, (2) the *sunna*, (3) the doctrine of the four schools, and (4) *ijmā'*. This constitutes their *fatwa* or decision. The authors of these *fatwas* are called *muftīs*, i.e., givers of *fatwas*, and occupy a place of honour among the *'ulamā*. In Turkey the *'ulamā* are called *hoja*; in India, *mulla*.

But to this idea that all judgments are shut up to the *ijmā'* of a bygone age modern Muslims take the strongest exception. It is to them a crime committed against Islām by the *'ulamā* in the name of religion.

Adherents of the Hanafī school are found in Turkey, Central Asia and North India. They number approximately 130 millions. The Shāfi'is, who come next with 58 millions, were soon pushed out of their early home in Irāq and settled in Southern Arabia, East Africa, South India and the Indian Archipelago, Palestine, the Hejāz and Lower Egypt. Ash-Shāfi'ī's tomb is in Cairo, and in Al Azhar, the celebrated mosque of that city, his teaching is regularly expounded. The Mālikis now number 16 millions only, and are found in the West, in the Sudan and all Northern Africa (with the exception of Lower Egypt), and in the districts of Arabia bordering the Persian Gulf.

The system of Ibn Hanbal has almost disappeared. It is significant that there is now no *muftī* of this school at Mecca. His followers are said to number about 6 millions; they cherish his memory chiefly because of the importance he attached to tradition. For this reason the revolt of the Wahhābis, the puritans of Islām, in the eighteenth century brought about a temporary revival of Ibn Hanbal's system in Central Arabia. But the fate of the school is sealed.

It is no part of the purpose of this introductory study to deal with *fiqh*, the technical term signifying the science of Islamic law. During the course of this chapter we have indicated the scope of this branch of Islamic learning. It includes all manner of religious, ceremonial, civil, and criminal law. It is sufficient to state that its entire content is based on the four foundations of which we have spoken above.

SECTION III

THE FAITH AND PRACTICE OF ISLĀM

Chapter I

THE CREED

The central dogmas of Islām are two, viz., the Unity of God and the prophetic mission of Muhammad. These are enshrined in the brief and familiar creed: "There is no god but God; Muhammad is the Apostle of God." The whole of Muslim theology has been built up around these two beliefs, and though there have been varying expositions of Islamic doctrine and in consequence a great variety of sects, yet all Muslims agree to accept these two fundamental dogmas of the faith, and to repeat the creed in this brief form.

The words of this creed are whispered into the ear of the new-born babe; they form one of the first sentences taught to the growing child; pious Muslims love to recite them on all possible occasions, and desire that they shall be the last to fall from their lips ere they die.

We have already seen how the Qur'ān is the chief source for the Muslim *sharī'at*, or *law* in its widest sense, and it is from the Qur'ān that this short creed is formulated. But its two parts nowhere occur there together; they are taken from separate chapters (xlvii. 21, and xlviii. 29), a fact which serves to illustrate what we have said above, that the teaching of the book is in no way systematised. The task of drawing up the articles of faith and arranging the doctrines of Islām scattered through its pages was left to succeeding generations. In this and the following chapter we shall be studying the results of their labours.

Islām demands of believers (1) *īmān*, faith, and (2) *dīn*, "religion," in the sense of works or practical duties. In this chapter we shall deal with the first only.

Muslim theologians define *īmān* as "confession with the tongue and belief with the heart." This confession may be made in two forms:

1. "I believe in God, His Name and Attributes and I accept all His commandments"; and more fully,

2. "I believe in God, angels, books, prophets, the last day, the predestination by the Most High God of good and evil, and the resurrection after death."

1. The first article of faith is *belief in Allāh*, viz., "I believe in God," though by far the more familiar form in which this is expressed is the first part of the short creed; as though the Muslim were to say, "I believe there is no god but God."

The greatest possible stress is laid by the Muslim on this aspect of his belief in God, viz., His *unity*. This is the doctrine known as *tauhīd*. God "is singular, without anything like Him; separate, having no equal." The Qur'ān is never weary of reiterating the formula which expresses this unity, and the short two-verse chapter (cxii.) which has this for its theme is significantly appraised as equal to one-third of the whole book:

"Say; He, Allāh, is one.
Allāh is eternal.
He begets not, nor is He begotten:
And none is like Him."

This Arabic name for God was not, as is sometimes claimed, a new form revealed to Muhammad whereby he, first, preached the Divine unity among the Arabs. In pre-Islamic literature, Christian or pagan, *ilāh* is used of any god, and Al-ilāh (contracted to Allāh) was the name of the Supreme Deity. Centuries before the time of Muhammad Arabs called the Ka'ba *Bait-Allāh*. *Ilāh* is probably only a variant form of the Hebrew names for God: *El*, *Eloāh*, *Elohīm*.

A large part of Islamic theology is concerned with the problem of the relation between the essence of God's nature and His attributes, which number seven, *sifātu's-sab'a*. The following is a brief summary of these attributes (*sifāt*):

(*a*) Life (*Hayāt*). Allāh's existence has neither beginning nor end. If He so wills, He can annihilate the world in a moment, or recreate it in an instant. If all the infidels became believers, He would gain no advantage; if all believers became infidels He would suffer no loss.

(*b*) Knowledge (*'Ilm*). Allāh is omniscient. He has knowledge of all things, hidden or manifest, in heaven or on earth. Events past and future are known to Him. He is free from all forgetfulness, negligence or error. His knowledge is eternal: it is not posterior to His essence.

(*c*) Power (*Qudrat*). Allāh is Omnipotent. If He wills, He can raise the dead, make stones talk and trees walk, annihilate the heavens and earth and recreate them.

(*d*) Will (*Irāda*). Allāh can do what He wills, and whatever He wills comes to pass. Everything, good or evil, in this world exists by His will. He wills the faith of the believer, and the piety of the righteous; the unbelief of the unbeliever, and the irreligion of the wicked. All we do, we do by His will. The will of God is eternal, not posterior to His essence.

(*e*) Hearing (*Sama'*). Allāh hears all sounds. He hears without an ear, for His attributes are not like those of men.

(*f*) Seeing (*Basr*). Allāh sees all things, even the steps of a black ant on a black stone on a dark night: yet He has no eyes as men have.

(*g*) Speech (*Kalām*). Allāh speaks, but not with a tongue as men do. He speaks to some of His servants without the intervention of another, even as He spoke to Moses. He speaks to others by means of Gabriel, and this is the usual way in which he communicates His will to the prophets.

But about the exact nature of these attributes and

the extent of the knowledge of them to which men can attain, there was, and is, great argument. The ultra-orthodox strictly prohibit too close an enquiry. It is, indeed, said to be impiety to enquire into the nature of God.

Nevertheless, on the basis of various interpretations of a certain verse in the Qur'ān (iii. 5), involving a question of punctuation, opposing schools of theology arose in Islām. The more orthodox, sometimes spoken of as the *Sifātians*, held that the attributes of God are eternally inherent in His essence, without separation or change. Concerning certain terms applied to God in the Qur'ān which were causing technical difficulties—such as "hands," "eyes," "face"—this school attempted no explanation but just accepted them as they stood.

The *Mu'tazilīs*, or "separatists," on the other hand, rejected the idea that the divine attributes are eternal. They also rejected the attributes of hearing, seeing, and speech as being accidents proper only to corporeal existence. They interpreted the attributes as mental abstractions, with no real existence in the divine essence; thus the "hand" of God was to be understood as an expression of His power and favour.

For a time these rationalists flourished at Baghdād under Khalīfas of like mind, until a shrewd reformer named Al-Ash'arī arose and brought about their downfall. This he did by enlisting on the side of orthodox Islām all the dialectical skill of the *Mu'tazilīs*. Ever since then the principles and methods of Al-Ash'arī have dominated the greater part of the Muslim world.

It really comes to this, therefore, that, as the first half of the short creed itself unceasingly proclaims, the fundamental conception of Allāh among orthodox Muslim theologians is negative. He is unique, as well as a unit, and He has no relation with any creature that partakes of resemblance. He is defined, though not entirely, by a series of negations; a point of view that has crystallised into a popular refrain:

" Whatsoever your mind can conceive
That Allāh is *not*, you may believe."

We may arrive at some understanding of the Muslim conception of Allāh by a consideration of the significance of the ninety-nine names Islām gives to Him.

These are very commonly classified in two groups of attributes:

The " terrible " attributes—*asmā-ul-jalālīya.*

The " glorious " attributes—*asmā-ul-jamālīya.*

The " terrible " attributes receive the greater emphasis not only in the Qur'ān and in the Traditions, but in the daily life of orthodox Muslims.

An analysis of most of these names indicates that,

Seven of them describe Allāh's Unity and absolute Being;

Five speak of Him as the Creator, or originator of all Nature;

Twenty-four characterise Him as merciful and gracious (to believers). These are indeed " beautiful " names and are used often in the Qur'ān. The names " Merciful " and " Compassionate " occur in the well-known formula called *bismillāh* at the head of every chapter save one, viz., ix.;

Thirty-six emphasise Allāh's power and pride and absolute sovereignty—these are the " terrible " attributes;

Five reveal Him as hurting and avenging; He is a God who leads astray, avenges, withholds His mercies, and works harm (cp. vi. 39; xxxii. 22; xiii. 33; xlv. 22).

Four refer, in a special sense, to the *moral* qualities in Allāh.

Such a classification of these names shows that while Muhammad had a pronounced view of the " physical " attributes of God, his ideas concerning God's " moral " qualities were defective. For instance, the Qur'ān says that " God is the best plotter " (iii. 47; viii. 30).

The treatment of the subject of *sin* by Muslim theologians throws further light on the conception of God in Islām. *What Allāh forbids* is sin. In consequence, the Qur'ān repeatedly lays stress on things that are *halāl*, "permitted," and those that are *harām*, "forbidden."

Theologians divide sins into two main groups:

(*a*) *Kabīra*, or "great sins": murder, adultery, disobedience to God or parents, shirking *jihād*, drunkenness, usury, neglecting Friday prayers and the fast of Ramdhān, forgetting the Qur'ān after reading it, swearing falsely or by any other name than that of God, magic, gambling, dancing, shaving the beard, etc. Such sins can only be forgiven after repentance.

(*b*) *Saghīra*, or "little sins": lying, deception, anger, lust, etc. Sins of this class are easily forgiven if the greater sins are avoided and if some good actions are performed. As the Qur'ān says: "Observe prayer at early morning, at the close of the day, and at the approach of night; *for the good deeds drive away evil deeds*" (xi. 116).

But the sin of sins is a heresy, *shirk*, i.e., the sin of "associating a partner" with God. This in Islām is the unpardonable offence.

An Unitarian writer has observed: "Islām saw God but not man; saw the claims of Deity, but not the rights of humanity; saw authority but failed to see freedom."

2. *Belief in Angels.* God has angels whose great desire and business it is to carry out His behests. They are sexless and neither eat nor drink. Some are in heaven, some on earth, and of these some have charge of men and record their deeds. There are four archangels: *Jibra'īl* (Gabriel), the medium of inspiration; *Mīka'īl* (Michael), who sees that all created things are provided with sustenance; *'Izrā'īl*, who receives the souls of men when they die; *Isrāfīl*, who will blow the trumpet on the last day. All these angels are sinless, though

Iblīs, the Devil, was expelled from Paradise for refusing to do homage to Adam (xv. 30-32).

These angels intercede for men. It is commonly believed that on the right side of every man is an angel who records his good deeds, and on his left one who records his evil deeds. Two fierce black angels, by name *Munkar* and *Nakīr*, visit the corpse in the grave and interrogate it, demanding answers to these questions: "Who is thy Lord?" "What is thy religion?" "Who is thy Prophet?"

3. *Belief in the Books of God.* A Muslim is required to believe that various books of revelation have been sent by God through the instrumentality of Gabriel to the various prophets upon earth. The following are said to have received such books, though there is a difference of opinion as to how many each received:

Adam (ii. 35) and his son Seth;
Idrīs, i.e., Enoch (xix. 57); Abraham (lxxxvii. 19);
The *Taurāt* (Pentateuch) to Moses (xxxii. 23);
The *Zabūr* (Psalms) to David (xvii. 57);
The *Injīl* (Evangel) to Jesus (v. 50).

The Qur'ān, the last of all and "revealed" to the last of the prophets, Muhammad, is to be followed to the Day of Judgment.

There are four views current among Muslims concerning the authority of the earlier books:

(*a*) *tarfī'*, lit. "taking up"; that they were taken up again to heaven, e.g., Jesus is supposed, by some, to have taken the "Gospel" with Him at His Ascension.

(*b*) *tahrīf*, "act of corrupting"; by which it is understood that the O.T. and N.T. have been tampered with.

(*c*) *tansīkh*, "abrogating"; that the previous books have been abrogated by the advent of the Qur'ān.

(*d*) That the Qur'ān is itself a sort of compendium of all necessary teaching in the Scriptures of the Jews and Christians.

This, in effect, reduces the professed "belief in the books of God" to belief in one book only.

4. *Belief in the Prophets of God.* God has sent many prophets into the world. Adam was the first, Muhammad the last. If we were to believe the Traditions some 2,400,000 prophets and 315 apostles appeared, but the names of only 25 of these are mentioned in the Qur'ān (cp. vi. 84-86). Six of these, Adam, Noah, Abraham, Moses, Jesus, and Muhammad, being the heads of their respective dispensations, are given special titles, and by these titles they are commonly spoken of by Muslims (*vide* p. 69). These are the greatest and most exalted of the prophets.

Muslim theologians observe a distinction between one who is a *nabī* and a *rasūl.*

A nabī, prophet, receives the highest form of inspiration (*wahī*), but has not necessarily to deliver the message he receives.

A *rasūl*, apostle or messenger, not only receives this form of inspiration but, in addition, is commanded to deliver God's message to men. Thus every *rasūl* is a *nabī* but not every *nabī* is a *rasūl.*

There are degrees of rank among the prophets (xvii. 57), Muhammad's being the highest of all. He is, in the words of the Qur'ān, *Khātimu'n-nabīyīn*, "the seal of the prophets" (xxxiii. 40); the last and the best.

A popular book on prayer, while expatiating on the value of the prayers offered in a mosque five times daily, incidentally bears witness to this notion of varying rank. Thus:

Morning prayer	=	20	pilgrimages	to Mecca	in the	company of	Adam.
Noon	" =	40	"	"	"	"	Abraham.
Afternoon	" =	60	"	"	"	"	Noah.
Sunset	" =	80	"	"	"	"	Jesus.
Night	" =	100	"	"	"	"	Moses.
Friday	" =	1000	"	"	"	"	Muhammad.

Each prophet is said to have been sent to his own tribe, whereas Muhammad was sent to all men. There is a tradition to the effect that Muhammad said, "I was raised up for all men, whether white or black."

It is the orthodox belief that the prophets are free

from sin. The view of the *Ash'arians* was that the power of sinning is not created in them, but the *Mu'tazilīs* deny this and say that they possess some inherent quality which keeps them from sinning. The most that any Muslim will admit is that some prophets, before their call, may have committed some of the "little" sins. They refuse to admit that any one of them ever committed one of the "great" sins, and consequently are caused a certain amount of perplexity by the testimony of the Qur'ān. There it is clearly stated that five of the six outstanding prophets were guilty of actions that required the forgiveness of God (cp. vii. 18-24; xi. 47-49; xxvi. 82; xxviii. 15). The one exception is Jesus, a distinction supported also by the Traditions. Bukhārī and Muslim commenting on iii. 31, say: "There is no child born but Satan touches it at its birth and therefore it cries at the touch, except Mary and her son." (Sahīhu'l Bukhārī, iii. 194; cp. Mashāriqu'l-Anwār, No. 929).

5. *Belief in the Resurrection and the Day of Judgment.* We shall consider these two articles of the creed together.

Four outstanding features characterise the Muslim view of the last things.

(*a*) *The sounding of the Trumpets.*

It is recorded that Muhammad said, "The last hour will not be till no one is found who calls on God." *Isrāfīl* will give "a blast on the trumpet, and all who are in the Heavens and all who are in the Earth shall expire, save those whom God shall vouchsafe to live. Then shall there be another blast on it, and lo! arising they shall gaze around them" (xxxix. 68). But some say that *Isrāfīl* will give three blasts; the first to terrify, the second to slay, the third to quicken the dead. The resurrection of the body is mentioned or suggested in several passages in the Qur'ān (xvii. 52; xxxvi. 79): but Muhammad did not know just when all this would take place.

According to the *ijmā'* of the learned, anyone who

doubts this article of the creed is an infidel. They are not agreed, however, as to the state of the soul during the time when the body is dead, nor concerning its revival. Muhammad will come first in order at the resurrection and will be the first also to enter Paradise.

(*b*) *The descent of the Books.*

After the resurrection men will wander about for forty years, during which time the books, which contain the records kept by the recording angels, will be given up. Men will rise up naked and confused; some will walk about, some stand for forty years looking up towards the heavens awaiting the books. They will perspire profusely through excess of sorrow. Each book will be given to its owner, into the right hand of those who are good, and into the left hand of those who are wicked. As the Qur'ān says, "Every man's fate have we fastened about his neck: and on the day of resurrection will we bring forth to him a book which shall be proffered to him wide open: 'Read thy book: there needeth none but thyself to make out an account against thee this day.'" (xvii. 14; cp. verse 73, and lxxxiv. 10-14).

(*c*) *The Scales.*

No Muslim can doubt this article of the creed since it is based on the Qur'ān, the *sunna*, and *ijmā*'. The Scales contain the good and bad deeds of men. The good deeds are "heavy," the bad deeds "light." The fate of the doers, both good and evil, is expressly stated in the Qur'ān (xxiii. 104-6; cp. vii. 7, 8).

Prophets and angels and, according to some authorities, believers also will be exempt from this trial. The Qur'ān makes frequent reference to the fire of hell, and popular books on the subject dilate on the awful torments of the doomed.

Hell has seven divisions, each with a distinctive name, purpose and terrors.

(1) *Jahannam*, the Muslims' purgatory; (2) *Laza* is the fire for Christians; (3) *Al Hutamah*, for the Jews; (4) *Sa'īr*, for the Sabeans; (5) *Saqar*, for the Magi; (6) *Al-Jahīm*

is the huge hot fire for idolaters; (7) *Hāwia* is the bottomless pit for *munāfiqīn*, hypocrites.

(*d*) *The Bridge.*

When the foregoing tests are concluded, a very narrow bridge, *sirāt*, lit. "road," has to be crossed (xxxvi. 66; xxxvii. 22-3). Concerning this the Prophet is reported to have said: "There will be a bridge sharper than the edge of a sword, finer than a hair, *suspended over hell.* Some will pass over it in the twinkling of an eye, some like a flash of lightning, others with the speed of a swift horse. The angels will call out, "O Lord, save and protect!" Some Muslims will be saved, some will fall headlong into hell, and afterwards be released. The infidels will all fall into hell and remain there for ever.

There is a wall, *Al A'rāf*, situated between heaven and hell. Persons whose fate is doubtful will sit thereon. They will look to heaven but will not be admitted; to hell and beg not to be sent thither. This subject gives the name to the seventh chapter of the Qur'ān (cp. vii. 44-5).

The *mushrik*, or one who ascribes plurality to God (*shirk*), will remain in hell for ever, because the offence and its punishment are alike eternal (xcviii. 5).

Muslims who commit the "great" sins, though they die unrepentant, will not remain in hell for ever on the basis of a verse in the Qur'ān, which says: "Whosoever shall have wrought an atom's weight of good shall behold it" (xcix. 7). Or, as Al Ghazāli puts it: "There will not remain in hell an attester of God's Unity . . . there shall not abide eternally in the fire a single believer" (*Ihyā 'ulumu'd-dīn*, Book II, Sect. 1).

On the other hand, the *Mu'tazilīs* teach that the Muslim who enters hell will remain there for ever; that the person who, having committed the "great" sins, dies unrepentant, *though not an infidel*, ceases to be a believer and hence will suffer as infidels do, but more lightly. Al-Ash'ari, however, says: "The sinner who dies unrepentant is at the mercy of God, but the Prophet will intercede for him, as he said: "My intercession is for those among my people who commit great sins" (Shahrastāni, *Al Milal wa'n-Nihal*, p. 73). Accordingly, it is the belief of the orthodox that Muhammad is now an intercessor on their behalf and that he will be on the last day.

The signs of the last day are several, e.g.:

(*a*) The appearance of *Dajjāl*, or Anti-Christ;

(*b*) The decay of faith on the earth;

(*c*) Tumults and seditions; war with the Greeks and Romans;

(*d*) The rising of the sun *from the west*;

(*e*) The second advent of Christ. As the Qur'ān has it: "Jesus is no more than a servant whom we favoured . . . and he shall be a sign of the last hour" (xliii. 59-61). It is believed that he will return to destroy *Dajjāl*, and will descend near the mosque at Damascus at the time of the afternoon prayer. He will re-establish Islām, live for forty years, and be buried at Madīna.

Popular treatises have vivid descriptions of heaven, (*Jannat*), which is described by at least eight names. Its sensual delights are portrayed in detail in these books. According to Tirmīdhi, the Prophet is supposed to have stated that there are one hundred degrees of felicity in heaven.

6. *Belief in the Predestination of Good and Evil.* The believer is required to confess that good and evil take place by the predetermination of God; that all that has been and all that will be was decreed from eternity.

Should any ask why God willeth and produceth evil, one can only reply that He may have wise ends in view which man cannot comprehend.

This whole subject has been hotly debated in Islām, giving rise to three well-defined schools of thought.

(*a*) The *Jabarīans* (from *jabr*, compulsion), who deny all free agency to man. God is responsible for all his actions.

(*b*) The *Qadarīans*, who deny *al-qadr*, or God's

absolute decree. These say that evil and injustice ought not to be attributed to God, but to man, who is altogether a free agent.

(*c*) The *Ash'arians* hold that God has one eternal will. In this they agree with the *Jabarians*. Nevertheless, they allow some power to man. This they call *kasb*, or acquisition, because when God wills a thing the man *acquires* (by a creative act of God) the power to do it. The orthodox Muslim is thus inevitably a fatalist.

CHAPTER II

RELIGIOUS DUTIES

ALONG with such "faith" there are certain "works" that are binding on the believer. These religious duties are *five* in number and because of their importance are known as *arkānu'd-dīn*, or "the pillars of religion."

1. *Tashahhud*, reciting the *Kalima*, a confession of faith.
2. *Salāt*, or *namāz* (Pers.), reciting the daily prayers.
3. *Saum*, or *roza* (Pers.), observing fast.
4. *Zakāt*, the giving of alms.
5. *Hajj*, undertaking the pilgrimage to Mecca.

All these are *farz*, or obligatory duties, based on definite instructions in the Qur'ān or the *hadīth*.

There are, besides, other duties which good Muslims should perform, but these are *wājib*, "necessary" rather than "obligatory." Some of these are:

(*a*) Undertaking the *'umra*, or lesser pilgrimage to Mecca.

(*b*) Obedience of a wife to her husband.

(*c*) Giving alms after a fast.

(*d*) Offering the Baqr-'Īd sacrifice.

(*e*) Reciting an extra prayer—*salātu'l witr* (i.e., three *rak'ats* after the obligatory night prayer).

(*f*) Supporting one's relatives.

Of these (*c*) and (*d*) are *wājib* for the rich. If performed by the poor they are styled *mustahabb*, "meritorious."

There are still lesser duties, based on the practice either of Muhammad or of previous prophets and "permitted" by Muhammad, e.g. (*a*) circumcision; (*b*) shaving off the hair from the head and body; (*c*) paring the nails.

In this chapter we shall deal only with the five "pillars."

1. *Tashahhud*, or *Shahādat*. This word comes from a root meaning "testify" and consists in a confession such as this: "I testify that there is no god but God; I testify to His Unity and that He has no partner: I testify that Muhammad is His servant and His messenger"; or more briefly the confession may be made in the words of the *Kalima*: "There is no god but God; Muhammad is the Apostle of God."

2. *Salāt* (*namāz*). Before a Muslim recites his prayers certain ablutions are prescribed which must be performed. These are of three kinds:

(*a*) *wazu*, the lesser ablution; (*b*) *ghusl*, the greater ablution, and (*c*) *tayammum*, a special purification by sand, in the absence of water.

(*a*) *wazu* is the ablution made before the appointed five daily prayers in accordance with four rules. Thus the following parts of the body are to be washed with water:

(1) The *face*, from the top of the forehead to the chin and as far as each ear;

(2) The *hands* and *arms*, up to the elbows;

(3) A fourth part of the *head* is to be rubbed with the wet hand;

(4) The *feet* up to the ankles.

The Shi'as, on the other hand, only wipe or rather rub the feet.

It is commonly believed that if any portion of the specified parts of the body is left unwashed, the subsequent prayer is robbed of all value. Nor is the performance of *wazu* quite so simple as it looks. Bound up with these four main rules are fourteen minor ones based on the *sunna* of the Prophet. Here are a few: To utter one of the names of God at the commencement; to clean the teeth; to rinse the mouth three times; to put water in the nostrils three times; to observe the proper order in washing the parts of the head and body; the space between the fingers of one hand must be rubbed with the wet fingers of the other; the beard must be combed with the fingers; to rub under and between the toes with the little finger of the *left* hand, drawing it from the little toe of the *right* foot and between each toe in succession, finishing with the little toe of the left foot.

The "little sins" are forgiven after such *wazu* followed by prayer. Muhammad is reported to have said, "He who makes *wazu* according to my *wazu*, and then makes two *rak'ats* (i.e., recites two sections in prayer), without being defiled between, all his former (little) sins will be forgiven" (*Sahīhu'l Bukhārī, kitābu'l-wazu*).

(*b*) *Ghusl* on the other hand is a bathing of the whole body after certain legal defilements. In this case water must be poured three times over the right shoulder, three times over the left, and finally three times on the head. Besides this there are three *farz* regulations: the mouth must be rinsed; water must be put in the nostrils; and the whole body must be washed. Not one hair must be left dry in the process.

(*c*) *Tayammum*, or purification by sand, is prescribed for special circumstances, viz., when water is not procurable within two miles; when one is sick and the use of water might be dangerous; when water cannot be obtained without encountering danger from an enemy, wild beast or reptile; when a person, delayed by some festival or funeral, has not time for the ordinary ablutions.

The sand is struck with open hands, and then the mouth and other parts are rubbed with them.

Having performed the necessary ablutions, the worshipper is ready and can proceed to recite the prescribed prayers. These may be said in private or in public, but those said in a mosque are more meritorious. The person and his clothes must be clean, and his face turned towards the *mihrāb*, or niche in the back wall of the mosque indicating the direction of Mecca. Prayer in a mosque is preceded by the *adhān*, or "call to prayer," which is loudly chanted by the *mu'adhdhin* from high up in a minaret of the mosque. This *adhān* sounds forth five times a day and is composed of short sentences which elicit similarly worded or appropriate "responses," sentence by sentence, from intending worshippers within hearing. Thus the *mu'adhdhin* calls out: "God is great; I confess that there is no god but God; I confess Muhammad is the Apostle of God; come to prayer; come to do good"; (and, in the morning, "prayer is better than sleep"); "God is great; there is no god but God."

During the course of the prayer certain postures are assumed and genuflexions made by the worshipper according to prescribed rules. The prayers themselves are a recitation, in Arabic, of certain passages from the Qur'ān, more especially the concluding short chapters, also the *Fātiha*, the opening chapter, together with some ascriptions of praise to God.

At prescribed intervals during the recitation of these prayers the worshipper utters the *takbīr*, or ascription of greatness to God (viz., *Allāhu Akbar*), followed by a prostration with forehead touching the ground. A completed portion of the prayers is a *rak'at*, and the worshipper offers two or more according to his originally declared *niyyat* or "intention."

At the conclusion of the *rak'ats* the worshipper says the *durūd*, or prayer for Muhammad, thus:

"O God! have mercy on Muhammad and on his descendants, as Thou didst have mercy on Abraham and on his descendants. Thou art to be praised and Thou art great," etc.

He then turns his head first to the right and repeats the *salām*, or salutation, to the assembled congregation, "The peace and mercy of God be with you"; then to the left with the same words.

A very beautiful gesture marks the conclusion of the prayer. Raising his hands as high as his shoulders, with palms upturned to heaven, the worshipper offers up a *munājāt*, or supplication, either in Arabic or in his own words, and then draws his hands over his face and on to his breast as if to convey the blessing received to every part of his body.

Tradition, and not the Qur'ān, has fixed the number of obligatory daily prayers as *five*; these are named and defined as follows:

Fajr, at dawn, before sunrise.
Zuhr, soon after midday.
'Asr, mid-afternoon.
Maghrib, soon after sunset.
'Ishā, after nightfall.

There is also a class of prayers styled *nafl*, "voluntary." The prayers on *Jum'a*, Friday (the Muslim Sabbath) take the place of ordinary prayers and are preceded by a *khutba*, or address delivered by the *imām*.

3. Saum (*roza*), or fasting; in particular during the days of the month called *Ramdhān*. Fasting is defined as abstinence from food and drink, perfumes, tobacco, conjugal relations, during the hours between sunrise and sunset. Meals are to be taken at night. One purposing to keep the fast says: "O Lord, I intend to fast to-morrow for Thy sake. Forgive my past and future sins."

On the conclusion of the fast he prays: "O God, I fasted for Thy sake and had faith in Thee, and confided in Thee, and now I break the fast with the food Thou givest. Accept this act."

It is a *farz* duty to fast during the month of *Ramdhān*. Young children and idiots are excused, while the sick and those on a journey may postpone it to another time.

There are other fasts also, such as that on the tenth day of the month of Muharram, but these are *nafl*.

The fast of *Ramdhān* is commenced with the first observance of the new moon marking the opening of the month and is rigidly kept; when, in the course of rotation, *Ramdhān* falls in the heat of summer the fast can be a severe trial to both body and temper.

Certain acts render the fast invalid: e.g., if, when cleansing the teeth, a drop of water should pass down the throat; if food is eaten under compulsion; if medicine is put into the ear, nose, or even on to a wound in the head; if a meal has been taken on the supposition that it was night-time; if after the night meal a portion of food larger than a grain of corn should remain between the teeth or in a cavity of a tooth; if food is vomited. In all such cases another fast must be kept.

Where the fast is wilfully broken certain alternative penalties are prescribed; the delinquent must atone by setting free a slave, or fast every day for *two* months, or give sixty persons two full meals each, or give one man two such meals for sixty days.

The aged and infirm must, in lieu of the fast, feed some poor person. In the case of women with child and mothers suckling a child and also sick persons, it is required that they keep the fast at some other time.

The fast is broken on the last day of *Ramdhān* after the sun has set, with a very light meal called *iftār*, lit. "breaking fast." Often a little water is drunk, or a date eaten.

4. *Zakāt.* In Islām two terms are used for alms-giving.

(1) *Zakāt*, i.e., legal alms; this is due, subject to certain conditions, from every Muslim; (2) *sadaqa*, or "offerings" made at the time of the festival known as *'Īdu'l-Fitr* at the end of *Ramdhān*, or just alms in general. We shall in this place deal only with *zakāt*.

It is a *farz* duty for every Muslim of full age to give *zakāt* on account of his property, provided he has sufficient for his own substance (ii. 40, 77, 104). The three conditions without which *zakāt* would not be compulsory are: that a person should be (1) in Islām; (2) a free man; (3) the possessor of *nisāb*, i.e., the fixed amount of "property." The amount of this varies according to the nature of the thing possessed.

When one's stock is required for daily use, such as grain for food, implements for work, the *zakāt* is not taken from it. Again, if a person owes a debt, the amount of the debt must first be paid, and the alms are to be paid from the balance. On the other hand, if a debt is due to God as the result, say, of a vow or in atonement for the neglect of some religious duty, it must *not* be deducted from the "property" on which *zakāt* is due.

As regards *cattle* the following rules are laid down; of sheep and goats nothing is given if the total number is less than 40. The owner has to give one for 120, two for the next 80, and one for every 100 after. While buffaloes are classed with sheep, the rules for camels, horses and cows are very intricate. Donkeys and mules are curiously exempt on the strength of a statement attributed to Muhammad: "There has not been sent down to me anything particularly about asses" (*Mishkātu 'l-Masābih*, Book 6, chap. i., Part I.).

This *zakāt* is to be presented to certain classes of persons as indicated in the following passage in the Qur'ān: "Alms are only for the poor," (i.e. paupers), "and the needy" (i.e., those in temporary distress), "and those who collect them, and for those whose hearts are made to incline" (i.e., to Islām), "and for ransoms, and for debtors, and for the cause of God and the wayfarer. This is an ordinance from God, and God is Knowing, Wise" (ix. 60).

It is of interest to note that the Khalīfa Abū Bakr abolished this giving of *zakāt* to converts, and the Khalīfa 'Umar said to some such persons, "This *zakāt* was given to incline your hearts towards Islām, but now God has prospered Islām." No Companion has denied this statement, by which we conclude that on the authority of the *ijmā'* of the community this order is "suspended."

Zakāt may be given to a slave to enable him to purchase his freedom, or to enable a poor person to undertake the *hajj*. Such care for their own poor is a prominent characteristic in many Muslims.

But *zakāt* must *not* be used for the building of mosques, funeral expenses, or for liquidating the debts of a deceased person; neither is it permitted to give it to parents or grandparents, children or grandchildren.

5. *Hajj*. Finally there is the *hajj*, or pilgrimage to Mecca.

This is a *farz* duty as laid down in the Qur'ān: "Proclaim to the peoples a pilgrimage: let them come to thee on foot and on every fleet camel . . . let them pay their vows, and circuit the ancient house" (xxii. 28, 30), also, "The pilgrimage to the temple is a service due to God from those who are able to journey thither" (iii. 91).

Baidhāwī, the famous commentator, says that the words "are able" were interpreted by the Prophet to mean the possession of food for the journey, and an animal to ride on. Imām Ash-Shāfi'ī concluded from this that if a man could not go himself he might send a substitute. Ibn Mālik held that if any man could walk and keep himself on the way, he must go. The Prophet is reported to have said that it is only necessary to make the pilgrimage once, any additional pilgrimages to the holy city are *nafl*. On the other hand, if a slave, while a slave, makes the pilgrimage he must make it again on obtaining freedom. So, too, if a child makes it, he must go again on coming of age.

Into the intricate prescriptions for the due performance of this pilgrimage we cannot enter here. It must suffice to note the three actions that are *farz*, and five that are *wājib*. The pilgrim is obliged:

(*a*) To wear no other garment except the *ihrām*; i.e., seamless garments specially reserved for the purpose. One of these is worn round the loins, the other is thrown over the shoulder. The head is left uncovered.

(*b*) To stand on Mt. 'Arafāt.

(*c*) To make the *tawāf*, or circumambulation of the Ka'ba seven times.

The *wājib* duties are:

(*a*) To make halts (*wuqūf*) in the outlying sanctuaries of Muzdalifa and Minā, with a sacrifice at Minā.

(*b*) To run along the course between Mt. Safā and Mt. Marwa.

(*c*) To perform the ceremony of casting pebbles at the pillar representing Satan.

(*d*) To make an extra *tawāf*.

(*e*) To shave the head at the conclusion of the pilgrimage.

The pilgrimage must be made in *Dhu'l-Hijja*, the twelfth month of the Muslim calendar.

During the circumambulation of the Ka'ba the pilgrim is expected to kiss the Black Stone, which is let into one of its walls. If on account of the crowd he cannot get near enough he must touch it with his hand, or with a pole, and kiss that which has touched the stone. At this time he says: "O Allāh, I do this, in Thy belief, and in verification of Thy book and in pursuance of Thy Prophet's example. May Allāh bless and preserve him! O accept Thou my supplication, diminish my obstacles, pity my humiliation, and graciously grant me Thy pardon."

The entire ceremonies connected with this *hajj* have, as we observed above, been taken over with very little variation from Arab paganism.

The '*umra*, or lesser pilgrimage, is optional but highly meritorious. It is not restricted to any special time of the year. It comprises the same ceremonies and obligations, excepting the sacrifice, as the great pilgrimage, but is confined to the visit of the Ka'ba and the sanctuaries around Mecca.

Subsequently the pilgrim makes the *ziyārat*, or "visit," to the tomb of the Prophet at Madīna. Henceforth the pilgrim is known and respected as a *Hājī*, one who has made the pilgrimage.

Chapter III

MUSLIM HIGH DAYS

During the course of the calendar year a number of high days or "holy days" are celebrated by Muslims. Special historical significance attaches to these; some are festivals, occasions of joy; others are days of solemn recollection and even mourning. There is, however, a tendency for them to become public holidays.

1. Baqr-'Īd, "the Cow Festival," is the most important of the Muslim feasts. (It is also called *'Īdu'l-Azhā*, vulg. *'Īdu'z-Zuhā*; in Persia, *'Īd-i-Qurbān*; in Turkey and Egypt, *Bairām*; i.e., the Feast of Sacrifice.)

This is the "sacrifice" made by the pilgrims in connection with the ceremonies of the *hajj*, and referred to at the close of the preceding chapter. While the pilgrims assembled at Mecca are offering it as one of the concluding rites of the pilgrimage it is faithfully observed simultaneously by Muslims everywhere. The authority for this sacrifice is an injunction in the Qur'ān, xxii. 33-38.

Its origin is interesting. Soon after coming to Madīna Muhammad observed that the Jews kept their great fast of the atonement, on the tenth day of the seventh month, as a memorial of the deliverance of Moses and the children of Israel from the hands of Pharaoh. Those were the days when he was kindly disposed to the Jews, so he and his followers also kept the fast. But when, in the second year, his relations with them became strained he substituted this feast of *Baqr 'Īd.* He did more than that. Part of the ritual of the pagan Arabs during their annual pilgrimage to Mecca had been the offering of animals in sacrifice. Muhammad now made his newly-substituted feast to fall on the tenth day of the month of *Dhu'l-Hijja*, that is, at the very time when the Arabs were offering their victims near the ancient sanctuary. This is only another proof of his remarkable foresight.

Muslims believe that great merit accrues to all who keep the feast, and this is borne out by a well-known tradition credited to 'Āyesha. She reported that Muhammad once said: " Man has not done anything on the *'Īdu'l-Azhā* more pleasing to God than spilling blood; for verily the animal sacrificed will come, on the day of resurrection, with its horns, its hair, and its hoofs, and will make the scales of his (good) actions " heavy." Verily its blood reacheth the acceptance of God before it falleth upon the ground; therefore be joyful in it " (*Mishkātu'l Masābih*, Book 4, chap. 49, 2; but cp. with this Qur'ān xxii. 38).

According to the commentator Jalāl-ud-dīn Assuyūtī, this sacrifice was instituted in commemoration of Abraham's willingness to sacrifice his son *Ishmael.* The story as given by Muslim writers is somewhat as follows: When Abraham founded Mecca the Lord desired him to prepare a feast for Him. The Lord commanded him to offer up his son Ishmael. In accordance with God's direction Abraham took his son to a place near the Ka'ba to sacrifice him and made several ineffective attempts to cut his throat. Ishmael then said to his father: " It is through pity and compassion for me that you allow the knife to miss: blindfold yourself and then sacrifice me." Abraham acted on this advice, blindfolded himself, drew his knife, repeated the *bismillāh* (" in the name of Allāh ") and, as he thought, cut his son's throat: but he found to his surprise that in the meantime Gabriel had substituted a sheep for his son. There is nothing in the Qur'ān to connect this sacrifice, as Muslims do, with the history of Ishmael; the latter's name occurs in the *Hadīth Sahīh* of Bukhārī. Nevertheless, Muslim writers, generally, maintain that the son was Ishmael, not Isaac, and that the scene of the sacrifice was on Mt. Minā, near Mecca, and not in "the land of Moriah" as stated in Genesis xxii. 2 (cp. 2 Chron. iii. 1).

The usual celebration takes place as follows. Prayers are said at the *'Īd-gāh*, or place of worship for high days. This is a spacious enclosure outside the city set apart for an occasion like this in order that the whole Muslim population of the locality may join together in one joyful act of public worship. At the close of the service the worshippers, in happy mood, salute and embrace one another and then settle down to enjoy the rest of the day in feasting and merriment. It is an occasion when people bedeck themselves and their children in new clothes.

The sacrifice itself is offered on returning to their homes. It is a *wājib* duty that every Muslim should keep this feast and sacrifice an animal for himself. This may be a sheep or a goat. It is a common practice for a number of Muslims (not more than seven) to club together to sacrifice a large animal, like a cow or a camel, between them. The animal sacrificed must be without blemish or defect of any kind.

When all is ready the head of the family takes a sheep, or a cow, *baqr* (as is often done in India), or a camel, to the entrance of his house, places it to face Mecca, and sacrifices it by repeating the phrase *bismillāh Allāhu akbar*, while cutting its throat. Any other mode of slaying the victim is *harām*.

Particular reference is made to this "invocation" in the chapter of the Qur'ān prescribing the sacrifice: "And the camels have we appointed you for the sacrifice of God: much good have ye in them. Make mention, therefore, of the name of God over them when ye slay them" (xxii. 34).

The flesh of the animal is then divided, one-third being given to relatives, one-third to the poor, and the remainder reserved for the use of the family.

2. 'Īdu'l-Fitr, the "festival of the breaking of the

Fast" (i.e., of *Ramdhān*). It is also called *'Īdu's-saghīr*, the minor feast, to distinguish it from the Feast of Sacrifice, *'Īdu'l-kabīr*, the great feast. It commences as soon as the one-month fast of *Ramdhān* is over, or more precisely, on the first appearance of the new moon heralding the tenth month of Shawwāl. The appearance of the new moon is proclaimed by some prearranged signal, such as the firing of a cannon or maroon. It is a time of undisguised relief and rejoicing. Friends hail each other with exclamations such as, *chānd mubārak!* viz., "a happy moon" (to you).

The festival which is celebrated on the following day is characterised by alms-giving, when *sadaqa* or propitiatory offerings such as flour, fruit, etc., are made to the poor in the name of God. Having made these offerings the people forgather either in the principal mosque, or as in the case of the great feast, at the 'Īd-gāh. When the congregational prayers are completed the *imām* takes his place on the second step of the *mimbar*, or pulpit, and recites the *khutba*. At the conclusion of the sermon he offers a *munājāt*, or supplication, in which the people join, for the remission of sins, the recovery of the sick, increase of rain, abundance of corn, preservation from misfortune, and freedom from debt. Feasting and merriment mark this day also.

3. Bāra Wafāt (i.e., *bāra*, "twelve," and *wafāt*, "death") is a festival observed in India (but not generally elsewhere) on the twelfth day of the third month *Rabī'u'l-Awwal.* It is a curious fact that Muhammad is believed by some to have been born and by others to have died on this day of the month.

(*a*) *Bāra Wafāt*, then, is in commemoration of his death. On the previous evening perfumed embrocation is made from sandal wood. This is placed in a vessel and carried in procession to the 'Īd-gāh, or to some other place where the *Fātiha* (the words of the first chapter of the Qur'ān) is said over it. It is then distributed to the people. This evening ceremony is a sort of public notice that on the morrow the feast day will be celebrated with the usual *'urs*, i.e., prayers and offerings. On the morning of the twelfth the Qur'ān is read in the mosque or in private houses; then food is cooked and *fātihas* are said.

Some persons possess a special stone, called *qadamu'r Rasūl*, or stone with an impress of the Prophet's footstep. On this day the place in which it is kept is elegantly decorated. People assemble in the house for a special ceremony, when selected persons recite the story of the birth, miracles, and death of the Prophet. Portions of the Qur'ān also are read and the *durūd* is repeated. The Wahhābis, a puritan sect, do not observe the *Bāra Wafāt* as it is not enjoined either in the Qur'ān or the *Hadīth*.

(*b*) It is becoming increasingly common in India to celebrate on this day the *birthday* of the Prophet, as is done in Egypt and other countries. Consequently the day is spoken of as *Jashn-i-Milād-i-sharīf*, "the feast of the noble birth." On these occasions poems are recited and addresses delivered describing the character and achievements of Muhammad.

4. Ākhir-i-Chār Shamba is the Persian for "the last Wednesday," i.e., of the second month, Safar. On this day a feast is held in commemoration of Muhammad's having experienced some mitigation of the illness which in the following month terminated his life. It was the last time he performed the legal bathing.

Sweet cakes are prepared and *fātihas* in the name of the Prophet are said over them. In some quarters the strange custom is followed of "drinking the seven *salāms*." For this purpose a banana leaf, or a leaf from a mango-tree, or else a piece of paper, is taken to a *mulla*, who writes seven short sentences from the Qur'ān on it, each of which contains the word *salām*.

While the ink is still wet it is washed off in water, and the mixture is drunk by the person for whom the writing was made. Peace and happiness are thus ensured for the future. It is a day of special rejoicing among the

Sunnis, but the Shī'as consider it unlucky and the Wahhābis, again, do not observe it because it is not enjoined.

5. Shab-i-Barāt is the Persian for "the night of record," and is observed on the fourteenth night of the eighth month, Sha'bān. Muhammad is alleged to have said that on this night God registers annually in the *barāt*, book or record, all the actions men are to perform in the ensuing year; and that all the children of men, who are to be born and to die in the year, are recorded. Some say that this night is referred to in the Qur'ān at xliv. 2. "On the night wherein all things are disposed in wisdom."

Muhammad enjoined his followers to keep awake the whole night, to repeat certain prayers, and to fast the next day. As a matter of fact, however, the time is marked by great merriment rather than fasting, and frequently large sums of money are wasted on fireworks.

6. Muharram, lit. "that which is forbidden," and so anything "sacred." This is the name of the first month of the Muslim year, but it now primarily suggests the period in that month observed by the Shī'as as *days of mourning* in commemoration, chiefly, of the martyrdom of Husain, the younger son of 'Alī, the fourth Khalīfa, by Fātima, the Prophet's daughter. They also mourn for 'Alī himself and his elder son, Hasan.

The ceremony, as conducted in India, is briefly as follows. As soon as the new moon appears, marking the commencement of the month Muharram, people assemble in the '*Āshūr Khāna* (lit. ten-day house) and pronounce the *Fātiha* over some sherbet, or sugar, in Husain's name. This is subsequently distributed to the poor. They then mark out a spot for the pits in which each night bonfires are lighted. Here every night during the festival fires are kindled and the people, old and young, fence with each other across its flames, simulating a fight, and calling out, "'Alī! Noble Husain! Noble Husain! Bridegroom! Friend!"

The *'Āshūr Khāna* is sometimes only a temporary structure, its walls being draped with black cloth, bordered with texts from the Qur'ān. It is kept brilliantly illuminated. Placed to one side of it are the *ta'zias*, or *tābūts*, wooden structures covered with tinsel and meant to represent Husain's mausoleum erected on the plains of Karbalā in Irāq, or else the Prophet's tomb at Madīna. Near to the *ta'zias* are placed imitations of articles supposed to have been used by Husain at Karbalā, e.g., a turban of gold, a sword, a shield, a bow and arrow. Amongst numbers of *'alams*, or standards, is one with a representation of a human hand fixed to the head of a pole. This is a popular emblem representing the *five* members of the Prophet's family: Muhammad, Fātima, 'Alī, Hasan, and Husain.

Each evening within this building dense crowds assemble to listen to *marthiyas*, elegaic poems, which are chanted by paid singers in honour of Husain. Some one will mount a kind of pulpit and recite the story of the heartless way in which the foes of 'Alī put him and his sons to death.

Such recitals so stir up the emotions of the people that they repeatedly rise from their places and with real or feigned grief beat their breasts, crying out, " 'Alī ! 'Alī ! Husain ! Husain ! " Yazīd, the Khalīfa responsible for the latter's death, is cursed.

On the seventh day processions are formed outside the building and the people parade the streets holding aloft a number of standards, reminiscent of those sad events. The chief of these is the standard of Qāsim. This is to represent the marriage of Qāsim, the son of Hasan, to the favourite daughter of Husain, just before the death of the latter. With this event in mind the crowds shout at intervals, " Bridegroom ! Bridegroom ! "

On the evening before the tenth day these *'alams* and *ta'zias* are taken out in procession. It is a scene of great confusion, with men and boys running about in quaint disguises. This is the carnival of the Muslim year.

The next day is *'Āshūra* (tenth). On this day the *ta'zias* are stripped of their trappings and conveyed to a large open spot, near a river or pond. The water represents the plains of Karbalā and serves to recall the agony of thirst experienced by Husain before his death. Into this water the *ta'zia* frames are finally thrown.

On the evening of the twelfth day people sit up all night reading the Qur'ān, and reciting *marthiyas* and verses in praise of Husain. On the thirteenth day a quantity of food is cooked and, after the *Fātiha* has been pronounced over it, it is given to the poor.

Now, the Sunnis, as a rule, view these celebrations with disapproval for reasons which will appear clear in our next chapter. Nevertheless, they, too, keep the *'Āshūra* as a special day. They consider it to be a most excellent day, in the belief that on it God created Adam and Eve, heaven and hell, the seat of Judgment, the table of decree, the pen, fate, life and death.

It will be convenient at this point to turn to a consideration of the different sects in Islām, since we have already said so much about one of them, the Shī'as.

CHAPTER IV

THE SECTS OF ISLAM

MUHAMMAD is reported to have predicted that his followers would split up into numerous sects. The tradition as it appears in the *Mishkātu'l-Masābih* runs thus: "Abdu'llāh-ibn-'Umar related that the Prophet said: 'Verily it will happen to my people even as it did to the children of Israel. The children of Israel were divided into seventy-two sects, and my people will be divided into seventy-three; everyone of these sects will go to hell except one sect.' The Companions said, 'O Prophet of God, which is that one?' He said, 'The religion which is professed by me and my friends'" (Book 1, chap. vi., 2). The prediction came true, except that in the course of the thirteen centuries the total number of the sects has considerably exceeded seventy-three.

It would be interesting to know to what extent Muhammad was aware of the real ground on which the disruption was to take place. Certainly the language of the tradition attributed to him does not suggest the actual cause, for it was not religion, nor doctrinal differences. As a matter of fact the various sects have always subscribed to certain broad religious views and, in consequence, are entitled to be called Muslims. These are (1) the short creed: "there is no god but God; Muhammad is the Apostle of God"; and (2) the belief that the Qur'ān is the final and perfect revelation from God and, as such, abrogates and supersedes all previous scriptures.

No, the rock on which Islām was split in twain was the question of the succession, that is to say a political affair;

and, indeed, it has, as a rule, been political disagreements which have given rise to its numerous schisms and heresies. Who was to succeed Muhammad? that was the question. The Prophet, as we have seen above (p. 31), died without having made any arrangement for his successor; nor was there any guidance on the matter to be found in the Qur'ān.

'Alī, Muhammad's son-in-law, a privileged person, laid early claim to the succession, and there were some from the first who supported him; but on three separate occasions his claims were overruled and the vote of the people went to others, namely, the first three Khalīfas, all of the Quraish tribe as the *sharī'at* clearly ordained. Here was cause enough for jealousy, intrigue and revolt.

The Sunnis

The Sunnis can, and do, claim to be the orthodox sect indicated by Muhammad in the tradition we have quoted, for a Sunni is one who follows the *sunna*, or custom of the Prophet. More precisely he acknowledges the first four Khalīfas as the rightful successors of Muhammad; he accepts the " Six Books " of Traditions, and he attaches himself to one of the four orthodox schools of jurisprudence. He considers the *ijmā'* of those four great *Imāms* to be binding on him.

In other words the Sunnis are traditionists, and as such have arrogated to themselves the title of *Ahlu's-sunna*, " the People of the Custom," although other sects likewise profess to follow the example of the Prophet.

Wherever, therefore, in these pages we have spoken of the " orthodox " Muslims we have had in mind the Sunnis, whose number far exceeds that of any other sect in Islām. They predominate in all Muslim countries, except Persia. A few years ago it was estimated that of the then total Muslim population of about 235 millions, nearly 215 millions were Sunnis, and that of this number more than 90 millions belonged to the Hanafī school of law.

The Khawārij

The statement that dissension arose in Islām over purely political affairs is well illustrated in the origin of the Khawārij, lit. "seceders," the oldest sect of all. We have already seen how a large body of them (12,000) deserted the Khalīfa 'Alī in the critical battle of Siffin with the pretender Mu'āwiya. On that occasion they had protested against 'Alī's agreement to settle the question of his own succession by arbitration, and bitterly denounced him for his weakness. But they took their stand mainly on the principle that the succession must not be looked upon as the exclusive privilege of a particular family or tribe, like the Quraish. They maintained that the Prophet's successor should be duly chosen by the votes of the Faithful from amongst the worthiest, not excepting negroes. In fact they were typical Beduin democrats.

This sect during the first three centuries of the *Hijra* were the cause of the shedding of a great deal of blood. They were fanatics and desperate fighters, so much so that *jihād* threatened to become with them a sixth "pillar" of Islām.

The sect has its representatives even in the present day, but under other names and with numerous subdivisions. They are chiefly met with in scattered groups in North Africa.

The Shī'as

But by far the most important heretical group, both in point of numbers and influence, are the Shī'as who, like the Khawārij, owe their origin to violent disputes about the succession. These Shī'as, lit. "followers," are the adherents to the cause of 'Alī. As Muhammad left no sons this group from the outset maintained that 'Alī was the first legitimate Khalīfa, or *Imām* as they preferred to term the "successor." The Shī'as stoutly deny that the succession can be open to election, and in consequence they reject (and often denounce) the first three Khalīfas as usurpers.

We have already spoken of the tragedy that befell the family of 'Alī—of how he himself was assassinated at Kūfa, his elder son Hasan murdered, and the younger, Husain, cruelly massacred at Karbalā by the order of Yazīd, the usurper whom Shī'as speak of as "the polluted."

Ever since then the tombs of Husain at Karbalā and of 'Alī at Najaf have been sacred ground, places of pilgrimage for the Shī'as, their Mecca indeed. Kāzimain and Sāmarrā, which contain the tombs of some of the twelve Imāms, are also numbered amongst their holy places. To these, as well as to Karbalā and Najaf, Shī'as like to convey the bodies of their dead.

The Shī'as have developed their reverence for the members of the Prophet's house to the extent of lowering, at least among themselves, the prestige of the Prophet. 'Alī is apt to be made more of than Muhammad, just as Husain is given greater honour than are his father and elder brother. Shī'as are at times profoundly moved by the recollection that Husain is supposed to have voluntarily sacrificed himself in order to effect a reconciliation between God and his followers.

In the case of Shī'as it is true that their particular views on this question of the succession led to the formation of strange religious doctrines which served to widen the breach between themselves and the orthodox. Nor was that all; disputations among themselves caused the party to split up into numerous subdivisions, some say about seventy in number, each hostile to the other.

We must now briefly consider some of these later developments. The Shī'as are also called *Imāmiyyas*, because they give the successor of Muhammad the title of Imām and not Khalīfa, in the belief that the Muslim religion consists in true knowledge of the *Imām*, or rightful leader of the faithful. For this reason they arrogate to themselves the title (claimed by Sunnis also), *Al-Mu'minīn*, or "true believers."

In support of their views on the succession they claim that the Prophet, under the direct guidance of God, declared 'Alī to be his successor, and for their peculiar views about the Imāmate they find support in the following passage in the Qur'ān: "When his Lord made trial of Abraham by commands which he fulfilled, He said, 'I am about to make thee an *Imām* to mankind': he said, 'Of my offspring also?' 'My covenant,' said God, 'embraceth not the evil doers'" (ii. 118). On the basis of this verse the Shī'as contend that the Imāmate, or Khilāfat, is a divine institution and that, since the covenant "does not embrace evil doers" the divinely appointed leader must be without blemish and without capacity to sin.

There is a further curious idea, generally prevalent among all classes of Muslims, that long before the creation of the world God took a ray of light from the splendour of His glory and united it to the body of Muhammad. Now the Shī'as contend that this light of Muhammad (*Nūr-i-Muhammad*) descended from the Prophet direct to 'Alī, and that from 'Alī it passed on to the true Imām. In this way 'Alī and his successors came to be looked upon as almost divine.

It followed that the Shī'as believed that the Imām must be a direct descendant of the Prophet. This practically shut up the succession to the Fātimids, i.e., the children of 'Alī by Fātima, so that offspring by other marriages contracted by 'Alī were rigorously excluded. The Shī'as stoutly opposed the claims of the Abbāsids, the descendants of Abbās, Muhammad's uncle.

Such views involved the Shī'as in a great deal of persecution, particularly at the hands of the Abbāsids, and, in consequence, they invented the doctrine of *taqīya*, "guarding one's self," or more explicitly religious dissimulation (cp. Qur'ān iii. 27). According to this doctrine a Shī'a feels justified in resorting to prevarication in order to escape religious persecution. He may even represent himself to be a Sunni. He feels little hesitation in making use of such a practice because he believes that in doing so he is merely obeying the command of the *hidden* Imām.

This strange idea of a hidden Imām was another doctrine they were driven to invent. Including ‘Alī there were twelve Imāms. It is believed, however, that the last of these, Abū'l-Qāsim, known as Al Mahdī, or "the guided one," disappeared in 940 in a cave in Sāmarrā. He is said to be still alive and able to guide the believers. At the end of the age he will reappear and convert the world to Islām. Allegiance to him is a cardinal principle among the Shī‘as. It should be noticed that he is much more to the Shī‘as than is the Khalīfa to the Sunnis. He is not only Muhammad's temporal successor, but a sinless and infallible teacher. It follows, therefore, that this Imām has the sole right to decide controversial matters. In his authority the Shī‘as believe they have found something much more reliable than the *ijmā‘* of the people.

Shī‘as who believe in these twelve Imāms are called *ithna-‘ashariyya*, or "twelvers." They constitute the majority of the Shī‘a sect. About seven millions of them live in Persia where the Shī‘a faith is the state religion. Another five millions of them are to be found in British India, with their headquarters in Lucknow.

A few further characteristics of the Shī‘as as a whole may be briefly mentioned here.

They reject the "Six Books" of Sunni *hadīth*, replacing them by five collections of their own which they call *akhbār*. These are another set of traditions in which the *isnād* admits only the testimony of the members of the house of ‘Alī, the Imāms, and their followers. The sole object of these collections is to support the claims and cause of ‘Alī.

The Shī‘as in opposition to the Sunnis believe that there can still be *mujtahids*. Their doctors claim the right to be the interpreters of the hidden Imām, and, in that capacity, they share his infallibility. One result of this doctrine is that among Shī'as there can be no question of different "schools" or diverse opinion, as among the Sunnis. But even with them the road to progress is closed inasmuch as the decisions of the *mujtahids* must be in strict accord with the Qur'ān and with the *akhbār*.

Another practice that separates the Shī'as from the Sunnis is *mut'a*, or temporary marriage, on payment of a sum of money. Such a union may be dissolved after a period stipulated between the parties. The orthodox doctors severely condemn the practice as tantamount to adultery.

The Ismā'īlīs

Another prominent subdivision of the Shī'as is the Ismā'īlī sect, in many respects very similar to the "twelvers." They trace their origin to the fact that on the death of the sixth Imām, one of his younger sons, Mūsā, was nominated for the succession and not the eldest son, Ismā'īl. The greater number of the Shī'as accepted this decision, holding Ismā'īl to be not a fit person, but a smaller group upheld the claims of Ismā'īl and thus caused further dissension in the Shī'a ranks.

They terminate the line of the visible Imāms with this Ismā'īl, or with his son Muhammad, taking the two together as the seventh Imām, and for this reason they are also known as *sab'iyya* or "seveners." They say that the succession of hidden Imāms commenced from the death of this Muhammad.

The sect spread to North Africa where it received the support of the Fātimid dynasty. From Hākim bi-Amri'llāh, the sixth Khalīfa, sprang other sects, the most famous of which are the Druses of Syria. The "seveners" are found in small numbers in India, Afghānistān, Arabia, Persia, and other places.

The Bohras

The Bohras are a subdivision of the Ismā'īlīs, chiefly residing in Bombay and Baroda. According to the census of 1921 they number slightly more than 153,000. They are mostly the descendants of Hindu converts, though a few claim to be of Arab origin. The sect in India owed its origin to the work of missionaries from Yaman, Arabia. The head of the sect finally left Arabia and came to live in Baroda in the year 1539. In 1588 a schism took place in their ranks owing to rival claimants to the leadership, the new parties being called after the names of the rivals, Dā'ūdīs and Sulaimānīs. The *dā'ī*, or head of the Dā'ūdī branch, resides at Surat and that of the Sulaimānī in Yaman; but the latter has a representative in Baroda. Little is known of the religious beliefs of these people, because they practise great secrecy. They keep themselves aloof from other Muslims, and have separate cemeteries and mosques. The Dā'ūdī Bohras offer prayers only three times a day: morning, noon, and night.

The Khojas

The Khojas are another subdivision of the Ismā'īlīs, residing chiefly in the Panjāb, Sind, Kathiawar, Bombay, and Poona. Groups of them are to be found in East Africa, Arabia, and Persia. Their numbers are slightly less than those of the Bohras. The history of their origin goes back, as does that of the Bohras, to dissension following the death of a Fātimid Khalīfa of the eleventh century A.D. in Egypt. Leaders, *dā'īs*, of this sect came to India several centuries ago and settled in outlying parts like Gujarāt, Sind, and Multān. These men tried to adapt their peculiar doctrines to prevailing Hindu beliefs; thus one of them endeavoured to prove that 'Alī was the long-expected tenth *avatār*, " incarnation," of Vishnu!

There are two groups of these Khojas, commonly spoken of as the Panjāb Khojas and the Āghā Khānī Khojas. The main difference between these groups is in the matter of leadership, otherwise their religious beliefs and practices are almost the same. The Panjāb Khojas, the smaller party, do not recognise the Āghā Khān as their spiritual leader, but turn instead to the *pīrs* of the Chishti and Qādirī orders, though both of these are of the Sunni persuasion.

The main body of the Khojas, including most of the scattered groups outside of India, recognise the Āghā Khān as their head. The present Āghā Khān III. is the grandson of one of the same name who fled from Persia and arrived in Sind in 1840. These Āghā Khāns have always claimed to be the lineal descendants of 'Alī, through Ismā'īl, the seventh Imām in direct succession. The present Āghā Khān is immensely wealthy and is well-known in Europe and England as an owner of race-horses.

He is a leader in Muslim reform movements, and has always been a strong supporter of Aligarh University. To this and other causes he has made handsome donations. He is almost worshipped by thousands of devotees who help to maintain him in a life of luxury by their gifts. But there is evidence of a spirit of revolt in the ranks of these Khojas, and at intervals groups have seceded. As recently as 1927 a party of the discontented at Karachi, styling themselves "The Khoja Reformers' Society," addressed an open letter to the Āghā Khān protesting against his worldly mode of life in face of the poverty and illiteracy of the Khojas, and demanding drastic changes in the management of the affairs of the community. The letter contained such demands as these: that the Āghā Khān should disclaim and repudiate all divine honours paid to him; and that he should put a stop to, and refuse to accept, all "offerings" made to himself.

Bābīs and Bahā'īs

Reference must here be made to two other groups because of the affinity exhibited by their central teaching to the Shī'a doctrine of the Imām. Strictly speaking, however, these are not "sects" of Islām but rather a revolt from it.

To understand their origin we must go back many centuries to another idea cherished by the early Shī'as. They believed that the twelfth or hidden Imām, the Mahdī, held intercourse with his followers through a succession of mediums each of whom was called a *Bāb*, or "door" (i.e., of communication). This intercourse is said to have continued for sixty-nine years, when the last *Bāb* refused to appoint a successor.

After the lapse of nine centuries this theory and claim were revived in Persia in the person of one Mirzā 'Alī Muhammad, who gave out that he was the *Bāb* and that in him dwelt the mind of the Mahdī and the prophets. Born in Shirāz in 1820, he soon showed himself inclined to religious meditation, and proceeded, while still young, to Karbalā, where he earned for himself a great name for piety and learning. In 1844 he proclaimed himself to be the "Door" of communication between the Faithful and the hidden Imām, saying: "Whosoever wishes to approach the Lord his God and to know the true way that leads to Him ought to do it through me."

He settled down in Bushire, gathering around him a large body of disciples, among whom were some influential men. Zealous disciples preached his doctrines throughout Persia and gained for him such a following that the *mullas* rose in opposition.

The *Bāb* propounded his doctrines in a collection of books called the *Bayān*, which manifests a style similar to that of the Qur'ān. In this he sets forth, though often obscurely, the inner and veiled meaning of religion. Generally speaking, his teaching is marked by a more liberal spirit than anything hitherto known in

Islām. One main theme of his teaching was that God is unapproachable; man can only approach Him through some appointed medium. For this purpose a Primal Will, distinct from God, becomes incarnate in the prophets. This Primal Will has spoken in the *Bāb*, and will speak yet again in "Him whom God shall manifest."

His attitude to Islām can be gauged by the emphatic way in which he declared that no revelation is final. Other prophets will be sent as mankind progresses and requires fuller teaching. There is no real disagreement between the earlier prophets, rather each new manifestation is more complete than the last.

Such teaching naturally aroused widespread opposition which, in 1848, took the form of severe persecution at the time of the coronation of the new Shāh, whose Prime Minister hated the Bābīs. After long imprisonment the *Bāb* was condemned to death and executed in July 1850. He seems to have been a man of noble character with a zeal for religious and social reforms, so that such persecution merely served to strengthen his cause.

Unfortunately two years later some Bābīs, on their own initiative, formed a plot to assassinate the Shāh. This act exposed the whole community to renewed and relentless persecution. There followed such a slaughter as perhaps is unparalleled in the history of the world. During the successive outbreaks of persecution these unfortunate people invariably exhibited wonderful heroism and devotion to their faith. Thus closed a chapter in the Bābī movement.

The *Bāb* in 1849 had nominated as his successor one Mirzā Yahyā, to whom he gave the name *Subh-i-Azal*, "The Morning of Eternity." This man remained for some years the recognised head of the Bābī community. The persecution following the attempt on the Shāh's life drove him, however, to Baghdād, where, a year later, he was joined by his half-brother and senior in years, Mirzā Husain 'Alī Bahā'ullāh, who had just been released from prison. But ten years later the Persian

Government had them both deported to Constantinople, whence, once again, the Turks moved them to Adrianople. Up till now Bahā'ullāh had done nothing more than attempt to revise the works of the *Bāb*, and for a time he continued to subordinate himself to his younger and less assertive brother, but his own influence grew so rapidly that we find him in 1866 proclaiming himself to be no other than the person to whom the *Bāb* had referred in that mysterious phrase, "Him whom God shall manifest." Mirzā Yahyā and his followers naturally protested, and a violent quarrel ensued which led to blows. The Turkish Government intervened and deported them; Bahā'ullāh and his followers were sent to the Turkish penal settlement at Akka (Acre) near Haifa, in North Palestine, and Yahyā to Cyprus, where he died in 1912.

The *Bāb* had really only intended a reform of the Shī'a Imāmate, and Mirzā Yahyā aimed at nothing more than preserving the pure Bābist doctrine, but Bahā'ullāh took an independent line and proclaimed himself the messenger of a new dispensation. He announced that he was the emanation of the Deity, the Apostle of the final revelation, no longer for the Shī'as or Islām alone, but for all mankind. He thus reduced the original *Bāb* to the subordinate position of a forerunner of the final faith, Bahā'ism. He too set forth his doctrines in a book, modelled on the style of the Qur'ān; besides which he sent a series of official letters to the heads of governments setting forth the substance of his teaching.

The clean break made by Bahā'ullāh with Islām can be shown by the reforms he introduced; prayer is to be offered only three times daily, and while doing so one should not face towards Mecca; the fast of *Ramdhān* is abolished, also the wearing of the veil by women; traffic in slaves is forbidden; intercourse with persons of all other religions is enjoined; music is allowed; *jihād* is abolished.

It must be acknowledged that Bahā'ism raises women

to a higher level than they occupy in Islām and at the same time aims at restricting many of Islām's social evils. It encourages liberty of thought and urges that kindness should be shown to all. It has already done much to shake the complacent idea in the minds of many Muslims in Persia and elsewhere that Islām is the last word in temporal and spiritual matters.

On the death of Bahā'ullāh in 1892 his eldest son, Abbās Effendi, or as the Bahā'is prefer to call him, 'Abdu'l Bahā, "The Servant of the Splendour," succeeded him as head of the community. Like his father he also came into conflict, in 1898, with his half-brother, Mirzā Muhammad 'Alī, who claimed that he, and not Abbās, had been appointed to the leadership by Bahā'ullāh.

Abbās lived in Haifa virtually as a prisoner, and proceeded, after the manner of his father, to emphasise the cosmopolitan, pacificist, and humanitarian character of the new religion. Bahā'ism is patently an eclectic system that borrows freely from other faiths. At the same time it claims to realise the highest ideal, to sum up the best tendencies of Christianity, Judaism, Buddhism, Islām, Freemasonry, and Theosophy! The centre at Acre-Haifa became in Abbās' lifetime a place of pilgrimage for his more devout followers, and has since come to have an attraction for Bahā'is similar to that of Mecca and Madīna for Muslims.

Reliable statistics for the Bahā'is are not available. There are only a few hundreds in Syria. "The numbers of the adherents of the movement in Persia have been grossly exaggerated by travellers and others" (vide *The Moslem World*, Oct. 1931).

The movement was introduced into America in 1893 by a Syrian Christian, Dr Ibrāhīm George Khairullāh, a convert to Bahā'ism, who advocated the claims of Bahā'ullāh. This man on visiting Acre in 1898, that is to say, after the quarrel between Bahā'ullāh's two sons, transferred his allegiance to Muhammad 'Alī, but on his return to America failed to get the majority of the

Bahā'is to do likewise. Subsequently Abbās Effendi sent missionaries thither to advocate his own claims, and in 1912 he went in person. There followed the spectacle of two rival factions each denouncing the other. Nevertheless, the support which Abbās then gained from his American disciples greatly helped in his propaganda work.

He died at Haifa in November 1921. The position he had gained for himself may be judged by the fact that the British Government had conferred a knighthood on him, and that amongst those present at his funeral was the High Commissioner for Palestine. He left only daughters, and so a grandson, Shauqi Rabbāni, was proclaimed as his successor, but he does not seem to have received much support from the community.

The Bahā'is carry on an extensive propaganda in many countries and now claim to have thousands of adherents in America, Germany, and Russia, with several centres in India, where even Muslims are said to be joining the new faith. An observer of this movement in America, however, writes of having gained the impression that "a number of excellent people have had their hopes raised by men who had no message for them." Certainly the claims made on behalf of the dead 'Abdu'l Bahā in literature now current are, to say the least, preposterous: "'Abdu'l-Bahā is the chosen instrument of God . . . the 'Centre of the Covenant.' . . . All who have had spiritual contact with him realise that in reality he is the point of divine guidance in the world to-day. . . . As the life blood goes from the heart to each organ of the body . . . so from 'Abdul . . . goes forth the spirit of the love of God, to each of the members of the multitude." This looks uncommonly like a revival of the theory of a hidden imām.

Chapter V

SŪFISM

Sūfism is that mode of the religious life in Islām wherein the chief stress is placed on the activities of the inner self rather than on the performance of external ritual; in other words, it is the name given to Islamic mysticism. It owes its origin, on the one hand, to an effort to break away from the unsatisfying idea of a purely transcendent God, and on the other, to an attempt to recover from the failure of the Mu'tazilīs, or free-thinkers, to solve certain philosophical difficulties by the aid of pure reason.

Dissatisfied with the Qur'ān and the *sunna* as guides to a knowledge of divine truth, and unable to accept the principle of the use of pure reason, the Sūfīs formulated yet another basis for the discovery of divine truth, viz., *kashf*, or "illumination." *Kashf* is that direct and immediate apprehension of divine things which the soul gains, not from an inspired book nor by some process of reasoning, but through experience. This principle of *kashf* forms the basis of the teaching of the Sūfīs, whom we may call the mystics of Islām.

It is claimed that the system is not opposed to the *sharī'at*, yet in some respects it is. The two differ mainly in that the *sharī'at* deals with the outward and visible profession of religion, whereas Sūfism seeks to regulate the inner life of the soul. By way of explaining their separate functions the Sūfī says that the knowledge of religious truth is of three kinds: that which is received *from* God, that obtained *with* God, and that acquired *of* God. The knowledge received *from* God is that based on the *sharī'at*, the revealed law, made obligatory by

God Himself. That which is obtained *with* God is the knowledge of the mystic path. Finally, that which is acquired *of* God, called *'ilmu'l ma'rifat*, or *gnosis*, is the knowledge of God possessed by prophets and saints. This last kind of knowledge cannot be acquired by ordinary means, but results from Divine guidance and illumination.

Early History of Sūfism

Three well-defined stages mark the progress and developments of Sūfism.

In its earliest phase it took the form of an ascetic movement. The Umayyad Khalīfas and the nobles of their day, in their utter disregard for the *sharī'at*, were so unlike the four rightly-guided Khalīfas that pious Muslims in disgust withdrew from the world to find peace of soul in a life of seclusion. These hermits were the earliest Sūfīs of Islām. By them poverty was regarded as a meritorious condition, and renunciation the surest means of gaining Paradise. At first the good things of the world were renounced in the hope of obtaining rewards in the hereafter, but at a later stage the renunciation was made wholly for the love of God. Such selfless devotion to the Divine Being came to be looked upon as the characteristic feature of true Sūfism.

We shall give an account of two of the more famous Sūfīs of this earliest period, viz., Ibrāhīm bin Adham, and Rābi'a, both of whom lived in the second century of the *Hijra*.

1. Ibrāhīm was at one time the king of Balkh. His great wealth is indicated by the fact that when he walked abroad forty golden scimitars and forty golden maces were carried before and behind him. But being by nature religiously inclined he was led to renounce his throne and all the world's pleasures for a life of absolute poverty. Many stories are told of how he found satisfaction in poverty. On one occasion, after having nothing to eat all day, he passed the night in prayer, offering

400 *rak'ats* in thanksgiving for his utter destitution. A second day followed in like fashion and again at night he offered 400 *rak'ats* in thanksgiving. Thus a week went by and then, feeling the pangs of hunger, he cried, "O Lord, 'twere better now if Thou wouldst give me something to eat." At that moment a young man appeared and, asking him if he required food, took him to a certain house. The occupant, a man who had formerly been one of the king's slaves, at once recognised his master and exclaimed, "Sire, I am your slave, all that I have is yours." Ibrāhīm humbly made reply, "I set you free, and freely bestow on you all that is with you—only permit me to go away." Then hastening out of the house, he prayed: "O Lord! I promise not to ask anything from anyone in future, save from Thee. I asked Thee for bread and Thou didst offer the world to me!"

Ibrāhīm made the pilgrimage to Mecca on several occasions and remained there once for a number of years. Yet he never drew water from the well *Zamzam*, because the bucket had been the gift of some king and he scrupled to use it.

Once he overheard a *darwesh* bemoaning his poverty, and remarked, "I presume that you purchased your poverty for nothing." The *darwesh* exclaimed, "What! is poverty also sold?" "Yes," replied Ibrāhīm, "I bought mine at the cost of the kingdom of Balkh, and it was cheap at the price!"

2. Rābi'a was a woman, a native of Basra, who died at Jerusalem in A.D. 801. She was born in the poorest of homes and was left an orphan when only a little girl. A famine scattered herself and her sisters, of whom she was the fourth, as her name indicates. She was sold for the sum of six dirhams. As a slave she used to fast during the daytime while working for her master, who exacted from her hard labour. In the night time she spent long hours in prayer. Observing her ascetic mode of life her master freed her, and thenceforth she devoted

herself to the love of God, living a life of extreme poverty.

It is to her that Sūfism owes the conception of prayer as free and intimate intercourse with God. Thus, to the prescribed prayer which was regarded as, in itself, a meritorious act, there came to be added this kind of free prayer as a means of gaining access to God's presence.

Rābi'a never faltered in her vow of asceticism. Again and again her friends offered her assistance but she as often declined it, being content to look to God for the supply of her needs. Her reply to those who desired to help her was: "Verily, I should be ashamed to ask for worldly things from Him to Whom the world belongs; how, then, should I ask for them from those to whom it does not belong?"

Some of her prayers illustrate the statement made above that, in course of time, the vow of renunciation came to be taken not as a means of obtaining rewards in the world to come, but just from love of God. We give two of them: "O my Lord, whatever share of this world Thou dost bestow on me, bestow it on Thine enemies; and whatever share of the next world Thou dost give me, give it to Thy friends. Thou art enough for me." Another runs as follows: "O my Lord, if I worship Thee from fear of hell, burn me in hell, and if I worship Thee from hope of Paradise, exclude me thence; but if I worship Thee for Thine own sake, then withhold not from me Thine Eternal Beauty."

Speculative Elements in Sūfism

The second phase in early Sūfism coincided with the period from the accession of the Khalīfa Harūnu'r-Rashīd, 786, to the death of Mutawakkil, 861. During these years Hellenic culture greatly influenced the current of Islamic thought. Plato and Aristotle were translated into Arabic and eagerly studied. There resulted a strong rationalistic movement in Islâm under the influence of which Sūfism took on the form of a theosophy. Certain new elements, such as gnosticism, ecstasy and pantheism, now became characteristic features of Sūfism.

A brief description of two of the great Sūfīs of this period may be given here.

1. *Zū'n-Nūn Misrī* (860) of Egypt, is one of a number of famous Sūfis of the period who contributed greatly to the system from their immense learning, and who superimposed a speculative element on the more practical asceticism. This man was renowned for his great learning, devotion, and communion with God. He would wander amidst the ruined monuments of Egypt, studying the inscriptions and endeavouring to decipher their mysterious hieroglyphics. He is held in high reputation also as a chemist. At length he was charged with heresy and imprisoned by the Khalīfa Mutawakkil. When, however, the latter learned of his remarkable learning and sanctity he had him released and himself became his disciple.

It was this man who first introduced into Sūfism the idea that the true knowledge of God is to be obtained by means of *wajd*, or " ecstasy." He used to say, " The man who knows God best is the one most completely lost in Him."

Another outstanding figure of this period was *Abū Yazīd*, or Bāyazīd, of Bistam, a town in the province of Qumis, near the S.E. corner of the Caspian Sea. His grandfather had been a fire-worshipper and his father a nobleman of the town.

Bāyazīd is revered as *Sultānu'l-'Arifīn*, the king of gnostics. He first propounded the doctrine of *fanā*, or " extinction." He said, " Creatures are subject to *ahwāl*, or states, but the gnostic has no state because his vestiges are effaced and his essence is annihilated by the essence of another, and his traces are lost in the traces of another." In consequence he used at times to exclaim in a state of ecstasy: "Glory to me! how great is my majesty"; and, "Verily I am God; there is no God except me, so worship me!"

Both these expressions are to be found in the Qur'ān, and it is frequently said that in using them he was merely quoting from it. Nevertheless other similar expressions, and his views regarding the annihilation of man's essential nature, prove that in reality he held pantheistic views. The following prayer of his is often quoted: "O God, how long will there be 'I' and 'Thou' between me and Thee. Take this away, that my 'I' may become 'Thou,' and 'I' be nothing. O Lord, as long as I am with Thee, I am more than all, and when I am with myself I am the least of all."

How Sūfism won Recognition in Islām

The Sūfism of the earliest period was favourably received inasmuch as its main doctrines followed the line of orthodox Islām, but with the admixture of these foreign pantheistic elements later Sūfism had to struggle for recognition. It was not until the time of the renowned Imām, Al Ghazālī (1058-1111), who inaugurated the third phase, that Sūfism in its modified form was finally established.

This man, otherwise known as Abū Hāmid Muhammad, a native of Tūs, near Meshed, in Khurāsān, Persia, occupies a unique place in the history of dogmatic theology in Islām. Though left an orphan at an early age, he diligently prosecuted his studies at various places of learning and soon proved himself to be a genius. He was appointed as Professor in the Nizāmiyah College at Baghdād (the "Oxford" of the Muslim world of those days), where he lectured for four years before retiring from the world as a Sūfī.

"In his biography he speaks of how from his youth up he was possessed of an intense thirst for knowledge, which impelled him to study every form of religion and philosophy and to question all whom he met concerning the nature and meaning of their beliefs. When he endeavoured to distinguish the true from the false he could find no sure test. He decided that he could not trust the evidence of his own senses. If the senses deceive, may not the mind do likewise? Perhaps our life is a dream full of phantom thoughts which we mistake for realities.

"For two months he was thoroughly sceptical. Then God gave him light; he regained his mental balance and was able once more to think clearly. He now concluded that his thinking faculty must serve as his guide to truth. He thus set himself to examine the foundations of belief as represented in four classes of people who were devoting themselves to the search for truth, viz., the scholastic theologians, the teachers of esoteric doctrines, philosophers, and Sūfis.

"Scholasticism, he admitted, while an excellent corrective against heresy, could not cure the disease from which he himself was suffering, i.e., lack of religious certainty. The propounders of esoteric doctrines, though claiming to possess the truth, failed to satisfy him. As for the philosophers, all of them, materialists, naturalists and theists alike, were branded with infidelity and heresy. In any case his religious instinct would not permit him to worship at the shrine of pure reason. Thus Sūfism remained as his last hope. Having carefully studied the writings of the mystics he became convinced that this was the right path for him. He came to see that the higher stages of Sūfism could not be mastered by mere study, but must be learnt by actual experience. After a long and painful struggle with himself he cast aside all worldly ambition, and in 1095 left Baghdād to wander forth in Syria. At length he found the peace his soul craved. He died in 1111" (Nicholson, *A Literary History of the Arabs*, p. 381).

He became a dominating figure, and it is due to his influence that Sūfism became assured of a place within

Islām. It was he, also, who secured for philosophy and philosophical theory (hitherto regarded by the orthodox *'ulamā* as heresy) more honourable recognition. Since his time three principles are recognised as interwoven in the system of Islām: *naql*, or tradition; *'aql*, or reason; and *kashf*, or illumination. "Tradition" represents the authority of the Qur'ān and the *sunna*; "reason" is the basis of analogical reasoning and philosophical theology; and "illumination" is that direct revelation made upon the mind of the Sūfī.

The Main Characteristics of Sūfism

The entire system of Sūfism centres round the twofold question: How is man to gain the experience of God's inward presence; and what is God in relation both to the individual and to the universe?

The answer of Sūfism to the first question is contained in the teaching concerning *At-Tarīqat*, the Path, which will be dealt with in the next chapter. The answer to the second is contained in the doctrine of *ma'rifat*, or gnosticism, which describes God in terms of pantheistic and monistic philosophy and not in terms of the monotheism of the Qur'ān.

All the mystic teachers describe at length the organs of spiritual communication with which man has been endowed by God. These vary in number in the different "Orders," but the following three are found in every list: *qalb*, the heart; *sirr*, the soul; and *rūh*, the spirit. These are said to be located in the human body, but actually have no material existence. The first is on the left side of the breast, the second on the right, and the third between the two. The *qalb*, which "knows" God, though mysteriously connected with the physical heart, is not a thing of flesh and blood, and, contrary to the Western conception, is the seat of the intellect and capable of knowing the essence of all things. A tradition represents God as saying: "My earth and heaven contain Me not, but the heart of My faithful servant containeth Me." The function of the *sirr* is to "contemplate" God, and that of the *rūh* to "love" Him.

In regard to their speculations concerning God, Sūfis may be divided into two main groups. The larger of these is composed of Pantheists, to whom everything is God and of the same essence. For these the creed, "There is no god but God," means that besides Allāh there is no existence. They are called *Ittihādiya*, i.e., monists, or alternatively, *Wahdatu'l-wajūdiya*, i.e., pantheists.

Those forming the second group, in their anxiety to conform to the monotheistic teaching of the Qur'ān, explain away the pantheistic expressions of mystic writers, interpreting them in the sense that the existence of the universe and all that it contains is so far transcended by the reality of God that these things count for nothing. Sūfis of this class are called *Ilhāmiya*, "inspired."

Generally speaking, however, the Sūfis regard God as pure Being, so that, from the philosophical point of view, they are nothing less than pantheists. "But this is not materialistic pantheism, which dignifies with the name of "God" the mere sum totality of the universe. Sūfism is a spiritualistic pantheism which sees in the universe naught but a dim reflection, "as in a glass darkly," of the Infinite Attributes of that Invisible, Omnipotent, Omnipresent Spirit of whom alone reality and existence can be predicated." To the Sūfī everything speaks of God; "There is nothing that does not celebrate His praise" (xvii. 46). He is everywhere and in everything; "We (God) are closer to him than his neck-vein" (l. 15). Said a Sūfī, "Show what God is not, and I will show you what He is."

"From the philosophical point of view God is pure Being, from the mystical and devotional point of view God is Absolute Beauty, of which all earthly beauty, whether it be of form, or thought, or action, is but a dim reflection. Our finite minds cannot comprehend the Infinite: we can but speak in metaphors, according to one or another aspect in which the Infinite Being reveals it to us. Having regard to His power some call Him "King"; meditating on His loving-kindness, others call Him "Father.' Overwhelmed by His Beauty, the Sūfī conceives of Him, above all things, as the eternally Beautiful. Hence Sūfī hymns borrow the impassioned language of the lover. He is all-Beautiful and the whole universe is the mirror of His Beauty."

It is said that seventy thousand veils separate the absolute Being, or Beauty, from the world of matter and sense. The Sūfī in his journey along the Inward Path breaks through these veils and passes in time through seven "stages," during each of which ten thousand are encountered. In his progress his conception of the Absolute Being changes from that of an objective reality to One having identity with himself and with the universe. The changes in the position thus reached may be expressed thus: At the first the simple creed, "There is no god but Allāh," implied three things: there is no agent but Allāh, there is no object of worship save Allāh, and there is no existence save Allāh. In the later phase the creed took the form, "There is no god but Thou." In the final stage the creed becomes, "There is no god but I." This is the final goal of the Sūfī's journey along the Path. We shall consider this in more detail in the next chapter.

Chapter VI

THE MYSTIC PATH AND RELIGIOUS ORDERS

Sūfism speaks of advancement in the spiritual life as a journey, and the seeker after God as a *sālik*, or "traveller." Its teaching is intended to guide the traveller to the attainment of the perfect "knowledge" (*ma'rifat*) of God, the only Reality diffused through all things. Subsequently, the wandering soul is led onwards by slow "stages" (*maqāmāt*), and through the experience of certain "states" (*ahwāl*), along a Path (*at-tarīqat*), to the desired goal of union with God, called *fanā f'il-haqīqat*, absorption (lit. "extinction") in Reality.

The first requirement for one desiring to become a Sūfi is to place himself under a *Shaikh*, or spiritual leader, and to take the vow of obedience (*bai'at*). He thus becomes a *murīd*, "aspirant," or disciple. The *Shaikh* is believed to possess secret power for the transmutation of the human body. Under his direction it becomes refined in the fire of spiritual passion (*'ishq*), the flame of which is fed by the fuel of *dhikr*, the act of "remembering" God, accompanied by prescribed breathing exercises.

Early Stages of the Journey

The early "stages" for the Sūfi have as their object his purification. These are repentance, abstinence, renunciation, voluntary poverty, and trust in God. Repentance must come first. This is described as the awakening of the soul from the slumber of indifference to awareness of his evil ways, and a sense of contrition for past sin. There are three elements in such repentance: remorse for disobedience; determination not to sin again; immediate abandonment of sin.

Rābi'a taught that sin was, in the highest degree, hurtful to the soul because it was the cause of separation between the soul and its Beloved. She held that contrition for sin as a barrier between the servant and his Lord, and not fear of punishment, could alone lead to true repentance. "Repentance," she said, "is purely an act of Divine grace coming from God to man, not from man to God. Only God has power so to touch the sinner's heart that he will turn away from his wickedness and repent."

For the sincere penitent forgiveness is sure, since repentance is a sign of grace. Sin and grace are incompatible in the same soul. As Al Ghazālī said: "Darkness cannot dwell with light, nor filthiness with the whiteness of fuller's soap."

Renunciation involving poverty is one of the primary virtues in the practice of mysticism. The Sūfī ideal is not merely the lack of wealth, but the absence of any desire for it. *Faqīr*, "poor," and *darwesh*, "mendicant," are names which the Muslim mystic is proud to own, since they imply that he is stripped of every thought or wish likely to divert his mind from God. Rāb'ia used to say: "The poor are the richest of God's creation: they dispense with the gift for the sake of the Giver."

Finally, we may mention the necessity for trust in God. This in practice includes the cultivation of patience in face of the many ills of life. It is no passive virtue, but rather a "making war upon the passions and seeking after victory." There are three stages in the cultivation of this virtue: to cease complaining, the stage of the penitent; to be satisfied with what is decreed, the stage of the ascetic; to love whatever the Lord does, the stage of the friends of God. The following incident illustrates the mystic ideal of patience and resignation. One of the early "saints" once visited

Rābi'a when she was ill and in great pain, and said, "If you utter a prayer, God will relieve your suffering." Rābi'a replied, "O Sūfyān, do you know Who it is that wills this suffering for me? is it not God Who wills it?" Sūfyān answered, "Yes." "Since you know this," said Rābi'a, "why do you bid me ask for that which is contrary to His will? It is not well to oppose one's Beloved."

The States of the Mystic

The "stages" must be distinguished from the "states" (*ahwāl*, sing. *hāl*). The Sūfis define a "state" as a condition, of feeling or disposition, which comes upon a man without his intention or desire, such as sorrow, fear, joy. The various "states" which the Sūfi experiences in his journey are variously enumerated, but it is generally agreed that they are the following ten: Meditation, Nearness to God, Love, Fear, Hope, Longing, Intimacy, Tranquillity, Contemplation, Certainty. These "states" are induced by God in the heart of man, who is unable to repel them when they come or to retain them when they depart.

The Path is not finished until the traveller has traversed all the "stages," making himself perfect in each of them, and has experienced all the "states" God is pleased to send. Then commences the higher ascent of the Path, Illumination, which the Sūfis called *ma'rifat*, gnosis, and *haqīqat*, Truth.

The Seven-fold Path

Besides these early "stages," the Path has a further "Seven Stages" (*maqāmāt*) marking the progress of the soul towards the final goal of perfect union with the Absolute Reality. These also are variously described by Muslim mystics, but in general the "seven stages" are as follows:

1. *'ubūdīyat*, the stage of "service"—in which the aspirant is exhorted to obey the Law and serve God.

2. *'ishq*, that of "love"—in which the Divine influence inclines the soul towards the love of God.

3. *zuhd*, "renunciation"—under the influence of Divine Love all worldly desires are expelled from the heart.

4. *ma'rifat*, "knowledge"—in which the aspirant contemplates the nature, attributes and works of God.

5. *wajd*, "ecstasy"—in which mental excitement is produced through contemplation of the only existing Reality, God.

6. *haqīqat*, "reality"—the heart is now illuminated with the true nature of God.

7. *wasl*, "union"—in which the mystic, as it were, sees God face to face. This "stage" immediately precedes the final experience of *fanā*, absorption in the essence of the Eternal Being.

Each of these "stages" is related to the seven planetary systems, the Moon, Mercury, Venus, Mars, Jupiter, Saturn, and the Sun. These encircle the earth, while beyond them are fixed stars, and beyond them again is the world of the Real (*Al-Haqq*).

Once again the "Seven Stages" are related to *four* main "*stages*" (*manāzil*, sing. *manzil*). These are *ash-Sharī'at*, the Law; *at-Tarīqat*, the Path; *al-Ma'rifat*, Gnosis; and *al-Haqīqat*, Reality. Each of them comprises two of the afore-mentioned "stages," save the fourth, which coincides with the seventh.

Finally, the four main "stages" are related to a further *four* main "*states*" through which the traveller must pass.

1. *Nāsūt*, humanity, the natural state of every human being, in which the disciple must observe the *Sharī'at*.

2. *Malakūt*, nature of angels, in which he takes the Path of the spiritual journey, *at-Tarīqat*.

3. *Jabrūt*, possession of power, for which there is *Ma'rifat*.

4. *Lāhūt*, Divinity, the state of absorption into the Deity, in which he attains Reality.

Dhikr

The Sūfī, in the course of his journey, performs special acts of devotion, technically known as *dhikr*, "remembering," and *murāqaba*, "watching," the significance of which will become clear as we proceed.

The *dhikr* is of two kinds: *dhikr jalī*, that which is recited aloud, and *dhikr khafī*, repeated in a low voice or else mentally.

These exercises are variously performed, but are described as follows by Shāh Wali Ullāh of Delhi (*vide* T. P. Hughes, *Dictionary of Islām*, p. 703).

Dhikr jalī.

1. The worshipper sits in the usual posture and shouts the word *Allāh*, drawing his voice as from his left side and then from his throat.

2. Sitting as at prayers he repeats the word *Allāh* still louder than before, first from his right knee, and then from his left side.

3. Folding his legs under him he repeats the word *Allāh* first from his right knee, and then from his left side, still louder.

4. Still remaining in the same position he shouts the word *Allāh* first from the left knee, then from the right knee, then from the left side, and lastly, in front, still louder.

5. Sitting as at prayer, with face towards Mecca, he closes his eyes, says *Lā*, drawing the sound as from his navel up to his left shoulder; then he says *ilāha*, drawing out the sound as from his brain; and lastly, *illa 'llāhu*, repeated from his left side with great energy.

Each of these stages is called a *zarb*, and they are recited many hundreds of times.

Dhikr Khafī.

1. Closing his eyes and lips, the worshipper says,

"with the tongue of the heart," *Allāhu sāmi'un*, i.e., "God hears"; *Allāhu Basīrun*, i.e., "God sees"; *Allāhu 'Alīmun*, i.e., "God the Knower." The first being drawn, as it were, from the navel to the breast; the second, from the breast to the brain; the third, from the brain up to the heavens; and then again repeated stage by stage backwards and forwards.

2. He then says in a low voice, *Allāh*, from the right knee, and then from the left side.

3. With each exhalation of the breath he says *lā ilāha*, and with each inhalation, *illa'llāhu*.

This third *zarb* is a most exacting form of devotion, performed, as it is, hundreds or even thousands of times, and is, therefore, considered the most meritorious.

Murāqaba, or watching, is a form of meditation designed to safeguard the divine illumination. At the outset the worshipper performs *dhikr* by reciting the phrases: *Allāhu hāzirī*, i.e., "God who is present" (with me); *Allāhu nāzirī*, "God who sees me"; *Allāhu Shāhidī*, "God who witnesses me"; *Allāhu ma'ī*, "God who is with me."

Having recited this *dhikr*, either aloud or mentally, the worshipper proceeds to meditate upon some verse or verses of the Qur'ān. The following give some idea of the line of thought considered by Muslim mystics to be the most devotional and spiritual.

"He (God) is first. He is last. The Manifest, the Hidden, and who knoweth all things" (lvii. 3).

"He is with you wheresoever ye be" (lvii. 4).

"We (God) are closer to him (man) than his neck-vein" (l. 15).

"Whichever way ye turn there is the face of God" (ii. 109).

"God encompasseth all things" (iv. 125).

"All on earth shall pass away, but the face of the Lord shall abide resplendent with majesty and glory" (lv. 26, 27).

In addition to the acts of devotion just mentioned

there are three other methods of "remembering" God, which are in even more common use. These are exclamations expressing joy and surprise which are used also as a form of devotional exercise.

(1) *Tasbīh*, viz., *Subhān Allāh*! "Holiness be to God!"

(2) *Tahmīd*, viz., *Al-hamdu li'llāh*! "Praise be to God!"

(3) *Takbīr*, viz., *Allāhu Akbar*! "God is great!"

These and similar expressions are also uttered with the use of a rosary (*tasbīh*), which enables one to keep count of the number of times the phrase has been repeated.

Religious Orders

The *sālik*, or traveller, from the very outset, attaches himself to one or other of the Sūfī "Orders," which are known as *khāndān*, "family," and *silsila*, "chain of succession." Their chief difference lies in this "chain of succession." The centre of every order is a *murshid*, "one who guides aright," or *pīr*, "elder," who is the successor or heir of the original founder of the Order. He is generally appointed by his immediate predecessor, though cases are known where such succession is hereditary. The residence of the *Shaikh* is called a *khānaqāh*, or monastery. The *pīr* with his disciples forms a *halqah*, or "circle."

All the orders, save one, trace their chain of succession back to Muhammad, through 'Alī. Thus it is claimed that the mystic Path is as old as Islām itself. Muhammad is said to have been the recipient of a two-fold revelation; the one embodied in the contents of the Qur'ān, the other within his heart. The former was meant for all and is binding on all; the latter was to be transmitted to the chosen few through these lines of succession. Hence it is that Muhammad's knowledge is described as being *'ilm-i-safīna*, the Book knowledge, and *'ilm-i-sīna*, heart knowledge. The former is incorporated in the doctrinal teachings of the *'ulamā*; the latter is strictly esoteric, the mystical teachings of the Sūfīs. Though these views are held by Muslims generally, it is nevertheless true to say that the luxuriant growth of the Sūfī doctrine and practice, which we described in the preceding chapter, is viewed with disapproval by orthodox Muslims.

Of the hundreds of different orders into which Sūfism is divided and subdivided there are *four* which have gained great prominence. These four, which have a considerable following in India, are the Chishtīya, Suharwardīya, Qādirīya, and Naqshbandīya.

The Chishtīya Order

This, the oldest *darwesh* order in India, was founded by Shaikh Abū Ishāq Shāmī, who died in A.D. 940. It was introduced into India by Khwāja Mu'īnu'd-dīn Chishtī, of Sīstān, in Southern Afghānistān. He entered India with the army of Shihāb-ud-dīn Ghauri, and after staying for some time at Delhi took up his permament residence in Ajmīr, where he died in 1236. Muslims from all parts of India visit his tomb each year to celebrate the *'urs*, the festival of the anniversary commemorating the death of the saint. This coincides with the sixth day of the seventh month, Rajab, of the Muslim year. The spiritual descendants of Mu'īn-ud-dīn have been among the most famous of India's saints. A few of these deserve brief mention.

Khwāja Qutb-ud-dīn, Bakhtiyār Kākī, was his *khalīfa* in Delhi, appointed in his lifetime. He died the same year as his beloved *pīr*, the year of the death of Altutmish, the Sultān of Delhi. The great veneration in which Qutb-ud-dīn was held may be judged by the fact that the Sultān himself had become one of his disciples and counted it a great privilege to wash the corpse of his master.

Qutb-ud-dīn was succeeded by Shaikh Farīd-ud-dīn Attar Shakarganj, widely known as Bābā Farīd. He died in 1265 and was buried at Pāk Pattan in the Panjab. His *'urs* is celebrated on the fifth of Muharram. He is famous as the author of a number of books on Sūfism, the chief of which is *Tazkirat-ul-Auliya*, "Lives of the Saints." He was succeeded by two notable disciples, Hazrat Nizām-ud-dīn Auliya of Delhi, and Hazrat Makhdūm 'Alā-ud-dīn Ahmad Sābir of Pīrān Kalīr.

Hazrat Nizām-ud-dīn was a native of Budaun, U.P., and was appointed, when only twenty years old, by Bābā Farīd to be his *khalīfa* in his lifetime. He was responsible for the subdivision of the Chishtīya order known as Nizāmiya. He died in 1325 and was buried in the suburbs of Delhi. His grave is another place of pilgrimage. He is better known as Mahbūb-i-Ilāhi, "the Beloved of God."

Hazrat Makhdūm 'Alā-ud-dīn was appointed second successor to Bābā Farīd, and took up his abode in Rurkī, also called Kalīr, but since the *pīr*'s death in 1291, Pīrān Kalīr. He subdivided the Chishtīya order still further by founding the order Sābiriya, named after himself. His *'urs* is held on the seventeenth day of the third month, Rabī'ul-Awwal.

The Suhrawardīya Order

This order was founded by Ziā-ud-dīn Abi Najīb Suhrawardī, who died in A.D. 1167. It was introduced into India by Shaikh Bahā-ud-dīn Zakarīyā of Multān, a disciple of Shaikh Shihāb-ud-dīn, who succeeded the founder. Bahā-ud-dīn died in 1266. His tomb in Multān is greatly revered. His spiritual descendants were active and successful propagandists of Islām.

The more famous saints of this order may be mentioned. Jalāl bin Ahmad Kabīr, commonly known as Makhdūm-i-Jahāniyān, Jahān-gasht, "Master of the Universe and World-Roamer." He is said to have made the pilgrimage to Mecca thirty-six times and to have performed innumerable miracles. He died in 1384. Another was his grandson, Abū Muhammad 'Abdullāh, known as Qutb-i-'Alam, "the Axis of the Universe." He died in 1453 and was buried at Batuwa in Gujarāt. A son of his, Sayyid Muhammad Shāh 'Alam, played an important part in the political and religious life of his time. He died in 1475 and was buried at Rasūlābād, near Ahmadābād.

The Qādirīya Order

The Qādirīya order was founded by Shaikh 'Abdu'l Qādir Jīlānī, better known as Ghausu'l-'Azam, "Succourer of the World," a title indicating the highest rank of all. He is venerated throughout India as Pīr-i-Pīrān, "the Pīr of the Pīrs," and Pīr Dastagīr, Pīr the Rescuer. His *'urs* is celebrated all over the Muslim world on the eleventh of the fourth month, Rabī-ul-Ākhir, and is known as *Gyārhwīn Sharīf*, "the noble eleventh." Shrines are erected in his honour to secure his beneficent assistance. He died in 1166.

The order was introduced into India by one of his descendants, Muhammad Ghaus, who settled at Uch, in Sind, 1482. An important *pīr* of this order was Shaikh Mīr Muhammad, or Miyān Mīr, distinguished as the religious teacher of Prince Dārā Shikoh, son of the Mughal Emperor Shāh Jahān. He was buried on the outskirts of Lahore. The Prince himself was the author of several books on mysticism.

The Naqshbandīya Order

This order traces its origin to Khwāja Bahā-ud-dīn Naqshband of Turkestān, who died in 1389 and was buried near Bukhārā. Khwāja Muhammad Bāqī Bi'llāh of Kābul introduced the order into India. He resided in Delhi, where he died in 1603. His *khalīfa*, Shaikh Ahmad surpassed his master in fame and sanctity and came to be recognised as the founder of a new order, known as Mujaddadīya, a subdivision of the Naqshbandīya. Shaikh Ahmad is also spoken of as Mujaddid-i-Alf-i-Thānī Imām-i-Rabbānī, by which is indicated that he was the reformer at the beginning of the second thousand years after Muhammad. He died in A.D. 1624 and was buried at Sirhind, in Patiāla State.

The Naqshbandīya Order has certain peculiarities. It does not favour *dhikr jalī*, though it practises *dhikr khafī*. We have seen that all the other orders trace their origin to Muhammad through 'Alī. This order, on the other hand, claims to go back to Abū Bakr, the first Khalīfa. Though hitherto not so successful in India as the earlier orders, it has witnessed a kind of revival recently in the Panjāb and Kashmīr. It is especially favoured by the educated classes.

Besides these four main orders there are others of independent origin known as *be-shara'*, i.e., without the law. Some of these are organised, but others are made up of wandering mendicants.

Further Characteristics of the Sūfīs

1. *The Class of Saints.* As already indicated, there is a class of saints in Islām, who, in accordance with the degree of their sanctity, occupy " ranks " in an *invisible* order. This is considered to be a Divine organisation, in which the ranks are bestowed by God Himself.

The highest rank of all is that of the *Ghaus*, or " Succourer of the Universe." There can only be one exercising this office at a time. Next in honour come the *Aqtāb* (pl. of *qutb*, " axis "). These are supposed to be the centres of influence around which all the greatness and grandeur of the world revolve. They are three in number. After these are five *'Amd*, or " pillars," the support of the universe. Then forty *Abdāl* (pl. of *badl*, " substitute "), the transformed ones, because their natures undergo a complete change, spiritually. Next come seventy *Nujbā* (pl. of *najīb*, a " noble "), and three hundred *Nuqubā* (pl. of *naqīb*, a chief). Finally, there are a number of *auliyā* (pl. of *walī*), the more ordinary "saints."

It is believed that the world would long ago have come to an end because of the sins of the people, but for the prevailing prayers and great merits of the higher orders of these "saints." The intercession of the *Ghaus* is never in vain, though the prayers of the lower ranks may prove unavailing.

2. *Karāmāt.* All the saints of Islām are believed to possess the power to work wonders. Nevertheless, according to the teaching of the great Sūfīs it is as much an obligation for a saint to hide his gift as it is for a prophet to show his openly. These "wonders" are of four kinds:

(*a*) *mu'jiza*, lit. "miracle," which is the sign of prophethood, and is a gift bestowed by God on prophets only;

(*b*) *karāmat*, lit. "favour" (from God) to work wonders;

(*c*) *maunat*, lit. "help," a term used for describing wonderful works performed by an ordinary person by mere accident;

(*d*) *istidrāj*, stealth, or deception, by which is meant the amazing deeds of the magician.

3. *Samā'* (lit. "hearing"), Music. According to the *sharī'at*, on the authority of the *sunna*, music is forbidden to Muslims. By certain of the Sūfī orders, however, it is permitted, subject to certain stipulations such as the following. The musicians may not be boys or women, but men who have reached middle age. The audience must be composed of such as are capable of using the music as an aid to devout thoughts. Only musical instruments like the flute may be used; other kinds are barred. Needless to say these conditions are not strictly observed in the present day.

The famous saint, Shaikh Farīd-ud-dīn, described *samā'* as "the hearing of harmonious sound which moves the heart and kindles the fire of love for God." The object of such music is to induce a state of ecstasy. Arrived at such a state, the Sūfīs (or *darweshes*), either individually or collectively, begin to perform *raqs*, or dancing. Concerning such performance, Nizām-ud-dīn Auliyā, of Delhi, once said: "When a *darwesh* claps his hands in a state of ecstasy, all the sins of his hands are removed, and when he shouts all his evil desires are destroyed." There are cases on record where Sūfīs, listening to such music, have actually died in a state of super-ecstasy.

Congregational *samā*ʻ is generally performed at the tombs of the saints, especially at the times of celebrating the ʻ*urs*.

4. *Devotion to the pīr.* Although Sūfism claims to be the means of obtaining an immediate experience of God, yet in practice the mediation of a *pīr* or *murshid* becomes a first necessity. A *pīr* is to be followed blindly, and is actually obeyed as much as the Prophet Muhammad. All the *pīr*'s wishes, even though they contravene the letter of the *sharī*ʻ*at*, must be fulfilled. The saying of a famous mystic writer illustrates this: "If thy *pīr* orders thee to colour thy prayer-mat with wine, do it; for thou art ignorant of the path by which he is leading thee." In fact, the final stage of the journey, absorption in the Deity, is considered not to have been reached until the aspirant has "lost" himself in his *pīr*.

5. *Ziyārat.* The practice of paying such great respect to *pīrs* is continued after their death. A shrine is erected over their graves, and, usually on Thursday evenings, small earthenware lamps (*chirāgh*) are lit and placed on the tombs. Flowers also are offered.

Such a shrine is called *mazār*, the place of visitation, or *dargāh*, the royal court. The tomb of a *pīr* who is also reputed to be a saint receives still greater honour, being a place of resort for large numbers of pilgrims.

A pilgrimage to such a tomb is called *ziyārat*, "visit," and is generally made with a view to receiving some temporal or spiritual benefit. The form the worship usually takes on the occasion of such visits combines such features as these: Sūras i., cxii., cxiii., and cxiv. are recited; these are followed by the repetition of certain prayers for the soul of the departed; finally the worshipper makes some personal requests. As a rule, a vow is made at the time, which must be paid at the tomb when the favour is granted. It is a common practice to tie bits of thread or pieces of cloth, etc., on gratings near the tomb by way of reminding the saint of the favour asked.

The more orthodox Muslims, in particular the Wahhābis, strongly condemn such practices as being *shirk*, polytheism, the worst form of sin.

SECTION IV

ISLĀM IN THE MODERN WORLD

Chapter I

ISLĀM IN THE NEAR EAST

Islām from its very beginning was a political movement as well as a religion. Through all its history, and in the theory of its laws, religion and the state have been inseparably united. If, therefore, we wish to consider the state of Islām to-day, we must enquire both about the political status of the countries where Muslims dwell, and also concerning the religious life of the Muslims.

External Politics

The last century has seen enormous political changes in Islām. A hundred years ago, or to be precise, in the year 1830, the great majority of Muslims lived under Muslim rule. The Ottoman Empire included not only the present territory of the Turkish Republic, but also Egypt, Libya, Arabia, Syria, Irāq, and the Balkan Peninsula. Greece eight years before had been part of the Ottoman Empire, but in 1830 was in the middle of its wars of independence. Westwards from Libya the whole of the rest of North Africa was in Muslim hands, and consisted of independent states. The century that has passed has seen, on the one hand, aggression of European powers against Muslim lands, and, on the other hand, wars of liberation by which countries have freed themselves from the Turkish yoke.

In 1830 the French attacked Algeria, and by 1847 completed the conquest of it as far as the edge of the desert. In 1878, after the wars between Turkey and Russia, the independence of the Balkan States was recognised, namely, Serbia, Montenegro, and Rumania; while Bulgaria was to be autonomous but under tribute to Turkey. The other European powers objected to this treaty, and certain changes in boundaries, etc., especially affecting Bulgaria, were made shortly afterwards. At the same time Bosnia and Herzogovina were ceded to Austria, and the island of Cyprus to Britain. It was between 1878 and 1883 that the French established their protectorate over Tunisia. In the early years of the twentieth century Morocco was the subject of diplomatic rivalry between France, Spain, Germany, and Great Britain, which almost led to the outbreak of a great European war in 1906. Eventually in 1912 France obtained a treaty with the Sultān of Morocco by which Morocco became a French Protectorate. Spain had to be satisfied with the second place, having nothing more than a sphere of influence along the north coast. The last stage of the aggression of the European powers in North Africa took place in 1911 when Italy invaded Libya (Tripoli) and annexed its two chief provinces.

It was only natural that these repeated aggressions should eventually rouse resistance. Italy was resisted in Libya, not by the Turks, but by the Sanūsi of the desert, who prevented them from consolidating their conquests. Their last oasis, Kufra, in the extreme south, was taken by the Italians in 1930. As soon as the Spaniards tried to occupy their Moroccan zone in 1909 they met with opposition from the Rifi, and in 1925 the opposition of the latter extended to the French area. After the conclusion of the Great War, while the Allies were still negotiating over the terms of the peace treaty with Turkey, the Greeks coveted the Turkish city of Smyrna because it was largely inhabited by Greeks, and the Allies unwisely allowed the Greek forces to occupy it, only stipulating that they should not advance beyond the city of Smyrna itself. But in spite of this agreement the Greeks pushed up inland, and proceeded to invade Asia Minor, or Anatolia as it is now called. The Turks had borne patiently the loss of their outlying dominions, Arabia, Irāq, Syria, and Palestine, as well as most of their territory in the Balkan Peninsula, but this threat to their Anatolian homeland touched them to the quick, and their General, Mustafa Kamāl, rose to the occasion and led the Turks to victory over the Greeks.

Meanwhile allied diplomacy was hindered by disagreement among themselves, and, on the British side, by the Khilāfat agitation in India. The result was the signing of a humiliating treaty by the Allies, who retired, shamefacedly, from Constantinople. Mustafa Kamāl as the saviour of his country has earned the title of *Ghāzī*, "victor," and the popularity he gained largely accounts for the fact that he was able to bring about sweeping changes in Turkey which Amanullāh a few years later was unable to carry through in Afghānistān.

The political state of affairs therefore now is that Turkey is a small but consolidated country, inhabited almost entirely by Turks. Rumania, Bulgaria, Yugoslavia, Albania, and Greece, which formerly were part of the Turkish Empire, are now sovereign states. Egypt has gained practical independence, though Britain temporarily exercises some sort of influence there. The declaration of the independence of Irāq is only a question of time. Arabia is entirely free from foreign control, and the greater part of it is subject to the rule of Ibn Sa'ūd. Palestine, Transjordania, and Syria are under British and French administration, but Britain and France only hold authority there by mandate from the League of Nations, and have to render an account of their administration to the League. In North Africa the power has passed over entirely to European powers: France, Spain, and Italy. Thus the last hundred years has seen not only the break-up of the Turkish Empire, but also a large amount of territory changing from Muslim to Christian rule. The change in Turkey itself is the most remarkable. For some time the Turks had hoped to become the leading power of a Muslim coalition. But the Great War proved to them that they could not count on the support of Muslims of other lands, and therefore they turned their faces westwards and decided to seek their future as a European nation.

Turning our attention now to Persia, we need to consider not one century but two. For during the last two centuries Russia has been gradually encroaching from the north, and within that time has annexed an area larger than the whole of Persia as it is now. West of the Caspian Sea, in the area of the Caucasus mountains, Russia has also been steadily advancing during the same period, with the result that a very large number of Muslims now live under the rule of Soviet Russia.

Internal Political Changes

While thus Islamic rule has ceased in many lands, one Muslim country has of its own accord thrown over Islām. In 1922 Turkey declared itself a Republic, and abolished the office of the Sultān, at the same time abolishing the "Capitulations," i.e., the rights of foreigners living in Turkey to be judged by foreign courts. For two years the ex-Sultān was allowed to remain with the title of Khalīfa as the religious head of the Turkish Muslims; but in 1924 he was expelled from the country, and the Khilāfat ceased to exist. In 1928 Turkey took the further step of abolishing Islām as the religion of the state, and in the same year adopted the Roman in place of the Arabic alphabet which had up till then been used for the Turkish language. These two steps were the final proof that Turkey was seeking her future on the lines of Western civilisation.

Great political changes have also taken place in Persia, resulting in the formation of the new Pahlavi dynasty, though the changes have not attracted as much attention in the world as the events in Turkey. In 1924 a movement in favour of a republic came to a head under a leader named Riza Khān, who by his ability had risen from the ranks of the Persian army to be Minister of War. Seeing, however, that the country was not ready for a republic, Riza Khān in 1925 allowed himself to be appointed Shāh in the place of Sultān Ahmad, who had been deposed. Sir Percy Sykes, writing only four years before, had said that the state of lawlessness and brigandage in the country was so bad that the abolition of the capitulations was unthinkable. Riza Khān realised the necessity of internal security, and within a very short time the country was freed of its brigands. Rapid improvement in communications by road, rail, and air have played a large part in establishing security in the country. The capitulations were abolished in 1928, and a missionary, writing in the same year, said, "So far there has not been the slightest difference noticeable in the comfort and privileges of foreigners in Persia since the capitulations have been abolished." In Persia, as in Turkey, there is the framework of democracy and parliamentary government, though in neither country is there as yet real political freedom, the voters only being allowed to vote for the Government candidates.

Religious Movements

The abolition of Islām as the religion of the state has given the impression that Turkey is more advanced in religious freedom than other Muslim lands. As a matter of fact it is not so, for, although freedom to change one's religion is permitted by the statute book, every difficulty is put in the way of missionary work. Except distribution of the Bible, practically nothing in the way of direct evangelistic work is possible. The Turks at the moment have very little interest in religion as they are too much engrossed in their social and political programme. The darvesh orders have been abolished but otherwise Islām may be freely practised. In the towns the outward observance of Islām has greatly diminished. The restrictions against religious propaganda are based on the idea that religions stir up communal strife and hinder national unity. There are no reform movements in Turkish Islām at present.

Interest in religion is much greater in Egypt, where there is complete religious freedom. Christian missions are carrying on vigorous evangelistic work, both amongst the Muslims and amongst the Coptic Christians. Signs are present of attempts to reform the Coptic Church by the better education of the clergy. Among the Muslims there have been some serious attempts to reform Islām, though not to the same extent as in India. The curriculum of al-Azhar University, formerly the great stronghold of Islamic orthodoxy, is being gradually altered to suit the requirements of modern education.

In Palestine the most conspicuous feature is the economic strife between the Muslims and the Jews. A remarkable instance of a new attitude towards Christianity was seen in 1927 when thirty Muslims in a certain village in Galilee asked to become Christians. They did not all persevere in their purpose, but even so it was a new experience in missionary work among Muslims in that country.

The present ruler of Arabia, Ibn Sa'ūd, is of the sect of the Wahhābis, whose religion is of a puritanical type, nearest akin of any Muslims to primitive Islām. The cult of saints, and the smoking of tobacco, are treated as innovations, and strictly forbidden. Missionary work can still only be carried on in the outskirts of Arabia.

In French North Africa the French Government is said to be encouraging the vernacular Berber language instead of Arabic, and the Muslims regard this as an attack on Islām.

Probably the most successful missionary work in any Muslim field is going on in Persia. A recent writer says that Persian Islām seems to be disintegrating without any serious attempt to reform it, but he notices the beginning of propaganda by Ahmadīyyas. The Bahā'i movement (not to be confused with the Bābi movement) has not fulfilled the claims made on its behalf and now seems to be making but little headway. The renewed sense of nationalism has induced some Persians to turn their attention to Zoroastrianism (the Parsi religion) which has never quite died out in Persia. Christian missionary work is allowed, and, in spite of restrictions of various kinds, is reaping a considerable harvest of converts. From all accounts the Persian Christian Church is a vigorous body, keen on the work of evangelism.

To sum up our brief survey, we would say that the great changes that have come over the Muslim world have stirred the minds of many so that they are more ready than ever before to accept new ideas. Of old they had believed that Muslim victories were a sign of God's approval of their religion. The loss of territory and prestige in recent years has no doubt shaken the faith of many in Islām. We must not, however, use this as an argument against Islām, for we know that worldly success is no criterion of the righteousness of a man or nation. But where men's minds are shaken, there is an opportunity for missionary work; and it is noteworthy that it is in countries like Turkey, where the Christian witness has been weak, that there is the greatest tendency to drift into materialism, but where the Christian witness has been strong there we find evidence of a tendency either to seek a better religion in Christianity or at least to try to reform Islām.

Chapter II

ISLAM IN INDIA SINCE THE TENTH CENTURY

(1) The Empire of Delhi

With the coming of the Muslims to India over nine hundred years ago, the immemorial systems, rule and customs of her people were subjected to a series of rude shocks, and in course of time underwent certain modifications. For nearly eight centuries the activities of her Muslim rulers practically dominate the pages of her history. But the old Indian life weathered the prolonged and, at times, severe storm, and still endures, little changed. The fact is, no true or permanent union has ever taken place between Hindus and Muslims, notwithstanding the valiant efforts of a man like Akbar.

Although the original conquerors were foreigners, viz., Turks, Persians, Afghāns and Mughals, the present Muslim population is almost as Indian as the Hindus, owing to the intermarriage of the invaders with Hindu women.

In the extremely abridged review of the period which we are compelled to make within the compass of two short chapters, the story must necessarily take the form of a rather dry chronicle of these kings, their courts and conquests.

The Arabs do not figure among the Muslim conquerors of India. It is true that, attracted by stories of the great wealth and luxury of India, they made a few raids by sea along the western coast in the seventh century, but as their object was plunder they left no permanent mark. A more spectacular expedition was conducted by Muhammad ibn Qāsim. This ardent youth of seventeen years marched at the head of picked troops from Chaldea, through Makrān, along the Persian coast, and penetrated into Sind, capturing Multān in 712. But he incurred the displeasure of the Khalīfa and was recalled and disgraced. This early "invasion" likewise was barren of result.

Mahmūd of Ghaznī, 997-1030

What the Arabs had failed to effect the Turks were destined to achieve. But their invasion of India was not due to a concern to spread Islām. It came about in this way. The Abbāsid Khalīfas of Baghdād sought to secure their position from intrigues by employing vigorous young Turks as a mercenary guard. Ultimately these Turks got the upper hand of their own masters and became so influential that they attracted others of their own race from the north in the search for wealth.

One such adventurer, Alptagīn, leaving the service of his master in northern Persia, penetrated into Afghānistān and set up a small kingdom with its centre at Ghaznī (962). Sabuktigīn, a slave who succeeded him, was the first Muslim to attempt the invasion of India through the lofty north-west passes used by the early Āryans and Alexander the Great. But though he met and repeatedly defeated Jaipal, the king of the Panjāb, he did not follow up his victories.

Sabuktigīn was succeeded, in 997, by his son Mahmūd, who besides possessing his father's energy and spirit was a Muslim fanatic. Elated by the Khalīfa's blessing on his succession, he there and then resolved to wage a *jihād*, each year, against the idolaters of Hindustān. He came very near to fulfilling his vow. It is calculated that between the years 1000-1026 he raided India *seventeen times*, traversing the ground between the Indus and the Ganges. We are largely dependent, it is true, on Muslim records for our information, and these assure us that Mahmūd was not cruel, and that he seldom indulged in wanton slaughter. Nevertheless, from them we learn that, in his day, he slew tens of thousands of Hindus and took crowds of slaves. The lure of loot made good fighters of his men. On one occasion he stormed the fortress of Kāngra (Nagarkot) where the Hindu grandees kept their wealth, and thus came into the possession of immense stores of treasure and jewels. Even when allowance is made for the exaggeration of Muslim annalists the spoils he took with him to Ghaznī must have been colossal.

Thus, again and again, he swept over the plains of Hindustān, conquering kings and their castles, razing temples and smashing idols, until he became the terror of the countryside. Little wonder that he earned such titles as *Ghāzī*, and *But-shikan*, "idol breaker."

Against such onslaughts the Hindus exhibited the pitiable spectacle of vastly superior numbers hopelessly weakened by jealousies and disunion. Their hurriedly-formed confederacies of kings, each responsible only for his own section, were utterly incapable of meeting these virile northerners rallying to one command. And Mahmūd could always appeal to the fanaticism and greed of his followers.

His realm by now included Khurāsān, in Persia, and rich territories to the west, so that his conquests and his wealth became notorious all over the East. Thousands of warriors from beyond the river Oxus came begging to be given the privilege of serving under him and fighting for the faith. With his forces thus augmented he came again to Hindustān in 1018, and crossing each of the rivers of the Panjāb in turn, stood before the walls of Mathurā, the ancient centre of Hindu worship. From its temples he gained vast treasures, having smashed to pieces immense idols of gold and silver. During this campaign the Rāja of Baran (Bulandshahr) surrendered to Mahmūd, and with ten thousand of his subjects accepted Islām. In subsequent raids Mahmūd overran Kanauj, Lahore, and Gwāliar.

His crowning achievement was the capture of Somnāth, in Gujarāt, in 1025-6. It is said that one hundred thousand pilgrims used to assemble at its costly temple, which was served by one thousand Brahman priests. Its fame and the wealth of its gems enticed Mahmūd to make the exhausting march across the Rājputāna desert from Multān. To the dumb amazement of its protectors he sacked the place, carrying off to Ghaznī the famous gates of the temple and treasure worth one million pounds sterling.

That act, more than any other, caused Mahmūd to be remembered and extolled throughout the succeeding centuries as the champion of Islām. It is to be noted that he made no pretence of subduing India (though he "attached" the Panjāb to his realm); and he could not have done so, even had he wished. His battles were with independent princes; he was not fighting with any recognised head. Besides which, after each campaign, he and his men longed for home, and they found Ghaznī and the rich lands to the west infinitely preferable to the hot plains of India.

This mighty conqueror was no less famous for his patronage of art and letters at his court in Ghaznī. Amongst those whom he attracted thither were Al-Bīrūnī, the chronologist, and Firdausi, the Persian poet, author of the well-known *Shāh Nāma*.

The Dynasty of Ghor, 1175-1206

The Ghaznī dynasty was short-lived. Falling into decay it was reduced to impotence by more virile invaders from the west, who however were content to remain in Persia. It was finally overthrown by fierce Afghān highlanders from Ghor (between Ghaznī and Herāt), who in pursuance of a feud sacked Ghaznī in

1155, putting all the males to death. Little remains there to-day to remind posterity of the reign of the Ghaznavids, save the tomb of Mahmūd.

The peace, if such it may be called, which India had enjoyed for more than a century was, once again, to be rudely broken. A nephew of the man who sacked Ghaznī eventually set up his throne there, viz., Mu'izz-ud-dīn, commonly known as Muhammad Ghorī. This man, like Mahmūd before him, was the scourge of India for thirty years.

He made it his first business to consolidate Muslim gains in India and rid himself of Muslim rivals. In this way he brought under his control the old Arab colony on the Indus, captured Multān and subdued Sind. In 1184 he ravaged the district of Lahore and fortified Siālkot. Thus established, he turned upon the Hindus, whom he and his fanatical Afghāns were only too eager to "send to the fire of hell." Attempting to seize and garrison Sirhind, however, he encountered fierce opposition from the warlike Rājputs. The two forces met in 1191, ten miles to the north of Karnāl, near to the historic battlefield of Pānipat. Strategy was met by strategy, but the Muslims were worsted and fled across the Indus.

The Sultān smarted under this defeat and, vowing vengeance, returned next year at the head of 120,000 troops composed of Afghāns, Turks and Persians. This time the Rājputs were overthrown with ruthless slaughter. Many of their chiefs were slain, even their Rāja being "sent to hell." This victory led to the annexation of Ajmīr and other territories in 1192. Qutb-ud-dīn, a slave of Muhammad Ghorī, was appointed viceroy of India. Eventually, on the death of his master, he founded the empire of Delhi.

In the meantime there was much fighting to be done in which the Sultān and Qutb-ud-dīn co-operated. They subdued the intervening country right up to Benares, whilst Khiljī Bakhtiyār, pushing still farther east, secured Bengal as a permanent possession for the Muslims.

Flushed with victory Muhammad Ghorī, like Mahmūd, now cast covetous eyes on the rich lands of Khurāsān. But suffering disaster there he returned to find anarchy rampant in his own realm. Ghaznī and Multān revolted, and enemies over-ran the Panjāb. Backed by the loyal Qutb-ud-dīn, the Sultān regained much that had been lost, but met his death at the hands of assassins in 1206.

Less famous than Mahmūd, Muhammad Ghorī yet left a more permanent mark upon India, and in particular gave her a viceroy who was destined to be the first of many Muslim sovereigns exercising their rule from Delhi.

The Sultanate of Delhi, 1206-1526

(a) *The Slave Kings*, 1206-1290

Qutb-ud-dīn was the first of thirty-four Muslim kings who ruled at Delhi from 1206 till the coming of Bābar in 1526. These kings fall into five successive dynasties. Since Muhammad Ghorī had no son, Qutb-ud-dīn the slave succeeded him and founded the "slave" dynasty, composed entirely of Turks. He had rendered notable service as viceroy, and as king he consolidated the gains already made. He was a staunch Muslim and a mighty "fighter in the way of God." He did things on a big scale. He was known as Lākh-bakhsh, "donor of lacs." A contemporary said of him, "his bounty was continuous and *so was his slaughter*." Yet he left some noble monuments, built with materials from demolished Hindu temples; the Jama' Masjid at Delhi and the Qutb Mīnār, said to be the highest minaret in the world.

Confusion reigned after his death in 1210, because rival slaves strove for the throne which his son was too incompetent to occupy. But Altamish (Altutmish), who had been signally loyal to Qutb-ud-dīn, seized Delhi and after a long struggle dispossessed a rival in Lahore in 1217. But shortly afterwards a new and unexpected danger appeared beyond the Indus. That terrible scourge, Chingiz Khān with his Mongol hordes, having conquered a large part of China and all the famous kingdoms of Central Asia, advanced with fire and sword through Persia and seized Ghaznī. Fugitives from far and near poured through the passes into India, whose people trembled with terror. But the danger quickly passed since the Mongols preferred the rich lands to the west. Altamish emerged more secure than ever. In 1225 he received the homage of the governor of Bengal and by 1234 had control of all India north of the Vindhya hills. The Khalīfa of Baghdād sent an embassy in 1229, recognising him as sovereign of India.

Altamish died in 1236 and there followed prolonged disorder owing to the fact that his sons, who should have ruled (some tried to), were incompetent or depraved. For three years, indeed, it was a daughter who occupied the throne (1237-40), but the scornful Turks finally put her out of the way. Meanwhile Balban, one of the corps of forty slaves trained by Altamish, gained prominence through his service as commander-in-chief to Nāsir-ud-dīn, third son of Altamish, the nominal Sultān. For twenty years, years of rebellion and attacks by the dreaded Mongols, he served his master well. He held the frontier against the Mongols, he suppressed Hindu disaffection, and kept a strong hand on scheming Turkish chiefs. It seemed only natural that when Nāsir-ud-dīn died in 1266, Balban should succeed him. His master had been soft but the new Sultān was ruthless. Yet the times demanded severe measures. He dealt mercilessly with all brigands, and in many ways brought lasting benefit to the kingdom. But it was the Mongols who caused him most concern, and lest they should break through again he organised a highly efficient army.

Meanwhile, Tughril, a favourite slave of Balban who had been appointed by him as governor of Bengal, thought the time opportune to make a bid for independence. Two armies having failed to bring him to his senses, Balban, now an old man, set out to punish him. Surprising him and his followers near Lakhnautī he took terrible reprisals. He had the sons, kinsmen and bodyguard of Tughril killed and their bodies exposed on gibbets, continuing the general slaughter of the inhabitants for over two days. He set up a son as governor, and, subsequently, descendants of his ruled in Bengal till 1339. Balban himself died in 1287, and was succeeded by a dissolute grandson. The latter was done to death in 1290 and so the slave dynasty came to an end.

(b) *The Khiljī Dynasty*, 1290-1321

The absence of a strong Sultān for some years after Balban's death gave rise to much lawlessness. Out of the chaos the clan of the Khiljīs, originally Turks but hailing from Afghānistān and really Afghān in character, emerged with some show of strength and contrived to put Jalāl-ud-dīn on the throne of Delhi. This was a set-back for the Turks proper, who had fallen into general disfavour. Jalāl-ud-dīn, however, was an old man of seventy and inconceivably gentle towards bandits and rebels. His nephew 'Alā-ud-dīn had him shamelessly assassinated in 1296, and reigned in his stead. He proved himself to be the only one of the six Sultāns of the Khiljī dynasty capable of ruling Hindustān, and in his reign of twenty years he considerably extended his kingdom. Nevertheless, he soon showed himself to be a cruel and blood-thirsty brute by the manner in which he disposed of all possible rivals or rebels. A lavish distribution of largesse from the treasure he had previously amassed while invading the Deccan secured him an immense army.

During his reign the Mongol hordes made repeated inroads into India from 1296-1305, and kept him in constant anxiety.

Wherever he went success attended his arms and he became inordinately wealthy. But he was guilty of breaking the law of Islām in keeping for himself far too large a share of booty taken in war. A contemporary describes him as anything but an amiable character. Intoxicated by success he styled himself "the second Alexander." But he was prevailed upon to turn his attention to matters nearer home. Sedition was rife even among the members of his own family. Having dealt summarily with these he so severely taxed his subjects that they were reduced to impotence. In particular, he ground down the Hindus so that at his command they were "ready to creep into holes like mice."

In 1303 the Mongols descended on Delhi and all but took it. The invasion revealed the weakness of 'Alā-ud-dīn's defences. He forthwith set himself to regulate the cost of supplies and to reorganise his forts and his armies, with the result that next time the Mongols engaged him in battle he crushed them with terrific slaughter. It should be stated here that a community of Mongols, from earlier days, had embraced Islām and settled near Delhi. Resenting the miserable plight in which they were kept they now conspired against the state. 'Alā-ud-dīn's fury knew no bounds. He had all the males, numbering about 30,000, butchered in one day. In his rage he turned all the women and children adrift.

Thus freed from fear of conspiracy and from attacks in the rear by Mongols, 'Alā-ud-dīn furthered his intention of reducing the Hindus by capturing from the Rājputs, Ranthambhor and Chitor, but only at great cost. The story has often been told of how the brave Rājputs immolated their females before going forth to do battle to the death.

Having previously opened the door to the south he now sent an army under Malik Kāfur to invade the Deccan. In 1308 Devagiri, near Poona, was captured, its shrines looted, and its rāja made a vassal. The following year Kāfur similarly took Warangal, in Telingāna, and forced its rājā to pay tribute. Enormous wealth was removed to the Sultān's court, now at Sirī. In 1310 Dvāra-samudra, on the Mālābār coast, was sacked. Thus the northern part of the Deccan acknowledged the overlordship of Delhi.

Throughout these years 'Alā-ud-dīn had ruled strongly, making intemperance and extravagance punishable crimes. But his very success and his violent temper led to his undoing. His sons took to drink and his nobles to squabbling. He himself succumbed to a lingering disease in 1316. There followed five terrible years. First a son, Mubārak, unspeakably dissolute, by his example inaugurated a period of reckless vice. He dealt with all offenders with unbelievable cruelty, until he was done to death by a minion of his court, a low-caste Hindu. This man, styled Khusrū Khān, outdid his master. There ensued "four months of the worst tyranny India ever knew." 'Alā-ud-dīn's guardian of the Panjāb, Ghāzī Malik (Taglak), a Kaurania Turk, seized the occasion to assert himself and had Khusrū beheaded in 1321.

(c) *The Taglak Dynasty*, 1321-1388

Ghiyās-ud-dīn Taglak, or Taglak Shāh as he was called, took prompt steps to restore order in his domains, and by a considerable reduction of the land-tax brought about a return of prosperity. The preceding years, however, had witnessed insurrection and disaffection in the Deccan and Bengal, and so he sent Prince Jauna on an expedition to recover the Deccan possessions. After a successful campaign he returned, and Taglak left him in charge at Delhi while he himself marched at the head of an army into Bengal where he received the homage of Nāsir-ud-dīn, a great-grandson of Balban. On returning to Delhi, however, he met his death (1325) by an accident, believed by some to have been planned by Jauna, who then ascended the throne as Sultān Muhammad Taglak.

The new Sultān was a man of ideas, with the trained mind of a scholar and an indomitable will; nevertheless, owing to his impetuosity and impatience, he proved a conspicuous failure. Despite his lavish gifts and high intentions his people grew to loathe him, and he, in turn, took diabolical revenge. Ibn Batūta, the historian, himself an eyewitness, describes the Sultān's barbarities in language that makes one shudder. His prodigality exhausted the treasury. He furnished huge armies, intending to conquer Persia and China, and then had to resort to insupportable taxation. The *raiyats* of the Doāb, mostly Hindus, abandoned their fields and fled to the forests, but the Sultān ringed them in like animals and massacred the whole lot.

Prince and people were now thoroughly wretched, and it was at this juncture that the Sultān conceived a great idea which, however, he carried out like a fool. So as to be nearer the centre of his vast dominions he resolved to make Devagiri his capital, renaming it Daulatābād. But he must needs insist that the entire population of the now extensive city of Delhi should make the transfer with him! It was a weary trudge of seven hundred miles so that multitudes died, if not of disease, of despondency. Taglak saw his mistake and did his best to get his people back and recondition them, but he had to "restock" Delhi by importing others. Ibn Batūta found Delhi more like a desert.

These remedial measures once more drained the treasury and drove him to think of another bold idea, in the execution of which he again showed singular want of sense. He issued a *copper* currency without foreseeing the consequences. Soon every Hindu house was a private mint and literally crores of illicit coins came into circulation. In high dudgeon the Sultān repealed his edict and called in the copper, paying his people back in silver and gold. Such fitful experiments made him unpopular, and he only became more so when, in exasperation, he sought ruthlessly to crush insurrection in all parts of his realm. At one time the territory under his sway had been more extensive than that ruled by any of his predecessors. It then comprised twenty-three provinces, lying between the Indus and Sonārgāon in Bengal and between Lahore and Dvāra-Samudra on the Mālābār coast. But now it began to fall to pieces as province after province gained independence. One of these, Bengal, remained separate till the time of Akbar. In putting down a revolt in Gujarāt in 1351, the distracted Sultān died of fever.

Firoz Shāh Taglak, a cousin, was pressed by the chiefs to accept the throne. Throughout the thirty-seven years of his reign there was not one rebellion. He presented the strongest possible contrast to Muhammad Taglak, being so kind and full of sympathy that he won the hearts of his subjects. Nevertheless, he undertook several prolonged and arduous and, for the most part, successful campaigns to recover lost provinces. One of these was to Bengal in 1353, where in a great battle 180,000 Bengalis are said to have been slain. While away from Delhi he was well served by his *wazīr*, Khān-i-Jahān, a converted Hindu, to whom in part his milder policy was due. Firoz Shāh had a passion for building, and brought several new towns into existence, such as Jaunpur, in honour of his cousin, the late Sultān. He gave his people the inestimable boon of a series of canals. He also made generous grants to learned men and to pious endowments. But he was unwise in rewarding his nobles with large tracts of land, as it enabled them to develop an independence that threatened the throne. From these feudatory chiefs the Sultān demanded and received a vast retinue of slaves. Not less than 180,000 of such slaves were in the pay of the government. He died in 1388 at the age of ninety.

(d) *Provincial Dynasties*, 1388-1526

A period of prolonged disorder followed. The despotism of former Sultāns had been forgotten under the mild Firoz and the spirit of independence was abroad. Revolt was encouraged among the old Hindu chiefships by favoured slaves who had been granted territory, for many of these were but nominally-converted Hindus. The next ten years saw the throne occupied by incompetent descendants and a series of puppet Sultāns, who rose and fell in quick succession.

Into this chaotic kingdom Tīmūr, a Turk of Samarqand, burst like another Chingiz Khān. His name became a byword in India, for though a Muslim he was, like Chingiz, the incarnation of ferocity. Not the lure of India's wealth alone, but the determination to " send to hell " the infidel Hindus and to purify the land of the defilement of polytheism brought him hither in 1398, with ninety-two regiments of a thousand horse each. Fearful stories are told of his atrocities. For instance, in one hour his forces slaughtered 10,000 Hindus in the Rājput fortress of Bhatnīr, whither they had fled for protection. The inhabitants of the Panjāb scattered in terror at his approach. On the 17th December he was encamped before Delhi. Before engaging in what was to prove the decisive battle he took the precaution of butchering in cold blood no less than 100,000 Hindu prisoners in the rear of his camp. The Sultān's army, outnumbered and outgeneralled, broke up and fled. Tīmūr, in mock piety, declared that he could not control his Turks. For three days Delhi was a shambles, only the quarter of the leaders of the Muslim religion was spared. He sacked Meerut and slew all the males, and then with hosts of women and children as prisoners, and untold booty, he made his way out of India through Hardwār, about March 1399. In despatching lacs of " infidels " " to the fires of hell " he had performed his vow, but he left famine and pestilence behind him. He had destroyed all semblance of government in North India, so that for fifty years there was no regular sultanate. True, certain princes, claiming descent from the Prophet, ruled over the diminished empire in succession, from 1414-1451, but they never assumed the title of Sultān.

The Lodī Dynasty, Delhi, 1451-1526

Eventually Bahlol Lodī, an Afghān and governor of the Panjāb, became Sultān in 1451. He recaptured Jaunpur which had become independent in the days of Tīmūr's raids, and placed a son, Bārbak, over it. A younger son, Sikandar, succeeded Bahlol in 1489 and annexed Jaunpur. He appears to have been a good ruler, though hostility to the Hindus was a marked feature of his reign. He restored Agra which Mahmūd had ruined. Sikandara, near by, is named after him. Ibrāhīm Lodī succeeded him in 1517, but soon came into conflict with other Afghān nobles who, resenting his treatment of them, besought the help of Bābar, king of Kābul. Bābar promptly responded, and in 1526 crushed Ibrāhīm Lodī at Pānipat.

Bengal

The briefest notice must now be taken of only five of the principalities in other parts of India that set up rule independent of Delhi. Bengal had long been independent, but itself had rival kings. One ruled at Sonārgāon, near Dacca, in East Bengal, and another at Sātgāon, near Hugli. But these were united in 1352. In 1446 the united kingdom had its capital at Lakhnautī, which was renamed Gaur and later Jannatābād, "Paradise Town." The kingdom included part of Bihār, Orissa, Tippera, Kamrup and Chittagong, but little is left on record concerning its various rulers from the time of Muhammad Ghorī in 1202 to its conquest by Akbar in 1576.

Jaunpur

Jaunpur, the territory of the "Kings of the East" as they were called, was by reason of its architectural monuments the most conspicuous of all these kingdoms. It extended north of the Ganges from Delhi to Benares on the borders of Bengal. The significance of this kingdom from the point of view of Muslim history lies in the fact that it was established at the centre of Hinduism. Ibrāhīm Shāh (1401-1440) gained for himself a great name as a benevolent ruler, and patron of art and architecture. The Atala Devi Mosque at Jaunpur is his masterpiece.

Mālwa

This state, now forming part of the Central India Agency, also sprang into existence during the convulsion caused by Tīmūr. One of Firoz Shāh's beneficiaries, Dilāwar Khān, a descendant of Muhammad Ghorī, made himself independent in 1401, and soon extended his authority over the ancient Hindu kingdom of Mālwa. With the aggressive states of Delhi, Jaunpur, and Gujarāt hemming it in, it took part in much fighting, especially with the Rājput kings of Chitor. The ruler of Mālwa was finally crushed by a king of Chitor in 1440. The Rājputs thereafter ruled Mālwa until it was annexed by Gujarāt in 1531.

Gujarāt

Protected to the north by the desert, and to the east by the Vindhya hills, the rich kingdom of Gujarāt had for long withstood Muslim invasion. We have seen that it was raided in 1024 by Mahmūd of Ghaznī who looted Somnāth, but it was not till 1297 that Delhi annexed it. Its emergence as an independent Muslim province was due to the revolt in 1396 of Zafar Khān, a converted Rājput, to whom Firoz Shāh had granted the territory.

He gradually extended his domains. It was his son, Ahmad Shāh (1411-1441), who really established the kingdom, building both Ahmadnagar and Ahmadābād. The kings of Gujarāt maintained a fleet to protect their ports, and were in constant conflict with the Portuguese. The Sultān of Egypt sent ships to assist them, since the Indian trade with Egypt was threatened. The Portuguese were finally successful and established themselves at Goa and elsewhere.

The Deccan

In the general revolt that marked the closing years of Muhammad Taglak's reign, an Afghān named Hasan Gāngū, who had risen to high command in the Muslim armies in the south, defeated the Sultān's troops and proclaimed himself king of the Deccan in 1347. He founded the Bahmanī kingdom, which comprised the gains from Hindus made by Muhammad Taglak. To the south of him stretched the great empire of Vijayanagar, the last stronghold of Hinduism in the Deccan. With this Hindu kingdom Hasan Gāngū and his successors were continually at war. The Muslims ceded no ground to the enemy, but, on the contrary, took full revenge for any raids made by the Hindus. Hasan Gāngū's son, Muhammad I, on one occasion raided and laid waste the Carnatic at the cost, it is said, of half a million Hindu lives. Subsequently, at the close of the fifteenth century, under a regency and in the absence of a single strong ruler, the disruption of this empire began to take place. Separate kings taking the title of *Shāh* ruled in the provinces of Bījāpūr, Golkonda, Biḍar, Ahmadnagar, and Birār. These petty kingdoms continued until the coming of the Mughals.

Chapter III

ISLĀM IN INDIA SINCE THE TENTH CENTURY

(2) The Mughal Empire, 1526-1764

Bābar, 1526-1530

Bābar, king of Kābul, was in the mood to respond eagerly to the invitation to invade India. He had from the first been an ambitious but disappointed man. The blood of Chingiz Khān, the Mongol (whence the Arabic form, *Mughal*), and of Tīmūr, the Turk, mingled in his veins, producing a character of extraordinary energy. He was notable, too, for his cultured mind and his patronage of art.

Though entitled to Tīmūr's throne in far Samarqand, Bābar had been repeatedly expelled thence. In recent years he had been finding what satisfaction he could in the modest kingdom of Kābul. But in 1512 he turned his eyes eastward and saw in Hindūstān the scope he desired for his soaring ambitions. After a punitive expedition into the Panjāb in 1524, he finally entered India with his army in November 1525. He fought a decisive battle with the numerically superior troops of the Sultān Ibrāhīm Lodī on the historic plain of Pānipat, on 21st April 1526. Over-confident of success the enemy was put to flight with great slaughter, and Bābar quickly seized Delhi and Agra, thus becoming the first Emperor of a new dynasty.

He was prodigal in the generosity with which he shared the immense spoils with everyone of his followers, his son Humāyūn receiving the chief share; nevertheless his men became restless and wanted to return to Kābul. But Bābar had come to stay, and in a short time there was a remarkable rallying to his support even from amongst the Afghāns, many of whom had resented his intrusion. The support was timely, for the Rānā of Chitor at the head of a vast confederate army of gallant Rājputs was marching against him. Bābar made the most elaborate preparations for a *jihād* against these infidels near Sikrī (afterwards named Fathpūr-Sikrī). The Rājput cavalry charges almost broke the nerve of the Muslims, but by a characteristic movement Bābar attacked them in the rear and overcame them with terrific slaughter. The flower of the Rājput race lay dead upon the field.

The Emperor, however, was destined to have further trouble with the hostile Afghāns in Oudh and Bihār. After a successful encounter near Kanauj, his army advanced to meet a large force of rebels around Jaunpur under Mahmūd Lodī, brother of the late Sultān Ībrāhīm. The enemy, however, scattered at his approach. Some of the chiefs offered him their allegiance while others betook themselves with their troops to swell the armies in Bengal. Crossing the Ganges in face of determined opposition Bābar's men attacked the enemy in front and rear and flank and gained another decisive victory which broke the Afghān resistance. He gave his last year to consolidating his empire, and to the writing of his famous *Memoirs*. Always a strong man he, nevertheless, broke up under the prolonged strain of his campaigns and the insidious effects of the use of wine and opium. He died in Agra in December 1530, but was buried as he wished in the hills of his beloved Kābul.

Humāyūn, 1530-1556

Bābar was succeeded by his eldest son, Humāyūn, a kindly soul but weak and vacillating, and quite unfitted to hold together the various parts of the kingdom which his father had never really conquered. His own brothers were disloyal, and Kāmrān, next in age, seized the Panjāb while professing to hold it for the Emperor. Nor were his brothers his only foes. To the east the Afghāns under Mahmūd Lodī were again manifesting a truculent spirit, and from the south Bahādur Shāh, king of Gujarāt and Mālwa, was actually advancing upon Agra.

Humāyūn's tactics, in circumstances of such danger, reveal his inherent weakness as a ruler. Proceeding first against Mahmūd he defeated him very decisively near Lucknow in 1531. Then, harassed by the fear of an attack on his capital he abandoned pursuit of this foe in order to get back to deal with the other menace. Marching into Mālwa he gained a hollow victory over its king and again left behind him a people unsubdued who threw off his yoke as soon as his back was turned. Meanwhile, in the north, Sher Shāh, a formidable Afghān noble, had become supreme on the borders of Bengal, and Muhammad Sultān had installed himself as king at Kanauj. Such was the net result of the Emperor's efforts.

After wasting a whole year in merry-making at Agra the Emperor at last roused himself to do battle with the rebels in Bihār. Sher Shāh, the chief of these, was, however, absent conquering Bengal which he had long coveted for himself. Before the Emperor could reach him he had transferred his booty and retinue to the once Hindu fortress of Rohtās. Arriving in Bengal only to find the devastation caused by the Afghān, Humāyūn with all his court and army wasted another precious six months in frivolity and worse.

Meanwhile Sher Shāh had cut off his retreat by closing every road into Bengal. Though well aware of the Emperor's plight his brothers did not go to his aid, but rather seized the occasion to assert their own claims. Forced to make a treaty the Emperor ceded Bengal and part of Bihār to Sher Shāh. Subsequently, the treacherous Afghān fell on the unsuspecting Mughals and slaughtered them almost to a man. Humāyūn was one of the very few to escape. A year later, May 1540, the Emperor again tried conclusions with Sher Shāh, but his dispirited and badly led troops were repulsed almost without a struggle. Once again Humāyūn only just escaped with his life.

Thereafter he lived a wandering existence for fifteen years, during which period his famous son, Akbar, was born in the year 1542. In 1547 Humāyūn took Kābul from the irreconcilable Kāmrān. Meanwhile Sher Shāh had been proving himself a capable and popular ruler in India. His policy of fair treatment for the Hindu prepared the way for the reforms of Akbar. While attempting, however, to subdue the Rājputs he met his death at Kālinjar in 1545. A period of disorder followed, of which Humāyūn took advantage in 1555 to return with Akbar to India. This he signalised by a great victory at Sirhind. Six months later he slipped down some steps in his palace and died at the age of forty-nine. It has been said of him that "he tumbled through life and he tumbled out of it."

Akbar, 1556-1605

Akbar was a lad of thirteen when he succeeded his father. At the outset he could only call the Panjāb and Delhi his own, and it cost him twenty years of hard fighting to recover for the empire such tracts as Ajmīr, Gwāliar, Chitor, Mālwa, Gujarāt, Oudh, and Bengal. Orissa, Kashmīr, and Sind only fell to him after thirty years. He failed to recover the Deccan.

There were those in the young prince's court who in view of the hostile forces around counselled retreat to Kābul, but Bairām, the Turkmān regent, took a strong line, knowing that the country was thoroughly disorganised. Nevertheless, the early occupation of Delhi by Hīmū, a Hindu upstart now supreme in Bengal, resulted in a critical battle on the field of Pānipat in November 1556. Akbar's army was victorious and thenceforth he became the attacker, and was never again attacked. Delhi and Agra welcomed him, and soon the north-west portion of India owned his sway.

In 1560 Akbar, no longer a mere boy, took the reins into his own hands. Shortly afterwards he firmly dismissed the regent and took steps to rid himself of meddlesome people in the palace. During these early years he exhibited a kindness and a sense of fairness towards all who were law-abiding that augured well for the future, but he could be terrible in his punishment of the rebellious. Not for him were the soft pleasures of the *harīm*. It is on record that he lived a regular and abstemious life and that he excelled in manly sports, such as polo and the chase. He seemed tireless on campaign and often infected his troops with his personal daring.

Akbar's conciliatory treatment towards Hindu chiefs was an important factor in his steady growth in influence and power, and their loyalty to him frequently offered a striking contrast to the attitude of seditious Muslims. His marriage with a Rājput princess confirmed him in his determination to show tolerance to all. Indeed, what with Hindu, Persian, and Mughal wives, and one an Armenian Christian, in his *harīm*, there was little fear that he would ever develop into a religious fanatic. On the contrary, he greatly increased his popularity among his Hindu subjects by abolishing the *jizya*, or Islamic poll-tax on "unbelievers," and another irksome tax hitherto levied on Hindu pilgrims.

It must not be supposed, however, that such conciliation won over all the Hindus. In particular the Rājputs of Chitor were still proud and defiant, and it was only after a prolonged and desperate siege that the famous fortress fell with great loss of life in 1567. But from that time practically all the Rājputs tendered their allegiance to this indomitable and highly respected fighter. Thus, with the hearty co-operation of loyal Hindu princes, the empire of Akbar was gradually extended throughout north India, and in the south up to the river Narbada.

The most notable Hindu in the Emperor's service was Todar Mal, a Rājput, who besides being a capable military commander proved himself a genius in finance. In 1582 he became Akbar's chief revenue minister. Since the Emperor had abolished several unpopular forms of taxation it had become imperative that the land-tax should be made to yield sufficient for the administration, without at the same time being unfair to the cultivator. Todar Mal, having made a most elaborate land survey, evolved a system of taxation that was both equable and popular. But he made himself unpopular with the more bigoted Muslims by demanding that all government accounts should in future be kept in Persian instead of Hindi, as heretofore. This innovation had the result of compelling Hindus to study Persian, and in course of time they stood on terms of equality with the Muslims themselves in competition for state service.

The more orthodox Muslims shook their heads also over the increasing " laxity " of their Emperor. He not only treated Hindus on equal terms with the " faithful " but held " broad " views on matters of religion, and in particular was greatly influenced by the free-thinker Abū-l-Fazl, a favourite in his court.

Akbar was in the habit of making pilgrimages to sacred shrines in the hope of securing an heir. In this connection his visits to the cave of Salīm Chishtī of Sikrī, near Agra, are of special interest. The son eventually born to him in accordance with the promise of the holy man of Sikrī was himself named Salīm. Sikrī was a place of constant resort. It is well known that Akbar dreamed in its luxurious surroundings of a universal religion. There, in his presence, prolonged debates often took place between representatives of various religions. It was clear that Islām no longer satisfied him. He gradually assumed for himself an authority over his subjects second only to that of the Qur'ān, and there were cynics who declared that *Allāhu Akbar* was now to be understood as " Akbar is God ! "

The fact is that he opened his mind to impressions from every side, and had evolved a kind of eclectic pantheism. He borrowed ideas equally from Brahman *pandits* and Portuguese *pādrīs*. Few really agreed with him in his eccentricities, but even horrified Muslims (and there were many) dared not openly speak against him.

He was comforted, however, in possessing men of real genius as his immediate counsellors. With Abū-l-Fazl, his chronicler, was a brother Faizī, worthy to be ranked among India's finest poets. But the last days of this noble-minded Emperor were filled with personal sorrow. Two of his sons died of drink, and Salīm, afterwards known as Jahāngīr, in a fit of jealousy had the trusted Abū-l-Fazl done to death. Akbar never recovered from the shock. He died in October 1605, and was buried at Sikandra, near Agra.

Jahāngīr, 1605-1627

The new Emperor, from being the petted darling of his father, had developed into a wilful, self-indulgent youth. More than once he had openly revolted against Akbar. He had a violent temper and was a notorious drunkard. Fortunately for the future of the empire he had toned down by the time he ascended the throne, at the age of thirty-seven. The chief factor in the reformation of his character was the strong influence of his beautiful and gifted queen, Nūr-Jahān, "the light of the world."

As Emperor he manifested a certain indolent good nature and sound common sense, qualities which enabled him to carry on the beneficent work of his father. Though more strictly a Muslim he yet continued Akbar's conciliatory attitude towards Hindus and Christians, and severely punished any proved guilty of oppression and intolerance. He likewise carried on the system of government instituted by his father.

In regard to our knowledge of his character and court

we are not in this case obliged to depend entirely upon Muslim annalists. Akbar's renown brought European travellers to the Mughal court in the early part of the seventeenth century, and from two Englishmen in particular, a sea-captain, Hawkins, and Sir Thomas Roe, ambassador of King James, we have much trustworthy information.

These men, in seeking to secure concessions for the English trade, were presented, in turn, to the Emperor himself. Their presence of course was strongly resented by the Portuguese who had already obtained a footing on the coast at Goa and elsewhere, and by the Jesuit *pādrī* at court, who did his best to prejudice Jahāngīr against them. Roe, eventfully, was successful in securing a firmer footing for the English factory at Surat, which Hawkins had been permitted to open.

These travellers show Jahāngīr to have been anything but an admirable character. To begin with he was inordinately wealthy. Hawkins estimated his income at 50 crores of rupees, or £50,000,000; and Roe ascertained that his viceroy at Patna drew a salary of nearly £80,000 a year, or about four times the pay of a British Viceroy. We are told, too, that the Emperor kept an army of menials numbering 36,000. The daily expenses of his court were 50,000 rupees, to which was added another 30,000 spent on the *harīm*—a small bill of £9000 or 3¼ millions a year.

But he was far from popular and his subjects stood in fear of him. In punishment as in sport he delighted in excessive cruelty. His daily life was far from edifying. After commencing the day with prayers and beads, he would "show himself," after the manner of the Mughal emperors, to his people, and receive their salutations. But many hours of the day and the first part of the night were given to feasting and drinking and the pleasures of the *harīm*. Roe, in particular, was often disgusted at his besotted condition.

It was under such circumstances that his capable

queen, Nūr-Jahān, became virtual ruler of the vast domain. A Muslim chronicler, Muhammad Hādī, declares that the Emperor was content to leave in her hands the affairs of state so long as he was allowed to make merry with a bottle of wine. Jahāngīr publicly acknowledged her worth by joining her name with his own on the state coinage.

Nūr-Jahān for long was liberal and just but her too-great power spoilt her, and in course of time her covetousness and favouritism aroused bitter jealousies and intrigues that darkened the last days of the reign. The Emperor's sons headed separate factions. Prince Khurram, the second of them, successfully removed from his path Khusrū, the eldest, who had proved fractious and seditious. Khurram was both capable and headstrong, yet Nūr-Jahān disliked him intensely, for she favoured a younger son by another wife. At length Khurram, already styled Shāh-Jahān, openly revolted against his father. The rest is soon told. Nūr-Jahān made a desperate but unsuccessful attempt to win over the army, and then when her husband died she retired to a life of complete seclusion leaving Khurram to ascend the throne. She died in 1547 and was buried by the side of Jahāngīr, at Shāhdara, near Lahore.

Shāh-Jahān, 1628-1658

Like his father the new Emperor was the son of a Rājput princess, and had indeed more Indian than Mughal blood in his veins. Having removed all rivals from his path he seems to have become a different man, for by all accounts he was the most popular of the Mughal Emperors, and in consequence his reign was one of singular prosperity. Encouraged in a more strict observance of the Muslim faith by his beloved wife Arjumand Bānū, otherwise known as Mumtāz-i-Mahal, he was just a little intolerant of Hindus. But he was a sound judge of character, and whatever prejudices he may have had these did not prevent him from employing many Hindus as his trusted generals.

The Mughal Emperors had made it a rule that, on the death of nobles and officers to whom grants of land and lucrative posts had been made, all their property and effects should revert to the crown. In this way the Imperial treasury was being constantly replenished. A European visitor to Agra in the time of Shāh-Jahān estimated that the treasure accumulated in the palace within the fort exceeded the enormous sum of £300,000,000. This same writer describes the extent and splendour of Agra in those days and the Emperor's immense army, the size of which may be gathered from the fact that it contained of cavalry alone, 144,000.

Shāh-Jahān was a great builder. Many beautiful edifices remain to this day in Agra as a memorial of his luxurious reign, but his masterpiece was, and is, the marble Tāj, commemorating his unchanging love for Mumtāz-i-Mahal, the mother of fourteen children. It was completed in 1648, 20,000 workmen having been engaged on it daily for several years. Yet even these buildings were eclipsed by the new palace which he erected for himself in Delhi. Several competent European judges of architecture have described it as being the most magnificent royal residence in the world.

To this splendid abode Shāh-Jahān retired in his declining years. Excess of wealth and all manner of extravagance had enervated the once vigorous man of action. He was still popular, however, and prodigal in the distribution of largesse. On his coronation anniversaries, following an old Mughal custom, he had himself weighed in massive scales against precious metals and gems of all kinds, and then distributed the equivalent of his weight of these to his people. But his own children now managed him. Anticipating trouble from the intrigues and jealousies of his sons he devolved his authority upon four of them, allotting to each the viceroyalty of a distant province. But this only accentuated his difficulties.

Aurangzeb, the third of these, a man who had proved himself an intrepid fighter, was assigned the troublesome Deccan. There with the help of Mīr Jumla, a brilliant Persian general, he recovered Bidar and Kulbarga and was about to annexe Bījāpūr, when he hastened north at the first news of his father's serious illness. There now ensued a desperate conflict between the four sons for the throne.

Shāh Shuja', governor of Bengal, quickly advanced with a large army into Bihār. Dārā Shikoh, his father's favourite, launched a surprise attack upon him at Benares and scattered his forces, and then turned to face the combined armies of Aurangzeb and Murād Bakhsh at Samūgarh. A bloody encounter, in which the three brothers displayed amazing bravery, ended in the rout of Dārā and his army. The latter had made the fatuous mistake of descending from his towering elephant, thus giving his men the impression that he had been slain. Aurangzeb now acted with despatch and cunning. First he imprisoned his old father in the palace at Agra. Then with Murād Bakhsh he pursued Dārā. On the way he intoxicated Murād and sent him away as a captive. When at last he got hold of Dārā he treated him shamefully and had him put to death as an "apostate." Shuja' was driven into the hills of far Arakan, and so Aurangzeb was left without a rival.

Aurangzeb, 1659-1707

The new Emperor was before all else a strict Muslim of the Sunni sect. His predecessors had exhibited no such scruples and, in fact, from Akbar onwards had owed much of their popularity and success to the tolerance they displayed towards the followers of other faiths. But with Aurangzeb religion was a passion, and government according to the standards of Islām a guiding principle.

Once again, for our very precise knowledge of this Mughal's character we are indebted to the memoirs of

Europeans, in this case two Frenchmen, Tavernier and Bernier, both of whom knew the Emperor intimately. In his more private life Aurangzeb was almost the *faqīr* he had once sought to be in his youth. He ate no meat and drank water only. He was a *hāfiz*, and twice copied out the entire Qur'ān in his neat handwriting, sending the ornate manuscripts to Mecca and Madīna. The one Islamic duty he did not (and dare not) perform was to leave his throne in order to make the pilgrimage to Mecca.

The story of his reign would have been very different had he followed the policy deemed wise by his fathers. He was now forty years of age and knew full well that the course he marked out for himself would alienate friends and foment opposition. But he was the bravest of the brave, and possessed a most resolute will. The thing he could not and would not do was to be false to his faith.

Yet he looked upon it as his supreme duty to further the welfare of his numerous subjects, and no detractor of Aurangzeb has been able to prove against him any act of injustice when viewed *in the light of the law of Islām*. This stern Muslim was a mild ruler and readily accessible to all, at least in the early part of his reign. But he kept his hands on the reins, for he was by nature inordinately suspicious. He, like others of his line, lived in dread of being poisoned. And this much must be said as against the praise of Muslims for this first of Muslims, that his courtiers and officers lived in fear of him, and that while all respected him none loved him. Made wise from personal experience he imprisoned his own sons, one for life and another for six years, because he suspected them of disloyalty.

Though he shunned the liquid ruby and would have none of those scenes of debauchery that had disgraced the private life of more than one Emperor, Aurangzeb nevertheless was sufficiently a Mughal to maintain a court of dazzling splendour. Delhi, the city of Shāh-

Jahān, was his favourite capital, and Bernier, who spent four years there, has left us in no doubt about its magnificence. The beautiful and famous Hall of Audience in the palace was often the scene of such amazing brilliance as to merit the inscription over its entrance: "If earth holds a haven of bliss, it is this, it is this, it is this." The famous Peacock Throne, constructed by Shāh-Jahān, was perhaps the most arresting ornament. Tavernier appraised its value at £6,000,000. It was supported by six massive feet, thought to be of pure gold. In it were set costly gems, rubies, emeralds and diamonds, the accumulated treasure from several campaigns.

Aurangzeb was more concerned, however, and with good reason, to keep an efficient standing army. He gathered round him a body of adventurers, raising them to power and affluence by the grants he made to them. They, in turn, to maintain their position and pay the customary dues to the crown, extorted all they could from the wretched peasantry who worked on their holdings. In fact the Emperor's professed regard for the welfare of his people stopped short of redressing the grievances of the oppressed poor.

The most notable military campaign, in a reign otherwise remarkably free from such undertakings, was that launched in East Bengal against the pirates of Arakan who were secretly aided by the Portuguese. Brigands from far and near flocked to Chittagong at the bidding of the King of Arakan to engage in marauding expeditions into the interior. Shaista Khān, the Emperor's uncle, successfully broke their power in 1666 and seized Chittagong, renaming it Islāmābād.

When twenty years of his reign had passed by Aurangzeb seemed to rouse himself from the tolerance he never felt and only half concealed. Provoked by the Brahmans of Benares he destroyed their temple of Vishnu, and then razed to the ground a shrine at Mathurā and on its site built a mosque. He had the idols brought to Agra where they were buried under the steps of a mosque, so that Muslims might feel they were trampling them underfoot! The Hindus were furious, and at length rose in revolt but were crushed with great slaughter. And then, nothing daunted, the Emperor committed, and *deliberately*, the incredible folly of re-imposing the *jizya*. It was a gratuitous insult to all Hindus, including the Rājputs. These last he doubly offended by demanding that the proud chief Jaswant Singh should send his two sons to Delhi to be " educated " under the Emperor's supervision. Jaswant's indignant refusal brought Aurangzeb into the field. The Rājputs were defeated but not dispirited. The war with them was prolonged and indecisive, but little did the Emperor realise that with every day he was alienating for ever the sympathies of these his best allies.

Aurangzeb now bethought himself of the still unconquered Deccan and turned southwards on a punitive expedition. But as though he had not enough foes already, there now appeared on the scene an unsuspected enemy in the Mahrattas, of the Konkan and Western Ghats. Used by the king of Bījāpūr as levies, these men, Hindus of the Sudra caste, emerged as tireless fighters in guerilla warfare. Their leader Shivājī, having established himself in the Konkan, actually ventured forth to try conclusions with the Emperor himself. Though gaining several successes at the expense of Aurangzeb, Shivājī was at length forced to make terms. The Emperor by treating him with contempt converted him into an inveterate foe. Shivājī died in 1680, " but his spirit lived in the nation he had created."

Aurangzeb, no longer trusting his own generals, now took command of the army himself. He made several ineffectual attempts to crush the Mahrattas, but as often as he turned from them they harassed his flanks. Aware of their confederacy with the Deccan he left them in the hope of cutting off their supplies by exterminating the kingdoms of Golkonda and Bījāpūr. He starved out the defenders of Bījāpūr after a blockade of one year's duration. But Golkonda proved to be no easy prey. Bribery at last succeeded when all other devices failed.

But the Emperor could hardly deceive himself into thinking that he had conquered the Deccan. The majority of the vanquished armies had no taste for service under him and went over to the Mahrattas. His forces just failed of success mainly because he no longer had the assistance of the Rājputs, and his own Muslim officers were not of the same mettle as those who ravaged Hindustān under Bābar.

The last view we have of the now aged Emperor is that of a gloomy and lonely soul. He returned to Ahmadnagar to die. All his zealous faith could not save him from the dread of approaching death. In his last letter to his sons, whom though suspecting he still loved, there was wrung from him a confession of his own failure. But in this at least he did not fail—to the end he remained true to Islām.

He was without doubt the most powerful of all the Mughal Emperors. He had commanded larger armies and more extensive territory than any of them, but with a will of iron. Now that he was dead forces were let loose that soon produced a general upheaval. His eldest son, Mu'azzam, having disposed of his brothers, ascended the throne as Bahādur Shāh, only to find Mahrattas, Rājputs, Sikhs, Jāts and, most significant of all, the English as hostile forces.

In the confusion of later years Delhi was sacked twice, once in 1739 when the Persians took away the Peacock Throne and immense treasure, and again in 1756 by the Afghāns. The Mahrattas fought a desperate battle at Pānipat in 1761 to win back Hindustān for the Hindus, but were repulsed with terrific slaughter. At length a decisive victory by the British at Buxar in 1764 reduced the last remnant of the Mughal power in Upper India.

Chapter IV

REFORM MOVEMENTS IN INDIA

Wahhābi Influence

In the eighteenth century there arose in the province of Najd, Arabia, an uncompromising *puritan*, Muhammad ibn 'Abd-ul-Wahhāb (1703-1791), whose teaching and example were soon to have a profound influence in India. An adherent of the Hanbali school, he sought to restore the golden age of the Prophet and his Companions. To this end he acknowledged only *two* sources of revelation, the Qur'ān and the early *sunna*. Further, he confined the scope of the principle of *ijmā'* to a definitely limited period and set his face against all innovations due to the exercise of *ijtihād*, whereby Islām had, in the interval, attempted to adapt itself to changing conditions. In particular, he disapproved of visits to Muhammad's tomb at Madīna and of the annual celebrations on his birthday (*maulūd*). He was equally opposed to the doctrines and practice of Sūfism.

After his death his followers pillaged the sacred shrines of the Shī'as at Najaf and Karbalā, and later, in 1803-4, captured the cities of Mecca and Madīna. They even looted the treasures kept at the tomb of the Prophet, and for years plundered the pilgrims, bringing about a cessation of the *hajj*. They were finally crushed by Muhammad 'Alī Pāsha, of Egypt. In modern times their successors under Ibn Sa'ūd, of Najd, once more occupied Mecca (October 1924), but showed more respect for ancient shrines.

The first signs of the presence of Wahhābi ideas in

India appeared in the Farīdpūr district of East Bengal, in 1804. In that year Hāji Sharī'at Allāh, of Bahādurpūr, founded the sect known as *Farā'izi*, i.e., observers of the "prescribed duties"; making it his business to purge Islām of the superstitions and corrupt beliefs it had assimilated through long contact with Hinduism. He pronounced India to be *dār-ul-harb*, "the abode of war," because it was under non-Muslim rule.

His son Dūdhū Miān carried on his work in the same district, where he built up an elaborate organisation. His chief success was among the agricultural classes, whose cause he championed. The *Farā'izi* sect is not much heard of these days, but its reform doctrines still persist in a sect known as *Ahl-i-Hadīth*, "the People of the Traditions."

Another zealot with Wahhābi tendencies was Sayyid Ahmad of Rāī Bareli. About the year 1819 he came forward to denounce the abuses that had crept into the faith and practice of Islām and soon gathered around him many disciples who hailed him as another *mujaddid*, or reformer for the new age. He made Patna his centre, but had a great following in Calcutta also. Returning from a pilgrimage to Mecca more zealous than ever, he proclaimed the need of *jihād*, since he, too, considered India to be *dār-ul-harb*. From that time the Muslims began to break up into two camps, and the cleavage remains to this day. The orthodox *maulvīs* opposed the drastic reforms of the followers of this *Tarīqa-i-Muhammadiyya*, or "Way of Muhammad," as Sayyid Ahmad called his sect, and nicknamed them "Wahhābis." He, in turn, called all Muslims who opposed him *mushrik*, polytheist. Ahmad's zeal led him to carry on a *jihād* against the Sikhs, and it was while fighting them that he met his death near Peshawar, in 1831. The movement survived him mainly because he had infused into his followers a passion for a free and reformed Islām. Not only so, immense pecuniary resources and an elaborate organisation (whereby emissaries for his cause covered the greater part of India) helped to insure for his reforms an abiding influence on Indian Muslims. It counted for much that he was lineally descended from the Prophet. His disciples paid him the utmost deference, believing him to be the promised Imām-Mahdī, who was to destroy *Dajjāl*, the Anti-Christ.

The Sayyid's propaganda work may be said to have been carried on by Maulvi Karāmat 'Alī, of Jaunpur, though he did not share his master's views on *jihād*. Some time before 1824 he had become one of the Sayyid's most ardent disciples, but he largely confined his activities to the more moderate and peaceful occupation of purging the popular Islām of East Bengal of its Hindu elements. Unlike his master and other Wahhābi leaders he fostered the relationship of the *pīr* and *murshid*, and ere he died, in 1873, could count his disciples in most of the villages. His relatives still carry on a peaceful propaganda in those districts and claim to have numerous disciples.

The ideas and activities of these Indian "Wahhābis" brought to birth two other sects, *Ahl-i-Hadīth*, "People of the Traditions," and *Ahl-i-Qur'ān*, "People following the Qur'ān." Neither numbers many adherents. The former repudiate any connection with the Wahhābi movement, yet, nevertheless, have similar aims as their manifesto indicates: "Whatever the Prophet Muhammad taught in the Qur'ān and the authoritative traditions, that alone is the basis of religion known as the *Ahl-i-Hadīth*." They denounce the prevalent homage paid to "saints"; they reject the four recognised schools of canon law, contending that the door of *ijtihād* is not closed and that it is incumbent on the *'ulamā* of each generation to seek for that generation their own interpretation of the Qur'ān and Traditions. And these reformers no less than their predecessors are seeking to rid present-day Islām of foreign customs and superstitions.

The *Ahl-i-Qur'ān*, on the other hand, reject all other

sources of authority save the Qur'ān, which they consider to be a sufficient guide in all matters. It was founded in 1902 by Maulvi Abdullah Chakrālawi of Lahore, who erected a mosque for the special use of his own disciples. The sect does not appear to exercise much influence.

Sir Sayyid Ahmad Khān (1817-1898)

The mention of this name takes us back to the middle of the last century. Here was a man of very different mould and outlook from that of the Wahhābi reformers. While no less loyal than they to the memory of Muhammad and the authority of the Qur'ān, he nevertheless, greatly daring, advocated an entirely new course of action for Indian Muslims.

Distressed at the sad and backward condition of his people he felt convinced that their salvation lay in a new attitude towards British rule and the revolutionising influences of the West. In the critical days of the mutiny of 1857 he remained loyal, as did many other Muslims, and when the storm had passed he sought to win the sympathy of Government for Muslims, to whose essential loyalty he bore witness.

His worth to Muslims and the cause of progress generally may be judged by the objects he set himself to achieve.

1. He strove to rid Muslims of the baneful idea that India was *dār-ul-harb*, insisting instead that it was *dār-ul-Islām*, since Muslims under the British were perfectly free to exercise their religion.

2. He believed that there was need of a change in the religious outlook of his people. He taught that the individual was not only free to do so, but was under a solemn obligation to exercise his own judgment in matters appertaining to the Islamic revelation. He stood for the supremacy of reason, and strenuously opposed the older school who demanded blind accept-

ance (*taqlīd*) of all that had been handed down. He maintained that current Islām was not the pure Islām of Muhammad's day; that Islām is Nature, and Nature, Islām. Further, having made a study of Christianity he ventured to reconcile the two religions, pleading especially for more sympathy from both sides. He showed considerable courage and enterprise in attempting a *Muhammadan Commentary on the Holy Bible* (1862-5), but this he did not carry beyond the first few chapters of Genesis.

3. He was a staunch advocate of new methods of education. To him it was clear that the old ideas of Muslim education were inadequate. He was not afraid, as were most of his co-religionists, that modern science would prove detrimental to Muslim beliefs. In 1869, during a long visit to England, he studied the educational systems then in vogue and came back fired with the desire to establish on Indian soil a college having the spirit of Oxford. He met with the most vehement opposition from leaders of the old school and was denounced as a *kāfir*, infidel. Nevertheless, backed by others of like mind, he had the satisfaction of inaugurating the famous Aligarh College in 1875. This, in 1920, was raised by charter to the status of a Muslim university.

4. Simultaneously he worked strenuously for certain social reforms. In particular he challenged two ideas then held by most, that *parda* was a necessity for Muslim women whereas education was not. To-day, at Aligarh, an intermediate college for Muslim girls functions in close connection with the University.

The lead Sir Sayyid gave in the direction of more liberal and progressive ideas was maintained after his death by men of his school; nevertheless there was also a reaction, as we shall see, in favour of preserving the older type of Muslim thought and life.

Men like Maulvī Chirāgh 'Alī, and the late Sayyid Amīr 'Alī of London, while seeking to defend Islām from what they considered to be unjustifiable attacks by

Christian writers, stoutly maintained, as Sir Sayyid had been in the habit of doing, that the reforms taking place in Muslim society under various Western influences, were not opposed to the spirit of Islām, nor detrimental to its best interests. Similarly, conspicuous scholars of our own day, like the late Mr Salāhuddīn Khudā Bakhsh of Calcutta and Sir Muhammad Iqbāl of Lahore, both students of the works of the leading European orientalists, have consistently maintained that the Islām of to-day is not the pure Islām of Muhammad's time, to which Muslims must revert. In consonance with this view, and with utmost candour, they would sweep away any traditions and legal ordinances that stand in the way. The late Mr Khudā Bakhsh fearlessly exposed many of the social evils in modern Muslim society—the ignorance in which most Muslim women are still kept; the vices of the rich; the neglect of children; legalised polygamy and the facile and callous practice of divorce. Said he, "We cannot have a very high regard for womankind with a system which sanctions four wives. Polygamy is destructive alike of domestic peace and social purity" (*Essays Indian and Islamic*, p. 231).

A further quotation from the same writer may be made at this place by way of contrasting his position with that of the unenlightened conservatives. "We do not despair of human progress . . . nor have we any sympathy with the class of men (unfortunately the larger portion of our community belongs to that class) who take it for granted that our religion and our social system admit of no corrective, or call for no improvement. Such a theory were subversive of all progress. . . . It would be the merest affectation to contend that religious and social systems, bequeathed to us thirteen hundred years ago, should now be adopted in their entirety without the slightest change or alteration" (*ibid.*, p. 219-20).

On the other hand, a society was formed in Lucknow in 1890 by the orthodox party, known as the *Nadwat-*

ul-'Ulamā, with the avowed purpose of conserving the older Muslim learning, making only such modifications in their curriculum as they considered safe. In 1895 they founded *Dār-ul-'Ulūm*, a college mainly for the training of religious teachers.

Sir Sayyid's keenness and personal devotion to the cause of improving the condition of Muslim society had far-reaching influence. It made possible, on the one hand, an interesting venture in South India, where, under an express *firmān*, order, of His Exalted Highness the Nizām of Hyderābād, there was opened in 1917 the Osmānia University. Two features in it are of great interest. It makes the fullest use of up-to-date Western works in the various branches of learning, and imparts this higher education through the medium of the Urdu language, the *lingua franca* of the Muslims of India.

On the other hand, his work roused Muslim leaders in all parts of India to new concern and activity on behalf of their fellows, as may be seen from the fact that each locality has its *anjuman*, or " association " for the promotion of Muslim education and the general interests of the community. Sir Sayyid was himself responsible for the initiation of some of these. In 1886 he founded the All-India Muhammadan Educational Conference, which promotes Western learning among Muslims. After his day the All-India Muslim League was established (in 1906) by those who felt they must go one step further than he had and devote themselves to the political interests of Muslims. Besides these there are a number of societies whose object is to consolidate as well as propagate Islām in India.

The Ahmadīyya Movement

We have reserved for more detailed consideration the emergence of another party which owes its existence, partly no doubt, to the upheaval of thought caused by the controversy with Christians seventy-five years ago, but which is evidence also of a reaction against the too-bold policy of the Aligarh reformers.

The founder of the Ahmadīyya movement, Mirzā Ghulām Ahmad, was born in 1839 at Qādiān, a small town in the north of the Panjāb. He had received a good education in Muslim learning and languages. About 1880 he concluded that he was called of God to a special mission, and in 1889 openly announced that he was the recipient of divine revelation and that he was authorised to initiate disciples of his own. From this time he began to expound a series of new doctrines.

He, too, found much to stimulate his thought, and furnish him with material for his doctrines, in Muslim predictions concerning the Imām-Mahdī, with which he joined Muslim expectations about the Messiah. The day came when, claiming that the Scriptures of Zoroastrians, Hindus and Buddhists alike prophesied the coming of a great world Teacher, he gave out that the hopes of the nations were to be fulfilled in himself. He was, further, the *mujaddid* sent by God for this century to restore the faith of Islām. He thus professed to be both the promised Messiah (in spirit, though not in person) and the Mahdī.

In order to make good his claim to be the Messiah he had to combat the idea current among Muslims as well as Christians that *Jesus* would return (as the Messiah). For this purpose he tried to prove that Jesus did not die upon the cross, but that he merely swooned and was revived by the application of an ointment, called *marham-i-'Isā*, "the Jesus ointment." Subsequently, so the Mirzā declared, he travelled to Kashmir, where, after conducting a mission to the inhabitants, he died and was buried. The Mirzā had the effrontery to claim that he had even discovered his tomb in the city of Srinagar. The tomb in question is said to be that of Yūs Asaf, and has hitherto been revered as that of a Muslim "saint."

The Mirzā thus, so easily, satisfied himself that the

one great obstacle to his claim to be the Messiah had been removed.

Likewise, on the ground that God, at intervals, sends "renewers" of religion, he claimed that in his capacity of Mahdī no other than Muhammad had made his "second advent." He was, in fact, "an image of the Holy Prophet." But here, too, a difficulty had to be removed. In the view of the orthodox the Mahdī is to be a man of war whose path will be red with the blood of "unbelievers." The Mirzā, on the contrary, professed himself to be a man of peace; accordingly the *jihād* he proclaimed, the only kind possible "under existing circumstances," was to be a spiritual warfare, involving at once loyalty to the British Government and abstention from the political activities of the All-India Muslim League.

In expounding his claims he allowed himself to use such language as this, "(God) has told me, not on one occasion but repeatedly, that I am Krishna for the Hindus and the Promised Messiah for the Muhammadans and the Christians. . . . Spiritually Krishna, and the promised Messiah are one and the same person" (*Review of Religions*, iii. 411). He also held that the door of inspiration is always open, that God even now holds communion with His good servants. It was on the basis of this belief that the Mirzā laid his claim to divine inspiration. He used language concerning himself which indicated that he thought of himself as, in some sense, a prophet; indeed, he went so far as to assert that he was superior to Jesus.

The Mirzā stirred up much opposition. He never ceased to upbraid the professional *mullas*, whom he charged with keeping the common people in the darkness and bondage of superstition. Nor could he tolerate the rationalists, such as Sayyid Amīr 'Alī and S. Khudā Bakhsh, who, by tracing some of the elements of the Qur'ān and Islām to pre-Islamic Arab cults, Judaism and Christianity, had weakened the claim and authority of the Qur'ān. But in regard to social reforms he sided with the conservatives. He repudiated the abolition of *parda*, and defended the Islamic law of polygamy and divorce.

Nevertheless the orthodox party whom he had come to " reform " branded him as heretic, blasphemer, enemy of the faith, and impostor. He was excommunicated, and he and his followers were forbidden the use of the ordinary mosques. Subsequently no less than four Qādiāni missionaries suffered the penalty of death for heresy in Afghānistān, two as recently as 1924, on which occasion orthodox leaders in India sent telegrams to the Amīr approving the measures he had taken in the interests of the faith !

The propaganda work carried on by the Qādiāni missionaries is perhaps the most characteristic feature of this community. It is claimed that its adherents now number over half a million, to be found in all parts of India, Burma, Ceylon, Afghānistān, Arabia, Egypt, Africa, Mauritius, Australia, China, England, France, Germany, and America. The whole of this work, together with an educational programme, is carried on by an elaborate organisation with headquarters at Qādiān, whither Muslims of this persuasion journey annually for their community meetings in December.

The Schism

Mirzā Ghulām Ahmad died in 1908, and was succeeded by a disciple, Hakīm Nūr-ud-dīn, as *khalīfa*, a man of different calibre who nevertheless successfully led the movement for some years. He died in 1914, but even before that date ominous signs were present which foreboded a serious quarrel. This broke out at the time of the election to the office of *khalīfa* of Mirzā Bashīr-ud-dīn Mahmūd, son of the founder. True, there were other differences among the more influential members of the community, but the rock of offence on which a violent split now took place was the insistence by this son, Bashīr-ud-dīn, and his supporters, that the original founder must be regarded as a *nabī*, prophet. We have already seen that the Mirzā did, in a modified sense, claim as much for himself.

At this a group, headed by well-educated men such as Khwāja Kamāl-ud-dīn and Maulvī Muhammad 'Alī, protesting that the Mirzā was no more than a *mujaddid* for this age, broke away and formed another branch with its headquarters in Lahore.

For the sake of clearness it is as well to speak of the adherents to these two sections as *Qādiānis*, disciples of the original founder (sometimes called *Mirzā'is*), and *Ahmadīyyas*, members of the Lahore party. Such distinction is, indeed, made by the Lahore group. In answering the inquiry of a recent correspondent about the position of Khwāja Kamāl-ud-dīn, the following statement was made in the columns of *The Light* (August 8, 1931). "A Qādiāni is one who looks upon Mirzā Ghulām Ahmad, the founder of the Ahmadīyya movement, as a prophet, and regards all those who do not accept him (as) outside the pale of Islām. . . . He (the Khwāja) belongs to the Ahmadīyya movement of Lahore, according to which the Holy Prophet Muhammad was the last Prophet and no prophet can appear after him; which considers everyone who recites the *kalima*, whatever school of thought he may belong to, a fellow-brother in Islām."

This party claims to base its title "Ahmadīyya" on the less familiar name of the Prophet, viz., *Ahmad* (cp. Qur'ān lxi. 6); that is to say, it does not connect it, as would the Qādiān group, with one of the names of the founder. *Ahmad*, it is explained, was the Prophet's name in the early and humbler period of his life when he suffered persecution. The name *Ahmadīyya* was accordingly adopted to indicate that Islām is at present passing through a time of trial.

The Lahore organisation is known as the Ahmadīyya

Anjuman-i-Ishā'at-i-Islām, or "Society for the diffusion of Islām," and has as its head Maulāna Muhammad Alī, M.A., LL.B. It, likewise, carries on an extensive missionary propaganda throughout India and in foreign countries. Khwāja Kamāl-ud-dīn has for years been at the head of their mission to England with its headquarters in Woking, Surrey, where there is a small mosque. Both of these leaders have published works intended to commend Islām to Western readers, and also some polemical writings against Christianity. Of these Maulāna Muhammad Ali's English translation of the Qur'ān with commentary, now in its second edition, deserves special mention. It claims to present the results of the best Muslim scholarship, but does not attempt to conceal its anti-Christian bias.

Both sections of the Ahmadīyyas have a very active press, and disseminate their views widely in English and Urdu journals.

Recently the main objects of the Lahore section were summarised in *The Light*, their English weekly. It is said to stand for: (1) a *liberal* Islām: it believes that *all* the religions of the world have a Divine origin; (2) a *united* Islām: it contends that there are present among Muslims no sectarian differences worth the name—*all* are agreed on the essentials; they observe the same periods for the prescribed prayers, recite the same number of *rak'ats* in each service, observe the month of fasting, offer *zakāt*, and make the pilgrimage (that is, of course, "all" except the *mullas*); (3) a *rational* Islām: the Qur'ān, not the books of the law, is their guide: so "Back to the Qur'ān" is their clarion call. They encourage the free use of *reason* and a free interpretation of the Qur'ān in the light of new world conditions; (4) a *free* Islām: at all costs the yoke of the *mullas* must be cast off; (5) a *perfect* Islām: thus making unnecessary a second advent of either a Christ or a Mahdī. Muslims must, and can, "generate" self-reliance. Islām, itself, possesses "an irresistible spiritual grace"; (6) a *triumph-*

ant Islām: it is the Muslim's duty to carry Islām to the ends of the earth. "Millions of people have yet to be approached and the light of Islām must be carried far and wide." Islām is to "triumph over all religions." Conversions must be made to Islām; mosques must be erected in Christendom; the *Unity* must be proclaimed in the realm of the *Trinity*

Notable Features

In conclusion we would make brief mention of certain outstanding features in the present situation.

1. From what we have said it will be clear that the older conservatism and this radicalism are at grips in a momentous struggle. The vast majority do not yet welcome these newer views and denounce the innovators as infidels. Both sides should excite our sympathy. While we regret the ignorance and bigotry which hamper the old school, we cannot but recognise that they often show the more devout spirit of the two, and that they still reverence the name of Christ. On the other hand the radicals, though frequently manifesting a bitter and uncharitable spirit, are yet honestly seeking to shake off old fetters and promote the cause of education and reforms.

2. During the last fifty years Muslims, having learnt their lesson from the West, have made great strides in the development of their own press. To-day there are issued in India by them alone over 230 periodicals. These are in ten languages, the work of over sixty presses scattered throughout the country. Lahore itself issues more than fifty of these publications. Their press covers every phase of Muslim thought and activity. At the same time it is frankly communal, and has one all-absorbing subject, viz., the defence and propagation of Islām.

3. The more educated Muslim women will soon prove themselves to be an influential factor in promoting

reforms in Islamic society in India. It was noticeable that they occupied a prominent place in the discussions at the recent gathering of the All-India Women's Educational Conference in Lahore (1931). It is clear that they resent the way in which, as if by tacit agreement, Muslim women have hitherto been kept illiterate, and they are now keen to support schemes for the education of the girls of their community.

Their attitude to *parda* is interesting. Comparatively few would entirely dispense with it, and of course the great mass have never thought of doing so. But while some vehemently oppose its abolition *on religious grounds*, others desire certain modifications whereby they may be more free to go out and see their friends, without, however, mixing in men's company.

While only a very few have entirely dispensed with the veil, there are many educated ladies who are no longer in strict *parda*. These are allowed out to *parda* parties, which are now frequent; others while out for a walk do not wear the veil but cover their faces with a parasol at the approach of men. In the matter of divorce, the view is expressed that the law should be more equitably applied. Practically unanimous support is given to the Sarda Act, which raises the age of consent in marriage. At present only a few speak out strongly against polygamy and divorce, but polygamy is not as prevalent now in India as is sometimes supposed. It is a luxury which the rich can afford, and a means of additional help on the farm to the more prosperous agriculturalist.

Educated women are proud of their religion and loyal to their Prophet. They are always ready to contend that Islām is the fulfilment of all religions, and that, in reality, it is not opposed to the essential truths of other faiths.

4. Perhaps the most significant contribution to Muslim thought at the present time is being made by Sir Muhammad Iqbāl, the poet-philosopher of Lahore.

He has studied philosophy in the West and seeks to combine the teaching of the Qur'ān with the tenets of Western philosophical schools. The keynote of his teaching, which owes much to the ideas of Nietzsche, is the development of personality, with the "superman" as the ideal. On the one hand, he scornfully denounces the teaching and practice of such Sūfis as advocate retirement from the world, and, on the other, derides in veiled language the ideal of self-sacrifice and the principle of non-retaliation. That it is the meek who inherit the earth is not a doctrine to which he can subscribe. There is something here that doubtless makes a powerful appeal to the educated youth of to-day, but it is not improbable that much of his thought is too subtle to be widely appreciated. In politics, he recently advocated the formation of a Muslim state in the north-west corner of India, comprising a number of districts with a predominantly Muslim population.

CHAPTER V

THE NEW APOLOGETIC

WE have seen the steps that have been taken in recent years to rehabilitate Islām and to introduce a measure of reform into Muslim society in India. In the present chapter we shall attempt a brief outline of the case for Islām as presented by the modern Muslim. The need for a new apologetic had been made urgent by the disintegrating influence of Western scientific learning on the minds of thoughtful Muslims who had been trained in the old traditional faith. Intercourse with European civilisation had also revealed the backward condition of Muslims generally. And, finally, as we shall have occasion to observe in our next section, contact and "controversy" with redoubtable exponents of Christianity during the last century had revealed a number of vulnerable points in Islām as popularly conceived.

Thus it came about that certain educated men, themselves indebted in no small degree to Western learning, undertook a new exposition of Islām and a new defence of its founder. These maintained that Islām and Muhammad had been misrepresented and were, consequently, misunderstood. It is customary for such to lay the blame for this not only upon European writers and Christian missionaries, but chiefly upon their own orthodox *mulla*s whom, in their exasperation, they upbraid in the strongest language.

Islām reinterpreted

It has been claimed, and with much truth, that India is the oldest centre of modernism in Islām, and it was

Sir Sayyid Ahmad Khān more than anyone else who led the way in the matter of a new exposition of the faith. Retaining his belief in the fundamental truth of Islām, he was nevertheless convinced that some radical reform was required in the manner of presenting it.

He appealed for a return to the pure Islām of Muhammad as set forth in the pages of the Qur'ān. In this counsel all types of Muslim modernists are agreed. The principles upon which he worked show him to have been a thoroughgoing rationalist; indeed he and others of his way of thinking have by some writers been called *neo-Mu'tazilīs.* These men vehemently repudiate the idea that the door of *ijtihād* is for ever closed. They contend that it is an essential principle of Islām that the Qur'ān can be made to yield guidance for each age and each new situation. The mistake in the past has been to adhere to the letter, and to attribute absolute values to details of secondary importance.

Exponents of this school maintain that Islām, of all religions in the world, is the one most in accord with the nature of man. Sir Sayyid himself had so stressed the affinity of Islām to nature that he and his followers were dubbed *nechari*, i.e., according to nature.

Moreover, it is said that Islām, in reality, is the universal religion that has been proclaimed from the first by all the prophets of mankind, and as such it is to be offered to men everywhere. One such apologist, indeed, insists that there is "no inherent antagonism between Christianity and Islām, if and when the sayings and doings of the founders of each are rightly viewed and understood in a simple and natural manner. Muhammad never ceased saying that he had come to attest and complete the mission of Jesus and His predecessors, who were God's messengers like himself. The greatest and the best rule of human conduct which Jesus laid down was "Love thy neighbour as thyself." This is quite consistent with human nature, and is the most comprehensive rule of conduct which has ever been laid down for the guidance of mankind. To my mind there is no better proof of the identity in spirit of Christianity and Islām than the confirmation of Christ's command by Muhammad himself, "No one will be a faithful Muslim until he loves his neighbour as he loves himself. For this reason I believe there is no difference between the two religions if the metaphysical doctrines engrafted on them both be eliminated. Thus Islām is but true Christianity writ short. Both recognise that the source of virtue is love" (quoted by M. T. Titus, *Indian Islām*, p. 209, from Sir Ahmad Hussain, *Notes on Islām*).

The late Sayyid Amīr 'Alī similarly makes clear his own attitude to the question by asserting that, "Except for the conception of the sonship of Jesus, there is no fundamental difference between Christianity and Islām" (*The Spirit of Islām*, new edition, p. 179). That is an opinion which is frequently expressed in the present day.

Muhammad in a New Light

Resenting the too-close scrutiny of the character of the historical Muhammad by Western critics and missionaries, and indignant at the way people have pointed out in him moral defects, modern Muslims have been roused to make a new defence of their Prophet. This has been attempted in a number of recent biographies and in frequent articles in magazines and periodicals. These have been published for the most part in the West for Western readers, but they have a circulation also in India, where the character of Muhammad has at times been assailed by Hindus.

It is a significant fact that, as a rule, the writers of these biographical reviews insist on comparing Muhammad with Jesus Christ, seeking to show at every point his superiority. And, indeed, they must be given credit for having at length discerned where the true issue lies. It is not now with them so much a question of this or that Book, nor this or that creed, but of Christ or Muhammad. It is the latter who is "The Holy

Prophet," "The Ideal Prophet," "The Ideal Character," "The Ideal Teacher"; and the object is to show him to be all this at the expense of Jesus.

But in order to maintain Muhammad at this level these advocates have found it necessary to reject as spurious a large number of traditions and records concerning him which have been current among Muslims for about a thousand years. Some of these depict him as falling far short of the ideal character.

Nevertheless, other facts concerning him which have often been cited as constituting serious blemishes in one claiming to be a prophet of God, are, by the new apologists, boldly retained, otherwise explained, and openly approved. Here we shall only mention two.

1. Thus since they cannot, they do not attempt to deny that he had many wives. He possessed at one time nine, besides concubines. The Qur'ān represents God as forbidding him to add to their number: "It is not permitted thee to take (other) wives hereafter, nor to change thy present wives for other women, though their beauty charm thee, except slaves whom thy right hand shall possess. And God watcheth all things" (xxxiii. 52).

They seek to justify his polygamy by pointing out that, with the exception of 'Āyesha, all of his wives were *widows* to whom he offered protection in the hard times of the early days of Islām. Again, confronted with the clear rule that no Muslim should ever have more than *four* wives (iv. 3), they say that Muhammad had married this large number *before* the rule was promulgated (cp. *The Spirit of Islām*, pp. 232-8).

2. They experience further embarrassment in connection with the wars he undertook, especially those against his former townspeople, the Meccans. Concerning this matter Sayyid Amīr 'Alī says: "The Quraish army was afield before Muhammad received God's command to do battle to His enemies." . . . At length this man, "who never in his life had wielded a weapon, to whom the sight of human suffering caused

intense pain and pity," was compelled, against his inclination, to repel the attacks of the enemy by force of arms, " and often to send out expeditions to anticipate treacherous and sudden onslaughts " (*The Spirit of Islām*, p. 61. See also above Sect. I., chap. ii., p. 26).

For the rest, these writers are at great pains to show that Muhammad was " the greatest and best of men, the man who brought to perfect expression the best of that which human nature is capable " (Khwāja Kamāl-ud-dīn, *The Ideal Prophet*, p. 8. But this is not the conclusion an unprejudiced reader would draw from the earliest sources; even the Qur'ān represents him as bidden to ask pardon for his sins, xl. 57; cp. xlvii. 21). He alone came with a universal mission. Both Moses and Jesus came with missions of limited scope and of limited object. But Muhammad " makes the whole human race his concern. . . . If Moses stands for liberty, and Jesus interests himself in sermonising upon love and meekness, Muhammad thinks of something else; without which liberty, love and meekness or any other human moral cannot work properly. There is something else in humanity which, if it remains undeveloped, will make a man a brute of the worst type. I mean wisdom, the power of reasoning and logic. . . . Muhammad stands for the development of (intelligence) " (*The Ideal Prophet*, p. 54).

It is claimed for Muhammad that " he used all the honest and honourable means that are open to others, and so his life is an object-lesson to those who have to work for success against heavy odds and under adverse circumstances " (*The Ideal Prophet*, p. 63). No attempt is made in this connection to meet the common criticism that he sometimes used unworthy means to rid himself of his opponents.

Finally, on the principle that none, not even prophets, can teach others what they have not themselves experienced, it is contended that Muhammad is a " model for men in every branch of life." Jesus, on the other hand, " could not find the proper occasions necessary to mould various other moralities into practical shape like Muhammad " (*The Ideal Prophet*, p. 18). What purports to be a children's catechism on Islām (published in Lahore) illustrates this idea as follows: " The person who did not subdue his enemies, nor had a wife and children, cannot be a model of forgiveness and coupled life. Men require a model for every branch of life and they cannot find such a model except in the Holy Prophet Muhammad. Jesus never vanquished his enemies, nor had he wife or children, therefore it is useless to take him as a model of forgiveness or married life." But quite obviously, " this is an argument against any 'universal' moral teacher at all, for it can equally well be argued that a married prophet like Muhammad would be unable to comprehend the problems of the celibate, a statesman (like Moses or Isaiah) unable to say anything to the peasant life of the world, and indeed that a universal morality could only proceed from someone who had both experienced, *and not experienced*, every possible experience, which is absurd " (W. Paton, *A Faith for the World*, p. 86).

In any case it is being assiduously proclaimed both in India and the West that to be Christlike is *not* the highest ideal for man, but to be like Muhammad; that the principles of Christianity tend to reduce man to impotence, whereas Islām, as no other religion, makes for virility, self-reliance, and independence.

The Qur'ān a Perfect Code

The most extravagant claims are made for the teachings of the Qur'ān, though there are Muslims who make the reasonable protest that legislation formulated thirteen centuries ago cannot possibly be considered as binding on Muslims to-day. Yet here is a specimen of the claim now made: " The Holy Qur'ān was not meant for one people or one age, and accordingly the scope of its moral teachings is as wide as humanity itself. It is the Book which offers guidance to all men in all conditions of life, to the ignorant savage as well as to the wise philosopher, to the man of business as well as to the recluse, to the rich as well as to the poor" (Maulāna Muhammad Ali, Pref. *Holy Qur'ān*, p. xiv.).

The author of this work is a pioneer in the endeavour to familiarise readers in English with the contents of the book. But there are large sections of the Muslim world who resent both the fact that he, a Muslim, should have dared to render the sacred language into English (and, in one edition, *without the Arabic text*) and, most especially, that he should have introduced into his commentary his own sectarian views. Egypt, in particular, is indignant at such action, and has refused to allow this particular translation into the country.

A few years ago a *wakīl*, "advocate," of the Jāmi'ul Azhar, Cairo, wrote as follows in a Cairo paper against such modernist tendencies: "Do these persons who venture to spread among non-Islamic peoples, here and there, English translations, really feel sure that they will be able to draw a clear line between Arabic Islām and English Islām? Is not the Qur'ān the abiding remnant of the Islamic community, after the great war has torn asunder the countries of Islām? after the Turkish Republic has demolished the throne of the Khilāfat, and thrown aside the chief capital of Islām, just as a corpse is thrown into the grave? Do these persons, who are smitten with such a fever of novelty and transition in their passion against the Holy Qur'ān in the garb of Arabic, really wish to see another battle-ground for the Islamic community, when they find in the Turkish Republic, a Turkish Qur'ān, and in the colonies of other governments, a French, or Italian, or Spanish, or Dutch Qur'ān, which translators will have to correct and revise, when they recognise a need for correction and revision, as is the case with the *Taurāt* and the *Injīl*?"

One cannot but feel a certain sympathy with a position

like that, because for the old school the Arabic Qur'ān is about the only bond left. Yet we miss this note of sympathy in a rejoinder made at the time in an issue of *The Light*, Lahore. "Don't insult the Qur'ān, please," let us say bluntly to this great theologian and through him to the legion of *mullas* who have degenerated Islām into a bundle of dogmas, rituals and ceremonies. If it is heresy to understand and fathom the profound wisdom treasured in the pages of the Holy Qur'ān, if it is heresy to imbibe the message of light and life contained therein, we would far rather be the foremost of heretics than the dull, mechanical *mulla*, with brain stuffed with words but with heart devoid of all spark of life.

"What after all is the good of the Quranic revelation? Is it at all intended to serve any useful purpose in the scheme of man's life? Or is it merely to be wrapped up in silk and satin and given a place of honour on a shelf high up against the wall, to be taken down only to be piously kissed and reverently replaced there? Or is it just to be crammed and recited, and that is enough to put us in the good books of God? Or, again, is it to work as a charm to cure diseases or to win the affection of the beloved? Downright insult we say, to all these notions, to a book out of which flowed the streams of life and light which led to the illumination and rejuvenation of a dead, dark and dismal world."

And indeed the future is with the translators, and not with those who are fearful about allowing the contents of the book to be printed in non-Arabic tongues. Some idea of the progress that has been made in this direction in recent times may be gathered from the fact that in India alone there are now to be had translations of the Qur'ān, in whole or in part, in *eleven* of the vernaculars.

The action of the Egyptian authorities in proscribing the Ahmadīyya edition of the Qur'ān is due, however, quite as much to the unorthodox tendency which characterises the accompanying commentary. Not only are particular Ahmadīyya views obtruded, but there is a marked breakaway from the interpretations of the older, and still greatly respected, commentators.

A single illustration, and one affecting a subject of considerable importance, may be given here to indicate this tendency. It is a doctrine commonly held by Muslims that certain verses of the Qur'ān abrogate other and earlier verses. Support for this is found in a number of passages, e.g., "Whatever verses we cancel, or cause thee (Muhammad) to forget, we bring a better or its like" (2,100). From the fact that Muslim doctors have hitherto compiled a list of about 225 Quranic verses that have on this principle been abrogated by other verses, we gather that the subject occupies a prominent place in their studies of the book.

But the rationalising Ahmadīyyas now affect to ignore entirely the view that has so long held the field, and so they translate the term *āyat*, "verse," as meaning "communication," and calmly assert that the passage refers to God's "abrogation" of the message of the Law given to the Jews. In so doing they put themselves in direct opposition to such great authorities as the Imāms Mālik and Shāfi'ī and the commentators Baidhāwī, Jalālain, Jalāluddin, Husain and others, ***but they do not tell their readers so.***

The present writer referred this novel interpretation in 1917 to Professor D. B. Macdonald, of Hartford Seminary, U.S.A., a recognised authority in respect of Muslim religious literature. In the course of a lengthy and exhaustive reply the Professor said: "I know of no evidence that the word *āyat*, or any of its plurals, can refer to our Scriptures; such is certainly not the Muslim use. . . . I have been unable to find the extant works of any author who denies the doctrine that one part of the Qur'ān has been abrogated by another and that, on the other hand, such has been the consistent agreement (*ijmā'*) of Islām from the first. . . . The Ahmadīyya position is an innovation (*bid'at*) in Islām of the gravest kind" (*The Moslem World*, vol. vii., pp. 420-3).

Further Modifications

Polygamy. The claim is commonly made that Islām gives woman rights, and that she occupies in Muslim society a place without parallel in any other religion. When, therefore, the Quranic sanction of polygamy is made the subject of criticism there are those who say that the passage in question (viz., iv. 3) "*permits polygamy under certain circumstances; it does not enjoin it nor even permit it unconditionally*" (Maulāna Muhammad Ali, *Holy Qur'ān*, in loc. cit. The italics are his).

Such claim that the essential teaching of the Qur'ān is monogamous, for while the law permits a man to take four wives, it is strictly on the condition that he can deal justly with all of them. This being practically impossible, the conclusion to be drawn is that the Qur'ān really means that a man should have but one! But there is a lack of consistency among Muslims about the matter. Others frankly justify the practice as a rational method of meeting the needs of human society, which, they say, are met in non-Muslim circles by more or less legalised forms of prostitution.

A few, nevertheless, are outspoken and candid. The late Sayyid Amīr 'Alī, for instance, went so far as to say "I look upon polygamy in the present day as an adulterous connection and as contrary to the *spirit* of Islām" (*The Spirit of Islām*, Calcutta, 1902, p. 216; but cp. S. Khuda Bakhsh, *Essays Indian and Islamic*, pp. 253-9).

Parda. Undoubtedly the practice of *parda*, if not doomed, is destined to very considerable modifications. The modernists now contend that it is a "pernicious poison," and a "dangerous overgrowth" in society. It is said to be a "libel" to make Islām responsible for it. Rather it was the Persians, after the time of Tīmūr, who grafted it on to Indian Islām. All of which serves to show which way the wind blows.

Jihād. There is no unanimity among Muslims about the use of the sword. Some in explanation of the Quranic injunction to "make war" (ix. 29) state that such recommendations were only valid in the time of the Prophet. Islām is essentially a religion of peace and toleration; in support of which they quote a verse which belongs to a considerably earlier date than the one given above, viz., " Let there be no compulsion in religion " (ii. 257). Rather, *jihād* is a *spiritual* warfare. As for Muhammad, his very nature was repugnant to fighting; he only fought in defence of his community, and that after thirteen years of persistent persecution.

On the other hand, even such writers make it clear that *jihād-bi's-saif*, " warfare with the sword," is, in India, only suspended. The command is not abrogated. The example of Muhammad in this matter also is still the rule of conduct. Though gentle by nature, he did not hesitate to use the sword in defence of the faithful.

New attitude to polytheistic faiths. An interesting change is to be observed in the attitude of some of these modernists towards the religion of the Hindus. Notwithstanding the fact that in the popular Muslim view these, and all polytheists, are definitely without the pale, having no part with *Ahl-i-kitāb*, yet now it is claimed, and on the basis of the Qur'ān, that all nations have had their prophets and their divinely inspired books (x. 48; xxxv. 22). Even Rām and Krishna, they maintain, ought to be reckoned among the prophets. Krishna was God's chosen one; he brought the message of Islām and was, in fact, a *Muslim*. Recently *The Light* committed itself to the following statement: " Were it not for the unfortunate communal strife which stands in the way of a dispassionate study of Islām, we are sure an intelligent race like the Hindus would have acclaimed the message of Islām as the self-same message of Lord Krishna." The writer then goes on to state that Nānak, Rām Mohan Roy and Keshab Chandra Sen recognised the essential unity of all religions and that Islām was a true religion from God. In assuring Hindus of a warm welcome should they embrace Islām he concludes with the truly amazing remark, " Krishna and other heroes of Hindustān are as dear to a Muslim as to a Hindu."

SECTION V

CHRISTIANITY AND ISLĀM

Chapter I

CHRISTIANITY AND ISLĀM IN INDIA SINCE THE SIXTEENTH CENTURY

The first serious attempt to propagate Christianity among the Muslims of India appears to have been made during the reign of Akbar (1556-1605). At his invitation representatives of all religions assembled at the royal court at Agra. It thus came about that the Portuguese Jesuits at Goa sent, at intervals, three separate missions to the Great Mughal. The first of these was withdrawn in 1583, having accomplished nothing. A similar fate attended the second, 1590-92. The third, which arrived in Lahore where the court then was, in 1596, is notable for the fact that at its head was Jerome Xavier, nephew of the famous Francis Xavier. This mission also met with no success.

Nevertheless, this Jerome undertook to prepare three books in Persian for the information of the Mughal Emperors. The third of these may be briefly mentioned here, viz., *Aina haqq numā*, "A mirror displaying the truth," which the author dedicated in 1609 to Akbar's successor, Jahāngīr. It is interesting to find that the first conversions took place in the reign of the new Emperor, who, though at first hostile to people of other faiths, gradually became almost as tolerant as his father. He accepted at the hands of the Roman Catholic priests a Persian version of the Gospels.

Concerning Jerome's book it has been said: "It is evident that the writer was a man of considerable ability and energy and that he spared no pains to recommend his religion to the Muhammadan . . . but he trusted much more to his own ingenuity than to the plain and unsophisticated declarations of the Holy Scriptures." (Dr Lee, Preface to Henry Martyn's *Tracts*, 1820.) Besides which the writer laboured under the disadvantage peculiar to Roman Catholics when he proceeded to seek support for his case by an appeal to saints' relics, prayers for the dead, and the worship of images. Incidentally we may note that even in his day he found himself compelled to defend (1) the Divinity of Christ, and (2) the integrity of the Scriptures.

One Zain-ul-Ābidīn replied to Jerome's book in 1621. The Muslim in a spirit of perversity forces Scripture to yield meanings to suit his purpose. In much of this he is the prototype of many an anti-Christian Muslim writer in the succeeding centuries. Thus, he declares that he finds allusion to Muhammad in the Pentateuch and the Psalms, and in Christ's promise of the Paraclete. In an argument against accepting the current version of the Scriptures he betrays his ignorance by saying: "We believe that the original was lost when Jesus ascended to heaven." He raises the question of the miracles of Jesus and declares that *the* miracle of Iṣlām is the Qur'ān. He utters a dignified and salutary rebuke, not unmixed with scorn, to the Jesuit concerning the use of relics and images: "We need not now notice your worshipping wooden images of the Virgin Mary and Jesus, whether such worship be intended as respectful to their persons, or for the purpose of paying them divine honours. . . . Since a word is enough for the wise, believing as we do that you are such, we shall content ourselves with the mere hint."

To this a very feeble retort was made in 1681, in Latin, by Philip Guadagnoli, a professor of the Theological College of the Propaganda of the Faith at Rome, who dedicated it to Pope Urban VIII.

This presentation of the Christian faith to Indian Muslims, as made by the Jesuits, was far from worthy or adequate, yet they alone were in the field up to the time of the British connection with India in the eighteenth century. But even when the British came there was no immediate improvement in the situation. We gather from a number of sources that Britain's representatives in those early years were careless of the spiritual condition of the peoples of India, why then should they give a thought to the Muslims? Too often they banished religion from their own lives and exhibited to all alike the spectacle of men without a faith. These "infidel conquerors" by their unworthy manner of life were in fact strengthening the case of the Muslims and confirming their contention that Islām is superior to Christianity.

The dawn of the nineteenth century broke with brighter prospects. The famous missionaries, Carey, Marshman and Ward of the English Baptist Mission, had already settled in Serampore, and a group of earnest Anglican chaplains were at work in and around Calcutta—Buchanan, David Brown, Thomason, Corrie, and notably, Henry Martyn.

Henry Martyn's advent in India, in 1806, opened a new chapter in the story of Christian contact with Muslims. Though he stayed but a short time—only till the opening of 1811—his career marked him out as the first missionary to Muslims in modern times.

At Dinapore and Cawnpore (1807-10), eager though he was to preach the pure Gospel of the Love of God in Christ, he soon became involved, to the great distress of his sensitive spirit, in a type of controversy with Muslims that has since become only too familiar. It is, nevertheless, difficult to see how it could have been otherwise with one of his ardent evangelical spirit.

With the prospect of such controversy immediately before him he expressed himself in words which we, in our day, will do well to lay to heart: "I wish that a spirit of enquiry may be excited, but I lay not much stress upon clear arguments; the work of God is seldom wrought in that way. To preach the Gospel, with the Holy Ghost sent down from heaven, is a better way to win souls." We now know that the example of his saintly life proved in the end to be the best testimony to the truth he preached, for however men differed from him they respected him and knew him to be what the Persians afterwards called him, *mard-i-Khudā*, "a man of God."

Discussions in India with *maulvīs* prepared him for further controversies in Persia, whither he went when compelled to leave India for his health's sake in January 1811. He had come to see very early that the New Testament must be done into Urdu for the Muslims, and he had the satisfaction of seeing this task completed ere he sailed. Meanwhile in his heart he cherished the further ambition that in Persia he would be able to perfect his translation of it into Persian. This too he lived to accomplish.

One of the main topics of discussion in which he engaged both in India and Persia was the question of *miracles*, especially the alleged miracles of Muhammad. Martyn took his stand in this matter on the clear and unequivocal testimony of the Qur'ān (cp. xxix. 48-50; xxviii. 48-9).

In Persia Martyn soon found himself confronted by no less a person than the Preceptor of all the *mullas*, Mirzā Ibrāhīm, who set forth his arguments against Christianity in an ably written book of moderate tone.

An example of the Mirzā's quaint method of reasoning may be given from his section on miracles. These, he argued, are subject to cycles which come and go. Thus, the miracles of Moses belong to the age of *magic* and were attested by magicians; the miracles of Jesus belong to the age of *physic* and physicians attested them; Muhammad's miracle, the Qur'ān, on the other hand, belongs to the age of *rhetoric* and Arab orators attested it.

The Mirzā also impugns the authenticity of the Scriptures and therefore, with commendable consistency, refrains from quoting the Bible in support of his case.

To this book Henry Martyn replied with three tracts in Persian which have been preserved. These deal respectively with (1) Miracles, in which he shows that the Qur'ān does not fulfil the requirements of a miracle; (2) Muhammad's mission; and (3) the errors of Sūfism. In the last of these he defends the principle of vicarious suffering; upholds the miracles of Moses and Jesus; and maintains the integrity of the Scriptures.

It has been pointed out that Martyn would have done better to have shifted the ground of debate to the more vital matters of the Christian faith, but the exercise of a little imagination will excite our pity for this lonely ambassador of Jesus Christ. He was then in a precarious state of health, a victim of consumption. Challenged as he was by this Muslim's attack he felt compelled as Christ's representative to make reply.

But Henry Martyn's work and worth, and his subsequent influence on the Christian enterprise among Muslims in India, are not to be judged by these tracts of his.

It has been well said of this brilliant scholar—in his day Senior Wrangler and First Smith's Prizeman at Cambridge University—that when only twenty-seven years of age he "inaugurated a new era of Christian evangelisation of the Muslim." For his undying fame rests rather on his translation of the New Testament into Urdu and Persian, whereby he laid the foundation of all subsequent work among Muslims. It was from this time that translations of the Bible into the languages of the Muslim world were, at intervals, undertaken and completed.

A reply to Martyn's tracts appeared from the pen of another Persian, Mirzā Muhammad Riza, in 1813, the year after Martyn died. This lacks the learning, skill, and good temper of the work of Mirzā Ibrāhīm, but it took full advantage of the weak arguments advanced by Martyn, e.g., the use he made of Qur'ān phrases to prove the greater excellence of Christ over Muhammad.

This reply, like that of Zain-ul-Ābidīn noted above, abounds in perversions of Scripture and unwarranted conclusions therefrom. The writer also displays at times amazing ignorance, as when he speaks of Plato sending a written message to Jesus!

More than twenty years later there appeared in the ranks of the missionaries in India an advocate of quite another type. This was the redoubtable Dr Carl Pfander, a German missionary who had been expelled from Fort Shusha, in Georgia, by the Russian Government. Prior to this he had acquired a knowledge of Persian and had made several journeys into Persia. It was there, in the city of Kermānshāh, that he published his first work, *Mizān-ul-Haqq*, "The Balance of Truth." It is significant that the opposition it aroused nearly cost him his life.

Dr Pfander joined the staff of the C.M.S. in Agra about the year 1835, and in course of time came to be looked upon as the champion of Christianity in the controversy with Muslims. He wrote several other works in Persian, all of which were afterwards translated into Urdu, but the *Mizān-ul-Haqq* was destined to provoke more discussion than any other book written for Muslims in the last century. Subsequently it was translated into almost every Muslim language in the world.

In this he defends the integrity of the Scriptures; explains the leading doctrines of the Bible; and refutes the claims of Muhammad to be the apostle of God and of the Qur'ān to be the Word of God. Two other books written by him require brief notice: (1) *Tarīq-ul-Hayāt*, "The Way of Life"; this deals with *sin*, its nature and consequences, and explains the way of salvation. It ranks higher than the *Mizān*. (2) *Miftāh-ul-Asrār*, "The Key to the Mysteries." In this the author deals with the exalted rank of Christ; His unique birth and miracles; the Divine Sonship and the Trinity.

Despite the vogue Pfander's writings once had it has

to be admitted that they chiefly serve to-day as a guide to something better. It was one of his failings that he either could not, or would not, issue a treatise on the Christian faith without turning aside to pass adverse criticisms on the teaching of Islām or the character of Muhammad. In places, too, his own arguments are weak, a fact of which Muslim controversialists took full advantage.

Some time before the middle of the century Dr Pfander found himself involved in determined controversy with the leading *maulvīs* of North India. This partly took the form of formal debates, carried on over a period of three years, in the Jama' Masjid of Agra. Amongst those who stood by in his support was Mr Valpy French, afterwards first Bishop of Lahore. On the side of the *maulvīs* were two of whom we shall have occasion to speak a little later—Safdar 'Alī and Imād-ud-dīn.

The results of these protracted discussions were both varied and interesting.

From the side of the Muslims books and pamphlets appeared in answer to Pfander's arguments. One Kāzim 'Alī was particularly perverse in the way he insisted that certain passages in the Bible had, and could have, this and no other meaning. Pfander soon found the man to be a bully and wisely declined to continue the discussion unless his opponent showed a fairer spirit.

Sir William Muir, who held a civil appointment in the district at that time, has recorded that the argument was conducted by the Muslims generally with ability and subtlety, but was marred by their customary wrong-headedness and by their refusal to perceive the folly of persisting to use what had already been demonstrated to be fallacious reasoning.

The interesting fact may be mentioned here that one of the champions on the Muslim side insisted that *human reason* must be the sovereign judge in all the matters under discussion.

We may note, too, that it was in 1845 that one of the Muslims put out a treatise called *Saulat-uz-Zaigham*, "The Lion's Onset," which was destined for years to remain the most popular anti-Christian work in North India. Its title alone speaks volumes. Sir William Muir said of it that it was a rambling, desultory attack, full of spite and animosity, careless of its arguments, but racy and attractive in style. It descended, too, to abusive and insulting language towards Christ.

Some of this Pfander had undoubtedly brought upon himself in that he had shown insufficient regard for the sensitive spirits of devout Muslims; nor had he always written so as to touch their hearts as well as convince the minds of his opponents. Nevertheless there was a more pleasing side to all this vigorous controversy, for three of the *maulvīs* participating in the discussions eventually embraced Christianity. Brief reference may be made here to two of these.

(1) Safdar 'Alī was baptized in Jubbulpore in 1865. He became Inspector of Schools in that district and wrote, amongst other things, a treatise called *Niyāz Nāma*, "A Letter of Entreaty," which sets forth for Muslim readers his reasons for his change of faith. It has its peculiar value not only as the work of a converted *maulvī*, but for the note of sympathy running through it.

(2) Another convert, a man of very different calibre, was Imād-ud-dīn, whom Robert Clarke baptized at Amritsar in 1866, the very year Dr Pfander left India. Imād-ud-dīn was ordained deacon in Calcutta by Bishop Milman in 1868 and later became chaplain to Bishop French in Lahore. In 1884 the degree of D.D. was conferred on him by the Archbishop of Canterbury. He died in 1901.

The story of his early search after truth has been told by himself and is most interesting. Imād-ud-dīn seemed destined to take the place of Pfander, for he became a doughty champion of Christianity and a great controversialist. He wrote over twenty works on a great variety of topics. One of these was a damaging delineation of the character of Muhammad. Another, his most notable book, was called *Hidāyat-ul-Muslimīn*, "Guidance for Muslims," in the course of which he vigorously defends the integrity of the Scriptures.

Unlike his friend Safdar 'Alī, he was a hard hitter, and though his writings had a powerful influence at one time, much of them, like some of Pfander's, cannot be used to-day.

There were other events which owed something to the influence of the Agra controversies, but as these have already been noticed in an earlier section of this book we shall only refer to them here very briefly.

(1) There was the emergence of a new Islām, new that is for India, a reformed Islām, in the person and teachings of that pioneer in reforms, Sir Sayyid Ahmad Khān, the founder of Aligarh College. Born in 1817, the Sayyid would have been about thirty years of age when the debates with Pfander were the talk of the day. A man of his insight and foresight must, it would seem, have been profoundly affected in his religious outlook by the upheaval in thought that was then taking place. The stress he afterwards came to lay upon *human reason*, as the sole criterion of judgment in religion, recalls one aspect of that early controversy.

(2) Another movement that began in the latter part of the century, partly no doubt as a reaction to the tumult caused by Pfander, was the one initiated by Mirzā Ghulām Ahmad of Qādiān (1839-1908), though he was only a boy when the debates took place in Agra.

Dr Imād-ud-dīn soon perceived that there was present in the teachings of these would-be reformers of Islām that which would produce new obstacles and opposition to the Gospel. With characteristic vigour, therefore, he set himself to refute the teachings of these men, and in particular to expose the arrogant claims of the Mirzā of Qādiān.

Meanwhile in the West, quite independently of the missionary enterprise and of the particular situation we have just been describing, a group of eminent scholars were undertaking the study of Islām and its sources: Fleischer, Flügel, Nöldeke, Goldziher, Sachau, Sprenger, Snouck Hurgronje, and others.

The stimulus thus given to such study, together with the demands made by the changing situation on the field, led a number of gifted and consecrated men here in India to seek to interpret Islām to the Christians of their day.

Foremost among these stands Sir William Muir, of the Civil Service, whose four-volume *Life of Muhammad* appeared in 1860. Among missionaries worthy of special mention were the Rev. T. P. Hughes (C.M.S., Peshawar), compiler of *The Dictionary of Islām* (1885), a volume of 750 pages, still a mine of most valuable information; Dr E. M. Wherry (A.P.M., Ludhiana), whose best known work is his *Commentary on the Qur'ān*, in four volumes; Dr St Clair Tisdall (C.M.S., India and Persia), author of *The Sources of the Qur'ān*, etc.; Canon Edward Sell (C.M.S., Madras), author of many works, the chief of which is *The Faith of Islām*, four times revised by him in forty years.

Side by side with these were eminent preachers of the Gospel to Muslims, men like Valpy French, Lefroy, Rowland Bateman, and Dr Pennell, to mention only a few. All of these have placed succeeding generations of Christians in India under a great debt of gratitude, and have enabled many a Muslim to see in true perspective not only his own religion, but the Christian Gospel also.

CHAPTER II

SOURCES OF STRENGTH IN ISLĀM

TIMES have changed and with the times we, who have entered into the labours of many who in their day and in their way were valiant for the truth, feel constrained, in the interests of truth, to look upon this great people and their religious convictions from a somewhat different point of view. In particular we are under a solemn obligation to cultivate an attitude of mind and heart that is determined to look for, and acknowledge, all that is really true and valuable in Islām.

It is peculiarly easy to adopt an unsympathetic attitude, and this for several reasons.

We are prone to see chiefly the externals of a religion other than our own, e.g., its formality and hypocrisy. These defects do indeed exist in Islām as amongst the people of other faiths, but it can only be blindness and prejudice that prevent us from seeing also its good things.

Again, we are too ready to endorse the opinions of others who worked years ago in this field before us. No doubt to some extent this is a wise procedure, but we need to be on our guard. Such was the angle of vision of many of these that much that they wrote was of a destructively critical nature, and it is not easy after reading that kind of writing to see the nobler things in Islām and Muslims. But apart from this, it should be a point of honour with us to form our own independent judgment.

And then we may be influenced, all unconsciously, by the suspicion which one fears still lingers in the minds of some, that Islām is essentially not of God. Have there not been those who have seriously suggested that Muhammad is the "anti-Christ" spoken of in 1 John ii. 22?

Surely the Christian preacher or teacher whose mind is swayed by such thoughts is not only unfitted by reason of prejudice to make a proper study of Islām, he is also thereby disqualified for the delicate task of leading a Muslim to see the truth as it is in Christ. A prominent Muslim recently said to the present writer: "A Muslim who respects the name of Jesus Christ is more likely to form a right judgment about Christianity than is a Christian about Islām, who enters upon his study with the conviction that Muhammad was an impostor"; and one felt bound to agree with him.

Our concern as followers of Christ when dealing with Islām and Muslims should be to seek to discover and fulfil, not to destroy and supplant. We should rejoice in every evidence we can find of the presence of God's Spirit in Islām, and in every witness it makes to His Being and Majesty. It is in this spirit, for instance, that we should take up the study of the Qur'ān, the book which, for thirteen centuries, has been the cherished and sacred possession of countless earnest souls. We need to bear in mind that He who would not break the bruised reed nor quench the smoking flax is our Master and Example in this as in every matter.

One of the most sympathetic and appreciative students of non-Christian religions in recent years was that distinguished scholar, the late Dr J. N. Farquhar. His views upon just this kind of study, although written with reference to Hinduism, are so apposite in relation to the study of Islām as to merit quotation here.

"Can there be," he asks, "any real doubt as to the attitude which the Christian ought to adopt? It is the quiet, sober, sympathetic, truth-seeking spirit of the scholar that gets to understand things in every province of human enquiry; and in the domain of religion, above all, the effort to learn needs the illumination of the heart to help in the task.

"If we look at the question from the point of view of our desire to win men for Christ, the conclusion must be the same. The more fully the question of the relative value of Christianity and the faiths of India comes into public discussion, the more need there is for a quiet, reasonable manner, and a will to see the best as well as the worst in the teaching and the traditional usages of the religions; harshness and condemnation can only repel." That, too, is an observation one feels constrained to endorse.

We are living in an age which calls for a bolder and more venturesome faith—faith to believe that other nations and peoples of other religions have a real contribution to make in the fulfilment of God's purposes for the world through Jesus Christ; and, not least, faith to cherish the conviction that, as Tertullian said, the human soul is fundamentally and naturally Christian.

How else are we to account for the innumerable fragments of truth to be found in other religions except on the ground that God's Spirit is quietly at work in the hearts and minds of men, notwithstanding human opposition and imperfection? So then we require patience, understanding and sympathy in our study, and with these faith to believe that there is something of real worth to the Kingdom of God at the heart of Islām.

One further point before we turn to the main subject of this chapter. There have been Christian scholars in the past who have turned from their study of Islām with the conviction that there is in this system no hope of progress. The chief reason for this conclusion would seem to be founded on some of the observed results in the history of Islām of the teaching of the orthodox doctors, viz., that the *sharī'at* laid down in the seventh century A.D. is binding upon each succeeding generation. The late Lord Cromer only expressed this thought in another form when he said: "Islām reformed is Islām no longer."

But we must resolutely refuse to allow any such feeling

of hopelessness to discourage us. It may have been Muhammad's intention (though plenty of modern Muslims doubt it) to lay down precise regulations for all time; it may have been the fact that Muslim *'ulamā*, through the centuries, believed and taught that God has no more light and truth to break forth from His word—nevertheless, if it is conceded that, as we have just ventured to assert, God's Spirit is even now at work within Islām, who are we that we should set limits to the developments that may yet take place among Muslims under the influence of that Almighty agency? There is, the present writer ventures to think, a Power at work within Islām that shall yet put to confusion the calculations of its most rigidly orthodox leaders, and, at the same time, rebuke the little faith of many a preacher of the Gospel.

Two facts cannot fail to impress the would-be student of Islām, and these should always be borne in mind by us since they are constantly present to the mind of the Muslim.

The Past History of Islām. From Muhammad's days down to comparatively recent times, Islamic history records the greatness and grandeur of many Muslim States. Is it surprising that Muslims point with pride to these periods in the history of Islām? There are the conquests of Muslim generals in and around Arabia in the first century of the *Hijra*; the achievements of Salāh-ud-dīn (Saladin) in Syria and Egypt at the time of the Crusades; the splendour of Sulaimān "the Magnificent," as he was called; the rise of the Ottoman Empire in Turkey; and last, but not least, the fame of the Mughal Emperors in India.

The Present Numerical Strength of Islām.—The world-population is now about 1800 millions (according to a statement that appeared in *The Times*, May 1929). Muslims, at the lowest computation, number 235 millions, or one-eighth of the world's population. It is conceivable that we may shortly have to alter that to "one-seventh" of the whole, but the available census figures in different lands do not warrant the extravagant assertion of Muslims themselves that they number 400 millions.

These are arresting facts and the Muslims would be less than human were they not to take pride in them *as facts*, and we may be sure that we shall never fully understand the mind of the Indian Muslims, especially in these days of change and strife, unless and until we make due allowance for the presence in them of this kind of legitimate pride.

Let us now turn to consider very briefly some of those elements in Islām which are among its sources of strength.

"Islām," writes a close observer, "remains vital because it is a religion. Before all else that it may be socially and politically, Islām is a system that, in its own way, serves to maintain the religious life of its followers. Were it not able to meet certain needs of the human spirit with influences that nourish a life of faith with men, it could not have become the force that it is to-day in the personality of so many millions of our fellow-beings" (Crawford, in *The Vital Forces of Christianity and Islām*, p. 126).

It is unquestionably true that Muslims find a measure of genuine spiritual *stimulus* in certain of their beliefs and practices. We shall attempt to set down here some of these.

1. There is the *simplicity* of the chief religious ideas in Islām.

(*a*) Islām produces in its adherents the profound conviction that there is only *one* God, a *living* God, the Creator and Ruler of all. That is a proposition the very simplicity of which has always proved restful amid the confusing claims of polytheism and saint-worship.

(*b*) Akin to this is the constant proclamation *Allāhu Akbar*, "God is Great"; which produces in sincere minds a feeling somewhat akin to that of the Hebrew psalmist who says: "O magnify the Lord with me, and let us exalt His Name together."

(*c*) Muslims are confident that God has revealed His will to men through prophets and that His truth is to be found in a *book*.

(*d*) They believe in the resurrection from the dead and in God as the God of the Day of Judgment.

(*e*) They believe in the efficacy of prayer to God.

There is in these tenets nothing distinctively Islamic, but we need to recognise that they are present as dominating convictions in the minds of zealous Muslims.

2. Another element of strength comes from the way in which the Islamic *forms of worship* stimulate into activity a man's religious nature.

(*a*) The forms of utterance in the daily *salāt* (*namāz*) are eagerly made use of as a channel for the expression of the mind's nobler impulses. Admittedly, the frequency of the repetition of these set prayers (five times a day) exposes the worshipper to the danger of formality, but, on the other hand, it tends to create a *habit* that has in it great possibilities for good. The *acted* and *spoken* prayer in the midst of an assembly has far-reaching influences; for instance, the genuflexions and audible utterances offer opportunity for the manifestation of humility and gratitude towards God.

(*b*) There is the effect, also, upon Muslims of the *adhān*, or call to prayer. Though perhaps only a small percentage of any community regularly answer the call, yet every Muslim who hears it must derive from it a feeling of pride and satisfaction; he is proud that the faith of Islām is, by that act, honoured and proclaimed.

(*c*) A similar influence is produced by the use of a common *qibla*. Every Muslim makes it his intention to face towards Mecca on each occasion of prayer. This yields a satisfaction similar to Daniel's who, before his open windows, prayed towards Jerusalem three times a day.

This habit of facing towards Mecca is a democratic and universal act of religious ritual which gives assurance and comfort to the Muslim, not only when engaged in prayer, but especially during his last illness when his bed is turned so that he may face that way. The same action brings comfort to the mourners as they lay the body on its right side in the grave, with the face of their dead turned towards the sacred city.

(*d*) The fast of *Ramdhān*, also, can have real religious value because of the heroic demand it makes on the will of the believer. It calls for a degree of self-control that enables a Muslim's faith to rise above lesser things.

(*e*) The *dhikr*, or act of remembrance (of God), is likewise a channel for the expression of religious emotion, through which Muslims attached to certain religious orders strive after communion with God. They claim that in this form of service heart and tongue are united in repeating the name of God.

3. Another feature making for strength is the *community-consciousness* among Muslims.

(*a*) It is this that binds together all Muslims, of all races, in all parts of the world. Whatever their differences in doctrine, or social custom, or race, they never lose the sense that they belong to a great brotherhood that, in reality, transcends these differences.

(*b*) This, in turn, is based on a principle, viz., the equality of all believers. Thus it is, for instance, that prince and peasant stand side by side in the same mosque as equals in the sight of the Great God.

(*c*) Consider also, in this connection, the moral effect of the circumstances attending the annual pilgrimage to Mecca. It is undoubtedly a wonderful stimulus to the pride and faith of Muslims to look upon so many fellow-believers gathered together on that site from many lands and peoples and tongues.

4. Further, there is the influence of the *Qur'ān*; first, upon its readers and then upon the illiterate masses who listen while it is being read, or recited, with unmistakable

reverence and charm. Though music is banned there is in the reading, or rather chanting, of this book something that supplies the place of music for the Muslim.

Associated with this exercise is another form of recital —the repetition, often with the use of a rosary, of the "most beautiful (99) Names" of God. Such meditation upon God is certainly one of the sources of strength in Islām.

5. Finally, there is the *idealisation of the personality of Muhammad.*

The trend in this direction, as we have seen above, is very marked at the present time. It is not an exaggeration to say that Muhammad is almost as prominently present to the mind of a Muslim as God Himself. The *kalima* is accountable for this. The assertion there that God is the God of their leader, whom they believe to be the last and the greatest of all God's prophets, is, in fact, the mainspring of much of the confidence and zeal of multitudes of Muslims.

In confirmation of this consider,

(*a*) The celebration and influence of the *maulūd* form of service at annual gatherings on the occasion of Muhammad's birthday. At these addresses are given and poems recited setting forth the story of the life, character and achievements of the Prophet. At intervals the audience intervene to chant a fervent *durūd*, or prayer to God for His favour to be shown to Muhammad.

(*b*) The significance of the doctrine of the *light* of Muhammad, a belief that has been cherished through many centuries. It is to the effect that God, at the creation of the world, set apart a portion of His own light that was destined at length to enter into Muhammad at his birth. Two other beliefs are associated with this one, viz., the pre-existence of Muhammad, and the supreme influence of his intercession in heaven on behalf of the Faithful.

From all of which we can readily perceive that Muhammad, thus represented as an ideal leader, is attracting to himself much of the moral enthusiasm and personal devotion of individual Muslims.

Finally, there are some general features within Islām, but not peculiar to it, which influence the thought and control the lives of many Muslims. We can do no more here than just tabulate them.

(*a*) There is their unshaken belief in a life after death, with its rewards and punishments. Thus, a *ghāzī*, one who fights in the cause of Islām, will face death cheerfully; a *faqīr*, one poor (in spirit), gladly suffers poverty; while those inclined to do evil are subdued by the thought of the terrors of hell.

(*b*) There is the Muslim's contempt for, and condemnation of, idolatry.

(*c*) The uncompromising attitude of the community, as a whole, to the use of intoxicants.

Chapter III

THE INADEQUACY OF ISLĀM

Having sought to discover and acknowledge elements of value and strength in Islām we shall not be so likely to lay ourselves open to the charge that we are incurably prejudiced when now we proceed, with equal candour and no less friendliness, to point out some of its defects.

In any case, the very claims of Islām make this further task necessary. It is common for Muslims to assert on a number of grounds that Islām is the best possible religion for all men and for all time, and in this way to put it forward as the serious rival of Christianity. We are thus obliged to scrutinize this system more closely to find out whether, in fact, it does possess a power for good over the lives of individuals and society such as Christianity has not got; for this is the only issue that really need concern us.

For our present purpose we ought to bear in mind that there are, broadly speaking, two schools of thought among Muslims: that of the reformed communities with their new interpretation of the Qur'ān and more progressive ways, illustrated by the Ahmadīyyas; and that great mass of the orthodox who, in India as elsewhere, still adhere to the faith and practice of Islām as these have been handed down through thirteen centuries.

Since we have already dealt with the views and teachings of the modern school in a previous chapter we shall confine our present remarks to the religion of the masses.

What, then, are the outstanding defects in the faith of the more orthodox?

The Character of Muhammad

It may seem strange that we should put first the consideration of Muhammad himself, but there is surely strong reason for doing so. Obviously, he is the channel if not the source of much that characterises Islām as we know it, and in particular of the contents of the Qur'ān, which in a very real sense is "the diary of Muhammad's life." What then of his character? Much as we should like to we cannot pass over this question in silence. The very prominence given by all classes of Muslims to their Prophet compels us to scrutinize him closely.

Yet there are current concerning him strangely conflicting views, some of them very damaging; though it is probably correct to say that, so far, no Muslim has ventured publicly to pass criticism on his character. In this connection the complaint has been growing in recent years that Christian writers, with their usual bias, have been making use of statements, detrimental to the character of Muhammad, that are to be found only in the works of unreliable Muslim authors. It has, therefore, become more than ever necessary to make sure that we do not use any sources that are generally recognised by the best Muslim scholars to be unauthentic. But it is equally true that we need to be on our guard against any tendency on the part of embarrassed Muslims to discount early Muslim writers merely on the ground that they record features in the character of their Prophet which do not meet with general approval to-day.

We shall, however, content ourselves here with making certain general observations on the attitude of Muslims themselves to the character of Muhammad.

1. A perusal of the writings of the earlier Muslim historians suggests to the unprejudiced reader that it does not seem to have occurred to them that the unworthy features in him which they have recorded (and which European writers have been blamed for quoting) were, in reality, moral blemishes. They even justify

them. They appear to think that what might indeed have been wrong in one of themselves could not be wrong in the Prophet of God. And it is but true to say that, until comparatively recent times, this was the view commonly held by Muslims as it is still the view of the orthodox. If proof of this were needed it can be found in the widespread popularity amongst them of collections of the Traditions like the *Mishkātu'l-Maṣābih*, which record of him things that could not be read in public.

2. In the course of the centuries the character of Muhammad has been gradually idealised, so that in popular biographies it takes on features not to be found in the historical Muhammad. It has often been pointed out, for instance, that various offices and titles properly associated only with the name of Christ have been, in the course of time, applied to the Prophet of Islām (cp. Zwemer's *The Moslem Christ*).

3. There is to-day a new sensitiveness among Muslims regarding Muhammad. They resent criticism. The Ahmadīyyas, for instance, are eager to prove first this and then that statement or tradition in Muslim writers to be unreliable, if it amounts to a blot on his character. But one may be permitted to ask who fabricated these records, if they are now to be set aside as spurious? It cannot be denied that they exist in the pages of Muslim authors. No Jew could have written them nor any Christian, but rather some Muslims who appeared to think that these things were either not untrue, or not unworthy of the Prophet.

4. On the other hand, where rejection of certain facts, on the ground, say, of the untrustworthiness of the author, is *not* possible, we find that the modern apologist for Muhammad seeks to justify them as being (though, it may be, contrary to the general expectation) features essential in the ideal prophet. Muhammad's wars are so defended.

In any case, we cannot escape the obligation to compare Muhammad with Jesus Christ, and, in that light, seriously minded and unprejudiced people all the world over, whose only concern is to follow the highest, have found in Muhammad what can only be described as grave moral defects.

The Islāmic Conception of God

The strength and weakness of the Muslim creed are nowhere so clearly portrayed as in the much-vaunted doctrine of the Unity of God. No one will grudge to Islām and Muslims the credit that is their due for this steady witness, down the years and amid the enervating influences of polytheism, to the truth that the God of all the earth is One God, the Living God.

But what does this extreme insistence on the Unity really amount to? What we have here is not monotheism in the commonly accepted meaning of that term, certainly not the monotheism of Judaism. The one and only God of Hebrew thought was, before all else, Holy and Righteous. It was upon His *character* that the Old Testament prophets laid greatest stress, and in this Christ was like them. But in Islām the stress has been to so extravagant an extent on the Unity that God's character has thereby both suffered and been subordinated. The Unity in Islām is primarily and essentially a mathematical unity.

Certain things inevitably follow from this. While there are notable exceptions among Muslims (and to this we gladly testify), yet the view of God most commonly held by the masses is one that produces fear and servility, also listlessness and formality in life and practice. Allāh is one to be feared rather than loved. Islām would propound the greatest commandment of all, as "Thou shalt *fear* the Lord thy God." In consequence, the tender passions of the human heart and the response of ardent love are rarely stimulated by the assurance that comes from a knowledge of real affection in God towards man.

Man is emphatically the *banda* (*'abd*), or "slave" of Allāh, and as such entirely dependent on His favour. For this reason multitudes of Muslims still perform their religious duties with a view to avoid the anger and chastisement of Allāh. Such a view produces a hard, and at times severe, disposition in men, one which not uncommonly looks with something akin to contempt upon those who believe that Love is the most characteristic feature in the Supreme Being.

Sin and Forgiveness

Sin, to the average Muslim, is not so much the doing of something that is morally wrong (though various faults, such as pride and covetousness, are definitely recognised as "sin"), but rather the doing of something forbidden. More precisely, sin is not ordinarily thought of as something to do with the state of man's nature but with infringements of prescribed ritual. According to the Qur'ān man is by nature weak but not tainted.

We have the singular fact, therefore, that the "unpardonable sin" in Islām is something quite other than we should have expected. It is not the offence against God's Holy Spirit of which Christ spoke, but (and here again we see the excessive influence of the doctrine of the Unity) *shirk*, the harbouring of a "heresy," the heresy of "associating a partner" with God; in the light of which both polytheism and Trinitarian views of God are alike *anathema*.

On the other hand, Islām makes ample provision in cases of failure to perform the prescribed ritual by enjoining certain "compensating" acts whereby such "sins" are cancelled. Such are the stated prayers, repetition of the "beautiful names" of God and the Muslim creed, almsgiving, fasts and the pilgrimage. By these also the believer "stores up" eternal merit.

It follows that genuine and deep-seated grief for sin in the strictly moral sense, and true repentance having in it the determination to turn from evil ways to holy living, are not often met with among Muslims who have this outlook. The forgiveness of sins, as we shall have occasion to observe a little farther on, is too easy a process, and for this reason—the real nature of sin, as essentially an affront to the Love of God, is not understood.

Prayer

The Muslim act of prayer is inclined to be formal and mechanical, a failing that besets others besides Muslims. But the danger is so much the greater in Islām because of the inviolable rule that prayer must be offered in Arabic. This means that for multitudes of people, more especially those whose mother tongue is not Arabic, prayer is apt to degenerate into an act in which the mind does not participate.

Once the required Arabic lines are committed to memory the need for mental exertion ceases. The worshipper suffers the inevitable penalty that comes from constant repetition. In short, prayer has become for such the performance of a duty demanded by God and not the spontaneous outpouring of the heart to Him.

Attitude to Women

This is a matter about which Muslims are both jealous and sensitive. In their reaction to widespread criticism on the subject it is now common to find educated Muslims declare that the legal system of Islām has given "rights" to women that no other religion has accorded to them. The late Sayyid Amīr 'Alī once committed himself in a public lecture in London to the statement that Islām had done more for the uplift of women than any other religious system.

The ideal, however, is one thing, the real quite another. We can but judge by what we know to be the facts, and it is in the light of facts—such as restrictions of *parda*, as commonly enforced, and the practice of polygamy and frequency of divorce—that some of the world's leading thinkers and travellers have stated that Islām's actual and customary treatment of women is a disgrace. It is a hopeful sign that there are now many honourable exceptions to this rule, and that here and there the more chivalrous spirits among Muslims are working patiently to bring about long-overdue amelioration in the lot of women.

Can it be doubted that the teaching of the Qur'ān (cp. xxiv. 23-33; iv. 29-30, 38; ii. 183) and the standards made familiar by certain of the Traditions have tended, in practice, to perpetuate their unhappy fate?

Education

It is notorious that orthodox Muslim doctors of the law have repeatedly opposed the cause of liberal education. There have been notable periods in the history of Islām when Khalīfas, Mughal emperors and men of affluence and authority have encouraged learning. Many modern Muslims, too, are zealous advocates of higher education, but the influence of Islām has generally been the other way.

The story of the Muslims of India is an illustration of this, notwithstanding the fact that special reasons might be advanced in extenuation. The backwardness of the Muslims as a community compared with the Hindus is very marked, although the two peoples have lived side by side for centuries. One of the real though not obvious reasons for such a situation seems to be this, that the doctrines of Islām, *as commonly believed and followed*, tend to discourage independent and progressive thought. It is as though their *'ulamā* had proclaimed: "Has not Allāh revealed *all* wisdom and *all* knowledge to men through the Qur'ān? Whatever of knowledge is not there is immaterial or contrary to the will of Allāh and need not and ought not to be studied."

The growing revolt of the younger generation against this point of view is a present-day feature full of promise.

Lack of Spiritual Power

But the most serious defect in the body of Islām is the absence of a channel for the inflow of regenerating power for men enslaved by sin, and, what is worse, the lack of a sense of the need for it.

Islām quite frankly does not claim to be a "spiritual religion" in the sense in which that phrase is used by Christians; that is to say, a religion which brings back lost man to God, and lifts the fallen up to Him. It has so stressed God as to do less than justice to man. It has failed to provide a way through which man's desire to sin is eradicated. It does not attempt to reach the foundations of human action in order to cleanse them.

There is in Islām no sense of the glorious redemptive purpose at the heart of God—no idea of God yearning to save men from the thraldom of sin—no idea of His purpose to make of man "a new creature" by the power of His Holy Spirit.

This is borne out by a recent statement in a journal belonging to one of the more progressive parties. The writer expressly stated that there is no such thing as "salvation" in Islām—the idea, an erroneous one, had been brought in (he said) from Christianity; rather, salvation was a gift to man at his birth (*The Light*, Lahore, 8th March 1931).

Further striking confirmation of what we have just been saying was furnished some years ago in the correspondence columns of this same journal. A correspondent had thus addressed its editor:

"I am a girl of twenty, and from the age of twelve I have done every sin that you can think of. In fact I have tasted of every leaf of the tree of life. Alas! there is nothing left for me but Hell when I die. I ask you sincerely what am I to do to be saved? I have put this question to a priest. He has told me to repent, but the truth is I cannot repent, as what I have done I have enjoyed doing, though it was a sin. Now will you advise me what I am to do so as to be saved from Hell?" And to this poor soul the editor replied: "Turn a new leaf. Lead a righteous life henceforward. This alone can wash off past sins. This is the only true atonement. Sins are washed off, the Qur'ān assures us (xi. 116), by good deeds and these alone" (*The Light*, August 1927). A stone for bread! What a confession of bankruptcy in Islām.

CHAPTER IV

CHRISTIAN DOCTRINES IN THE LIGHT OF MUSLIM PREJUDICE

THOSE who seek to present the Christian message to Muslims very frequently meet with a rebuff. It does not take them long to discover that these people entertain certain deep-seated prejudices about Christianity and are only too ready to voice them. Rightly to account for this we need, in the first place, to remind ourselves that Islām occupies a position relative to Christianity that is not shared by the other world-religions, inasmuch as it is subsequent to Christianity and was propagated in spite of, and in a sense as a protest against, it.

We have already seen that Muhammad had a controversy not only with the Jews but with the Christians of his day. That controversy, in some detail, is reflected in the pages of the Qur'ān, and occupies considerable space in the earliest Muslim writings; and its influence, with the main features still preserved, has persisted down the years, so that, as history proves, whenever close contacts are made between peoples of these two faiths it is apt to break out afresh.

It can be shown, however, that this characteristic and long-standing prejudice of the Muslims is ostensibly directed against certain doctrines rather than against the Christian message as such. That being so, a two-fold obligation rests upon us: we need to get down to the root-cause of their prejudice, and we ought to rethink and, if need be, restate our Christian beliefs so as to remove from their minds any possible cause of misunderstanding or offence.

We must go back, then, for the causes to the time of Muhammad and to the pages of the Qur'ān.

The Genuineness of the Bible

But before we enter upon a discussion of the doctrines in question we are obliged, by the very nature of the case, to deal with a pronounced prejudice against the Scriptures of the Old and New Testaments.

Muslims are assiduously taught to believe, and for the most part do believe, that the Bible now in circulation is not trustworthy, on the ground that it has been tampered with. Needless to say, this objection, as commonly stated, has nothing to do with the results of textual criticism, but reflects an old traditional attitude. Most Muslims in making it merely repeat what they have heard, and have no proof to offer; but others will seek confirmation from the Qur'ān. These often content themselves with saying: "Our book says so." We are thus led to enquire what it is that the book does say upon the matter.

In the circumstances it is rather surprising to find that the Qur'ān speaks here and there in very high terms about the Scriptures: (i) it declares that they were given by God: the *Taurāt* to Moses, xxxii. 23; the *Zabūr* to David, xvii. 57; the *Injīl* to Jesus, v. 50; (ii) it assigns high titles to them: "the Book of God," v. 48; "the word of God," ii. 70; "a light and direction to men," vi. 91; "a guidance and a mercy," vi. 155; and (iii) it is said to "confirm" and is sent to "safeguard" them; v. 50; ii. 83, 91; v. 52.

Bearing these passages in mind we may turn now to consider other verses on which Muslims are wont to base their charge that the Scriptures have been corrupted. The Arabic at the places cited yields such meanings as the following: (i) vii. 162: "the ungodly ones among them *changed that word into another* than that which had been told them." This is said of the

Jews of the time of Moses who intentionally mispronounced a word of the divine revelation, and so "changed" its meaning. (Cp. ver. 161; *hittat*, forgiveness, was the word given, whereas the Jews are declared to have said *habbat*, corn.) (2) iii. 72: "Some are there among them who *torture the Scriptures with their tongues*, in order that ye may suppose it to be from the Scripture, yet it is not from the Scripture." (3) ii. 73; "Woe to those who with their own hands *transcribe the Book* (i.e., corruptly) and then say, 'This is from God,' that they may sell it for some mean price." (4) iii. 64: "O people of the Book! why clothe ye the truth with falsehood? Why wittingly *hide the truth*?" (i.e., by covering up part of the text, e.g., with the hand while reading).

In reality these complaints rather prove the genuineness of the Scriptures as they existed in the time of Muhammad, for you cannot "transcribe corruptly" unless you have the correct text before you, nor can you "hide the truth" unless you have the truth. In any case such abuses do not affect the text of Scripture and therefore do not corrupt the Book.

No less a person than Sir Sayyid Ahmad Khān, of Aligarh fame, wrote a treatise in his day to show Muslims that the Qur'ān nowhere asserts that the Jews or Christians actually corrupted the text of their Scriptures. Early Muslim authorities, he said, recognise in theory two forms of *tahrīf*, corruption: viz., *tahrīf-i-lafzī*, "verbal corruption," i.e., corruption of the *text*; and *tahrīf-i-mānawī*, corruption of meaning or interpretation. He declares emphatically that the charges in the Qur'ān are of the latter type, of which he gives the following instances: making verbal changes while reading to convey to the ear words different from those written; reading only some passages and omitting others; instructing people in a manner contrary to God's teaching in His Holy Word and yet making them believe that this instruction is the true word; adopting an improper meaning of certain words of ambiguous or equivocal interpretation which does not suit the sense intended; misinterpreting passages that are mystical and allegorical (*The Muhammadan Commentary on the Holy Bible*, Seventh Discourse).

But what were the circumstances which gave rise to even these lesser charges against "the People of the Book," as Muhammad invariably called the Jews and the Christians? We have no alternative but to conclude that they were made originally by Muhammad himself. As we have said, he had a controversy with these people and one aspect of it is reflected in these passages of the Qur'ān.

Of the attempts made to reconstruct the situation as it existed for him, the following seems to be a fairly reasonable one. At Mecca Muhammad developed a sincere respect for the Jews and for their "Book." His own people had no such Book. In intercourse with them he learned something of its contents. Afterwards at Madīna he mixed freely with them, hoping to win them over in his support. From them he heard of, and became interested in, Old Testament prophecies regarding the Messiah, whom the Jews said was yet to come. Muhammad, claiming, as he had done from the first, God's authority for his mission, claimed also that the Scriptures foretold his coming (vii. 156; cp. lxi. 6). This the Jews vehemently denied (ii. 95); they knew from their Book that Messiah would be of the line of David. Seen in this light the complaints in the Qur'ān become intelligible. Muhammad, in effect, accused the Jews of "changing," "hiding" and "transposing" words, and of "twisting them with their tongues," whenever asked to read out to him passages alleged to have reference to himself. The outstanding fact is that in this, as in other matters, the Jews withstood him until, in exasperation, he removed them from his path. In a very real sense many of those Jews gave their lives for their Book.

In other words the early controversy was largely a personal one, involving the claims of Muhammad, and this aspect of it is present to the minds of many Muslims even to this day. Ignoring, or else being unaware of, the true significance of the charges made in the Qur'ān, such Muslims assume that the Bible once contained a number of references to Muhammad, which Jews and Christians, at some time or other, deleted.

The whole idea is of course absurd. It should be enough to ask what possible benefit could the Jews have gained by recourse to such an act. Rather, had their Scriptures contained any reference to Muhammad, they would have accepted him and so escaped much persecution. Besides, there is the fact that long before the time of Muhammad the Jews had become familiar with the claims of the *Christians*, to the effect that many of the Messianic prophecies of the Old Testament had received their fulfilment in Jesus of Nazareth; nevertheless they did not subsequently erase those passages, though they denied the Christians' interpretation of them.

In view of these things, and considering the strong assertion that the Scriptures have already been corrupted, it is curious to find Muslims still claiming that the Bible, *as it stands*, contains numerous references to Muhammad. But one cannot have it both ways.

The simple fact at the back of all this is that there is marked disagreement on many points between the Qur'ān and the Bible. What is more, the two have never agreed, for the Qur'ān from the first has differed from the Bible. This disagreement is a cause of embarrassment to proud and sensitive Muslims, who conclude that one of the Books must have been corrupted and is therefore untrustworthy. This, they hold, cannot be the Qur'ān, which, say they, belongs to an altogether superior category; therefore it is the Bible which is in fault. Not very sound reasoning, surely.

The Person of Christ

Notwithstanding the constant assertion that they respect and even reverence the name of Jesus, Muslims are quick to repudiate the high and unique claims which Christians make for Him. Jesus, "Son of Mary" (the common title given to Him in the Qur'ān), is for them but one of the prophets, and not the last nor the best.

Naturally it is not to be expected that they should give to Him a higher place than that which they assign to Muhammad, and in practice, as we have seen above (p. 104), they do not give Him as high. But such natural preference for their own Prophet is not the only or the chief reason why Muslims refuse to give to Christ a name that is above every name. It is rather their *jealousy for God*, as they understand Him, that provokes them to denounce as blasphemy any honour paid to Christ which, in effect, makes Him to be more than man.

This jealousy is rooted in the cardinal doctrine of Islām, *tauhīd*, the Unity (of God). So that this prejudice, also, goes back to the origins of Islām. "The unity of God is the one great theme of the Qur'ān . . . there is absolute unity in the divine nature . . . it admits of no participation or manifoldness . . . it denies all plurality of persons in the Godhead. . . . (Islām) refuses to acknowledge the incarnation of the Divine Being" (Maulāna Muhammad Ali, Preface to Holy Qur'ān, pp. viii.-ix.).

And as though the great stress laid by the Qur'ān on this doctrine of *tauhīd* were not sufficient to instil it into the mind of man, the offence of "associating a partner" with God (*shirk*) is further declared by the Qur'ān to be the one unpardonable sin. "Verily, God will not forgive the union of other gods with Himself! But other than this will He forgive to whom He pleaseth. And he who hath united gods with God hath devised a great wickedness" (iv. 51, 116).

It matters not that we, from our side, might strongly object to such crude language as altogether inapplicable to the case of Christ, the fact remains—in the mind of Muslims we come within the category of those so upbraided.

It seems certain that here, in the constant reiteration of the doctrine of the Unity of God and in the dreaded sin of *shirk*, we come upon the two main factors which produce in the Muslim so great a prejudice that he is not prepared to entertain any conception of the Divinity of Christ, or any explanation of the Incarnation. From this it follows that Muslims abhor the Christian doctrine of the Sonship of Christ. Only recently in South India an educated Muslim said to a Christian preacher, "Whenever you Christians speak of Jesus as the 'Son of God,' it makes our blood boil."

Another explanation of this resentment is that it seems to Muslims that in so speaking of Jesus we appear to belittle, ignore, and even deny the supreme doctrine of God's essential Unity. But there is much more behind this widespread feeling. There is the *denunciation of the Qur'ān.* Along with its declaration of the Unity of God the Qur'ān, with great vehemence, repudiates the very idea that God "has a son."

The relevant passages fall into two groups:

(1) Those that refer to heathen Arabs, and (2) those having reference to Christians. One instance from each group will suffice to show the kind of "sonship" Muhammad had in mind.

(1) vi. 100. "How when He hath no wife, can He have a son?" (cp. also x. 69; xxxix. 6; xliii. 81; lxxii. 3; cxii.).

(2) xix. 88-92. "They (Christians) say, 'The God of Mercy hath gotten offspring! Now have ye done a monstrous thing! Almost might the very heavens be rent thereat, and the earth cleave asunder and the mountains fall down in fragments . . . it beseemeth not the God of Mercy to beget a son!'" (cf. also ii. 110; v. 19, 75; ix. 31-2; xix. 36).

A study of all these passages makes two things clear: (1) that what the Qur'ān denounces is a *carnal* idea of sonship, and (2) that it charges both the heathen Arabs and the Christians of that day with being guilty of holding such views of God. The Arabs fully merited the rebuke. As for the Christians, the ground for such accusation may conceivably be found in the way Abyssinian Christians exalted the Virgin Mary to a position almost divine; and Muhammad, we know, had considerable intercourse with Christians of Abyssinia. Then, too, at an earlier date a sect in Syria had taught that the Trinity consisted of God, Mary, and Jesus! It may have been the fact that, even in Muhammad's time, some obscure sect still held such views.

Now it does not need to be argued that in no place is the phrase used in the New Testament in a carnal sense. Nor is it used as indicating that there is present to the minds of the speakers the thought of Jesus' birth, as having taken place in a special or supernatural manner. The simple and obvious fact is that the phrase is used as a title, a Messianic title. Only in Luke i. 35 is it used in connection with the annunciation of the birth of Jesus, and even there its significance is that of a name to be given to Him. In other words, the language is symbolic and not to be taken literally.

There is, however, much more in the New Testament use of it than that. The phrase conveys, and *is intended to convey*, the fact that Jesus' consciousness of God was a truly filial consciousness. His sense of sonship to the Divine Father was "deeper, clearer, more intimate, more all-embracing and all-absorbing than ever was vouchsafed to a child of man."

That is a *fact* that cannot, by any manner of reasoning, be eliminated from the gospels.

But it remains to be said that the gravamen of the Muslims' protest, like that of the Jews in the days of Christ, is directed not so much against the doctrine of the Sonship as against the deeper implication of such Sonship, viz., that there is identity of essence in the Father and the Son (cf. John v. 18, and x. 33). It cannot be denied that the phrase, as used in the New Testament, carries with it this implication.

Allāh, on the other hand, is *lā sharīk*, i.e., He has " no

partner"; if, then, the Christian view of Christ be admitted, Allāh would be sharing His Glory with another, He would "have a partner"—an impossible and blasphemous proposition for the Muslim. "Islām refuses to acknowledge the incarnation of the Divine Being."

Quite clearly again, it is his jealousy for God, as he conceives Him, that accounts for the Muslim's vehement repudiation of any idea of an incarnation. Just as he says: "It beseemeth not God to beget a son," so he would say, "Far be it from the God of Mercy to be 'found in fashion as a man'" (Phil. ii. 8).

That is to say, the Muslim considers it *derogatory* to the Glory of God to become incarnate, even though it be for man's salvation.

But his jealousy for God is based on an imperfect conception of the Deity. He feels that the Majesty of "the Lord of the Worlds" must be safeguarded at all costs. We, on the contrary, maintain that, far from it being derogatory to the Majesty and Glory of God to seek, by such means, to make Himself known to men *in a saving way*, this is Love's prerogative, for God is essentially Love. The glory of Power might be sullied by an act of condescension. Supreme Intelligence might hesitate to appear in lowly guise. Sheer Justice might demand some other way. But Love, true Love, *does stoop to save*, and, stooping, is not degraded.

And this is of the very essence of the Christian belief about Christ. We believe that God revealed *Himself*, His moral character, in His "Son"; that it is in Christ and through Christ and Christ alone that we know God as He really is; that it is "because men find in the soul of Christ the fullness of love that they find in Him the fullness of God."

The Trinity

Perhaps the most familiar object of Muslim attack is the doctrine of the Trinity. A Muslim paper has been known to set it out in the manner of a formula, thus

1 + 1 + 1 = 1; and then hold it up to ridicule with the remark that even a schoolboy would not make so silly a blunder in his sums, and if he did he would be spanked.

In this case, too, we may trace the extraordinary influence of the Islamic doctrine of *tauhīd.* It soon enters into the composition of the Muslim mind, for a baby is taught to respond to the word Allāh by raising one finger. Whereas there are certain statements in the Qur'ān, known to every Muslim, which are quoted in support of their protest against the Trinity.

" Believe in God and His apostle and say not ' Three ' : (i.e., there is a Trinity)—forbear ! it will be better for you. God is only one God " (iv. 169).

" They surely are infidels who say, ' God is the third of three,' for there is no God but one God : and if they refrain not from what they say, a grievous punishment shall light (on them) " (v. 77).

" God shall say—' O Jesus, Son of Mary : hast thou said unto mankind, " Take me and my mother as two gods, besides God ? " ' He shall say—' Glory be to Thee ! it is not for me to say that which I know to be not the truth ' " (v. 116).

But these statements indicate a conception which we ourselves would repudiate no less strongly than Muslims. The language of the Qur'ān contemplates not a trinity, but a *triad,* after the manner of the Hindu Brahma, Shiva and Vishnu, or the Egyptian Isis, Osiris and Horus. If Muhammad did get these ideas of his from Christians, it must have been, as we have suggested above, from the doctrine of some obscure sect which orthodox Christians would have repudiated.

We, too, believe that God is One God, and for this belief we have the example and approval of Jesus Himself. When asked to declare which was the first commandment of all, He quoted Deut. vi. 4-5: " Hear, O Israel, the Lord our God is One Lord : and thou shalt love the Lord thy God with all thy heart. . . ." If Jesus could endorse that, we can and should.

Now the Muslims may say, and with much semblance of truth, that the doctrine of the Unity which he holds has abundant support in the actual words of the Qur'ān, whereas the Christians have departed from the plain teaching of the Bible (as set forth, indeed, by the passage just quoted) and, instead, have propounded a doctrine not only offensive, but having little or no support in the Scriptures.

We are free to admit that the doctrine of the Trinity, as a doctrine, is not to be found in the original Gospel message. Nevertheless the gospels do contain elements which, afterwards, contributed valuable support to the doctrine when formulated. Rather we have here a wonderful conception which arose directly out of a vital and joyous experience of the early Christians.

They were compelled to think out for themselves the significance of Christ. They could place Him in no known category. Not His teaching alone, but His character, His works and His personal dealings with them proclaimed Him to be related to God and to the power, wisdom and love of God in some unique way, quite unlike anything hitherto known. And so they concluded that He belonged to the category of God, and signified their belief by calling Him " Son of God."

When He left them they experienced the indwelling of the Spirit. This was in accordance with Christ's own promise and they found that, as He had said, the Spirit took of the things of Christ and revealed them unto them. His words came true, for the Spirit carried on the work of Christ in the hearts of men, convicting them of sin and sanctifying them unto righteousness. So the early Christians called the Spirit "Holy," and by so doing virtually placed the Spirit, also, in the category of God. That is to say, they found in their experience that the " Father," proclaimed by Jesus, Jesus Himself, and the Holy Spirit were *ethically* one, and it was out of this experience that they formulated the doctrine of the Trinity.

After all, what matters most is not the doctrine but the experience, and that we can have, and do have, still.

The Crucifixion

It comes as a surprise to most to find that orthodox Muslims believe that Jesus did not die; consequently they meet our assertion with a plain denial, though, as we shall see in our next chapter, the form the denial takes with the modern rationalist is that it was *not on the cross* that He died.

Yet once again it is the Qur'ān that is responsible for this attitude, though there is considerable ambiguity in the language used in reference to the matter. The relevant passages are:

(The infant Jesus speaks from the cradle), " The peace of God was on me the day I was born, and will be in the day that I shall die, and the day I shall be raised to life " (xix. 34).

" There shall not be one of the people of the Book but shall believe in Him before His death, and in the day of resurrection He will be a witness against them " (iv. 157).

" When God said, ' O Jesus, verily I will cause thee to die, and will take thee up to myself and deliver thee from those who believe not ' " (iii. 48).

" And for their (i.e., the Jews) saying, ' Verily we have slain the Messiah, Jesus, the son of Mary, an apostle of God.' Yet they slew him not and they crucified him not, but they had only his likeness. And they who differed about him were in doubt concerning him: no sure knowledge had they about him but followed only an opinion, and they did not really slay him, but God took him up to Himself " (iv. 156; cp. also v. 117).

Various arguments are put forward by Muslims on the strength of these passages.

1. The orthodox, on the basis of iv. 156, hold that Jesus did not die, but was taken up, *while yet alive*, by God to heaven. These argue that Jesus could not have

died so shameful a death, for then he would have been "accursed of God" (Deut. xxi. 23), an impossible fate for a prophet of God. What actually happened, they say, was that another was made to appear to them like Jesus (cp. the phrase, "his likeness"); this other they crucified, while God took Jesus, unscathed, to heaven. But the Muslim completely loses sight of the fact that the gospel narratives show that Jesus *voluntarily* suffered this shame.

2. The remaining passages seem to suggest, on the other hand, that Muhammad supposed Jesus to have died a natural death, but that He continued in that state for only a short time, since it is also declared in places that "God took him up." As a matter of fact some of the older commentators say that death intervened for three hours only, others say seven (Commentary of Sir Sayyid Ahmad Khān, quoted from *Imām Fakhruddin Rāzī*, on iii. 48, cp. Baidhāwī *in loc. cit.*).

What, however, is quite clear from these verses is that the Qur'ān denies the death of Jesus *by crucifixion*. How are we to account for this? It is conceivable that Muhammad heard about, and was influenced by, the docetic doctrine of some Gnostic sects. Some of these, we know, propounded the theory that the authorities mistook Simon of Cyrene for Jesus and crucified him instead; according to others it was Judas Iscariot whom they crucified. Their views were undoubtedly adopted by later Muslim writers.

Now it is possible that Muhammad, out of regard for Jesus and with a view to clearing His name from the reproach which the Jews intended by such a death, welcomed this theory as true to fact. At any rate the language at iv. 156 does suggest an allusion to the early docetic view.

On the other hand, Muhammad appears to have considered *success* to be the invariable mark of all true greatness, so that the prophets, including Jesus, must of necessity have been "successful." How then could so great a prophet have been *crucified*? There must have been some blunder; the Jews who had lied so often must have lied about this; it was not Jesus whom they crucified but, as some Christians were known to assert, another whom the people mistook for Him.

The Atonement

Having denied the crucifixion it is not surprising to find that Muslims have no use for a doctrine of atonement. But the real explanation for their attitude is to be found not so much in the Qur'ān's denial of the crucifixion as in the typical Islamic conception of Allāh, set forth in the Qur'ān, whereby they declare that there is no need of any atonement.

The teaching of the Qur'ān in this respect is so clear and emphatic that it can be summarised very briefly as follows:

Allāh is Almighty—He can do what He likes.
Allāh is Merciful—He forgives whom He will.

That His might and His mercy are definitely lacking in certain moral qualities is borne out by the ordinary teaching of Islām concerning *sin*.

The principal terms used in the Qur'ān for sin are three:

(1) *dhanb*, 38 t.—a term signifying, chiefly, ceremonial offences.

(2) *ithm*, 29 t.—having almost the same significance.

(3) *khatā*, 5 t.—a term which, of the three, comes nearest to the idea of sin as missing the standard set up by God.

The more popular Muslim literature bears witness to this conception of sin; the ceremonial laws are so minute as to have become a burden, a veritable "yoke." And while it is true that the Qur'ān condemns such sins as pride, covetousness, etc., and that the doctors of the law have compiled a list of " great " sins, yet it is no less true that all offences, without exception, are dwarfed by the Qur'ān's denunciation of the sin of sins, the unpardonable sin, *shirk*, a heresy. This fact, by itself, throws much light on the Muslim conception of God's attitude to evil.

The mercy of God is further impaired by the Islamic doctrine of *fate*. The Qur'ān asserts that the fate of man, whatever happens, has been fixed by inevitable decrees. But while this doctrine is often urged, and quite legitimately, as a reason for resignation and patience, it is not by any means confined to such purposes. In the Qur'ān it is constantly obtruded in its crudest form, thus:

" Allāh will mislead whom He pleaseth, and whom He pleaseth He will place upon the straight path " (vi. 39).

" And whoso willeth, taketh the way to his Lord. But will it ye shall not, unless Allāh will it " (lxxvi. 30).

" Whom Allāh causeth to err, no guide shall there be for him " (xiii. 33).

" Every man's fate have we fastened about his neck " (xvii. 14).

" Had thy God pleased He would have made mankind of one religion; but those only to whom thy Lord hath granted mercy will cease to differ. And unto this hath He created them; for the word of thy Lord shall be fulfilled, 'I will wholly fill hell with jinn and men' " (xi. 120).

One might well ask, how is it possible for a Muslim, under the influence of such teaching, to come near in his conception of sin to that idea of it which we gain from Christ, viz., that it is an offence against the love of the Heavenly Father? Allāh is an arbitrary God, and man's very offences seem to be determined by an inexorable fate. And what, after all, are these offences? Apart from that terrible bogey, *shirk*, most of them are not the kind that harrow a man's soul. Contrast the quotations given above with these, for the like of which you will search the Qur'ān in vain:

"The Lord is not willing that any should perish" (2 Pet. iii. 9).

(God) "Who will have all men to be saved" (1 Tim. ii. 4).

"As I live, saith the Lord, I have no pleasure in the death of the wicked, but that the wicked should turn from his way and live" (Ezek. xxxiii. 11).

And when the Qur'ān does say anything about "salvation"—and it isn't often, e.g., the substantive *najāt*, salvation, occurs but once (xl. 44)—it does not convey the idea of moral and spiritual regeneration.

Our first task, therefore, is to help lift God's character out of the category in which Islām has placed it; to lead the Muslim to worthier views of Him, of His Holiness, His righteousness, and His Love. We can show him also that the measure of a man's penitence is the measure of his sense of sin; and it will be here, and in this connection, that we can prove both the need and the power of the death of Christ on the Cross.

We can show from our own experience that it is only through meditating on the meaning and the purpose of that suffering that one comes to hold worthier views of God and a more adequate conception of sin.

Chapter V

THE NEW POLEMIC

Alongside the new apologetic for Islām, which began to be formulated in the latter part of the last century, there emerged a new polemic with a pronounced anti-Christian tendency. Needless to say, this was not the work of Sir Sayyid Ahmad Khān or men of his stamp. Where he saw urgent need for rehabilitating Islām on a more rationalistic basis, others, in petulant mood, stooped to use unworthy means to further what they conceived to be their cause.

Prior to 1875 the controversy, as we have already seen, centred round the Books and Miracles, and concerned certain *doctrines*, such as the Divinity of Christ, the Trinity, and the Atonement. But from about that date the section known as Ahmadiyyas, or more precisely the one comprising Mirzā Ghulām Ahmad of Qādiān and his followers, began to employ other weapons of attack against the Christian movement. These weapons had been made familiar some time previously in the West through the writings of extreme and irresponsible critics like Strauss and Schmiedel, to whose ideas the polemical works of the Ahmadīyyas are clearly indebted.

For example, in regard to the Bible the views of men of the most extreme school of higher critics have been freely used to prove that the *text* of the Scriptures is unreliable, and their conclusions are brazenly represented as being the considered opinions of the foremost Christian scholars of the day.

The Ahmadīyyas have also sought to discredit Christianity by arguments of a more general nature, in which we may again trace the influence of extreme Western critics. Thus, Paul, not Jesus, was the "inventor" of the Christian religion; the ritual, feasts, and even doctrines of the Church bear the marks of pagan origin and the influence of the mystery cults; Christianity was never intended to be a universal religion, inasmuch as Jesus confined His ministry to the House of Israel. The decrease in attendance at church services in the West is cited as a proof of the waning power of Christianity. Social conditions also receive their share of condemnation. The position of women and the prevalence of divorce, especially in the United States of America, prove that Muslim women are in happier case; anyway legalised prostitution is far worse than the polygamy of Islām, etc.

Islām, the Ahmadīyyas maintain, is misunderstood in the West, largely because of the misrepresentation of Christian missionaries. It is thus part of their declared purpose to enlighten Christendom about the real facts, and, incidentally, to cripple the missionary enterprise of the Churches. "Europe and America," says one of their leaders, "the two continents that are at the back of the great movement of Christianity against Islām, are hopelessly ignorant of Islâm and they are directing this movement under the false impression created by the Christian missionary. . . . If we could only spread Islamic literature in these countries . . . we would be able not only to arrest the growth of the missionary movement but to deal it a death-blow at the very centre of its vitality." It is through the efforts of these Ahmadīyyas that mosques have been erected in London, Paris, and Berlin.

Changed Attitude to Jesus Christ

But the most significant feature of the new polemic is the attempt, originating with the founder of the Qādiānī community, to bring the name of Jesus Himself into disrepute.

Hitherto that name has occupied an exalted place in the regard of Muslims, and the passages in the Qur'ān that ascribe to Him special, not to say unique, honour (e.g., iii. 40; iv. 169) have had much to do with the maintenance of this attitude of respect through the centuries. But during the last fifty years the influence of this other factor has been steadily at work modifying the traditional point of view. True, the nobler minds among Muslims deprecate the line thus taken, nevertheless it is clear that others, not owning to the name of Ahmadīyyas, in their anxiety to prove Islām to be the superior religion, do not scruple to make use of this new weapon against Christianity.

The Mirzā of Qādiān, in defending his recourse to this kind of argument (which profoundly shocked many Muslims at the time), is said to have protested that it was not the *'Isā* of the Qur'ān that he was attacking but the *Jesus* of the Gospels; a remark that was as insincere as it was unreasonable. Three causes seem to have determined his course of action. (1) The movement he founded was part of the reaction in the body of Indian Islām to the upheaval of thought and feeling caused by the exposure of Islām and Muhammad in the public debates initiated by Dr Pfander. It is to be feared, that is to say, that this thing was done in the spirit of bitter resentment. (2) His own claim to be the long-promised Messiah led him to invent the preposterous story that Jesus did not succumb on the cross, but died a natural death in Kashmir. In this way the Mirzā sought to aim a deadly blow at the Christian faith. (3) He was shrewd enough to see that the supreme issue lay between the founders of the two faiths, and in this matter he has led the way for both sections of the Ahmadīyyas. The issue is now recognised by these to be, not so much a question of this or that Book, or this or that creed, but of Christ or Muhammad. It is as though they have determined that what Muhammad cannot be, Christ shall not be.

If further proof concerning the Qādiān leader's attitude

and purpose is required, it can be found in what we might term his "last legacy" to his followers. He is credibly reported to have said: "Listen, my friends, to my last injunction. I tell you a secret. Remember it well that you may upset all the arguments which the Christians put forward. Prove to them that in reality Christ, the Son of Mary, is for ever dead. Through the victory to be gained by this argument you will be able to wipe the Christian religion from off the face of the earth. There is no necessity for you to waste your precious time in other wearisome wrangles. Just concentrate upon the death of Christ, the Son of Mary, and by the use of powerful arguments reduce the Christians to silence. On the day that you succeed in proving that Christ joined the ranks of the dead and imprint this fact on the minds of Christians, you will know that the Christian religion has made its exit from the world" (*Izāla*, p. 116).

We know the steps this man took to achieve his object. He revived an early heresy to the effect that Jesus merely swooned on the cross; that He was taken down and revived, within forty days, by the application of an ointment, *marham-i ʻIsā*, and that eventually He travelled to Kashmir, where He died and was buried at the advanced age of 120. The Mirzā even gave out that His tomb is to be seen there to-day, in the capital, Srinagar (see above, p. 212).

Here is another statement in a similar vein, in this case appearing in an article by an Ahmadīyya of the Lahore branch, on the birth of Jesus, which reveals this same determination to "degrade" Him. "Islām and Christianity are engaged in a deadly struggle for world-mastery. It is therefore in the best interest of Islām that Jesus should be brought down from His divine pedestal. In crediting Him with a miraculous birth as well as a miraculous flight to heaven, the Musalmāns are only confirming the Christian contention that Jesus was divine, not human. It is, therefore, the crying call of the day to prove that Jesus was born in exactly the same way as any man is born, and that, like all the rest of mortals, He too had to drink the cup of death" (quoted from *The Light* in *The Moslem World*, Oct. 1929).

. . . . . .

We propose to deal very briefly with *four* aspects of the Ahmadīyya attack against Christ. In the last chapter we dealt with their denial of the crucifixion; here we shall consider their arguments against His supernatural birth, miracles, moral character, and resurrection.

It is to be regretted that Christian writers have, at times, used rather careless language in dealing with various articles of Christian belief, with the result that, on the one hand, some Muslims are honestly confused as to what things really are fundamental to the Christian faith, while others are only too ready to make great capital out of unguarded and incompatible statements.

Thus within the compass of one small book we find a prominent leader of the Ahmadīyyas asserting not only that (1) "the Christian religion laid its foundations on the death of Christ on the cross and his subsequent rising," but that (2) "the very basis of the Christian religion is laid on the exclusive sinlessness of Jesus," and that (3) "Christians find in his miracles proof of Christ's divinity." It will be a great gain when those who write for, and preach to, Muslims study to speak within the facts and carefully avoid all appearance of exaggeration. Nothing is to be feared from keeping strictly to the facts so far as we know them.

The Supernatural Birth

In the article from which we have culled the second quotation reproduced above, the Ahmadīyya writer seeks to prove, from the Qur'ān and the Gospels, that the birth of Jesus took place according to the ordinary course of nature. At the same time he admits that even now "the average Muslim gets positively shocked at the very idea that Jesus was born of a human father." He reproaches his co-religionists for their inconsistency, because, while holding to the view of a supernatural birth, they nevertheless refuse the conclusion that Jesus was divine. (The Qādiānīs, on the other hand, admit the virgin birth, but minimise its importance by claiming that there are parallel cases in pagan cults.)

After insisting that the relevant passages in the Qur'ān have been misunderstood by Muslims and Christians alike, and that the records in Matthew and Luke are not to be relied on, he goes on to say that the whole story in the Gospels is based upon Isaiah's reference to a *virgin*, whereas Dr A. B. Davidson has demonstrated that the Hebrew word used by the prophet does not yield that meaning. (Davidson quite rightly insists that the Hebrew word in question has been inaptly translated " virgin " ; it means rather, a maiden of marriageable age. Matthew got his word, not from the Hebrew, but from the Septuagint translation, which has *parthenos*.)

Now this is one of those subjects concerning which it is true to say that we gain nothing by claiming too much ; and exaggeration here is apt to confuse the Muslim as to the real issue. The fact is the question of the birth of Jesus does not vitally affect our Christian faith. Neither His " sinlessness " nor His " Sonship," nor yet His " Divinity," is bound up with the mode of His birth.

Moreover, we should be prepared frankly to admit certain difficulties in the matter, upon which the Ahmadīyya is inclined to dilate. For instance, it is true that (1) if sinful nature is transmitted to a child through its parents, it could equally easily be transmitted through one parent. (2) There is a remarkable silence about this subject in the rest of the New Testament. What Paul does say about it (cp. Gal. iv. 4) almost inevitably brings to mind passages in the book of Job (xiv. 1 and xxv. 4). These the Muslim, too, knows and quotes as conclusive in the case of Mary. (3) It is hardly possible to reconcile the narratives of the birth in Matthew and Luke. (4) The story of demigods, it is well known, had a wide diffusion among heathen peoples in those days.

But there is, here, much less reason for embarrassment than at first seems likely. (1) The silence of the New Testament is not really of great importance. It is quite conceivably accounted for by Mary's hesitancy to disclose the fact to the apostles until long after Jesus' death. And in regard to Paul's silence we need to bear in mind that, from quite an early date (cp. Acts ix. 20), he had proclaimed Christ's Divinity quite apart from any theory as to His birth. Besides, under the circumstances in which Paul proclaimed the Gospel to converts from paganism, the story of the supernatural birth would have been "strategically vulnerable as it was dogmatically unnecessary." (2) There is, after all, no absolute contradiction between the narratives of Matthew and Luke. They are written from two different points of view, the one from that of Joseph, the other from that of Mary. Yet they are in marked agreement on important matters such as these:

(*a*) The central fact of the supernatural birth itself.
(*b*) The location of it at Bethlehem.
(*c*) Its occurrence in the reign of Herod.
(*d*) Jesus' subsequent residence in Nazareth.

(3) It is highly improbable that heathen influence accounted for these narratives, for the following reasons among others. The New Testament, on the face of it, is free from such influence; and, despite the Mirzā's assertion, no ethnic parallel has been found by scholars to birth from a pure virgin; on the other hand, it is utterly unlikely, from what we know of them, that the New Testament writers should have stooped to use one of the very degrading features of pagan mythology.

Nor can we believe that this story is the "invention" of some Jewish Christians, for the Jews exalted marriage, *not* virginity.

But now in support of the claim we make for the

supernatural birth of Jesus we need to look squarely at certain other facts.

1. The case we are considering can by no means be dealt with as though it were that of an ordinary man. The very narrative of the life of Christ prevents us from doing that. No, we are speaking of One Whom we have come to regard as worthy of the Name that is above every name; One whose career (if we may make the assumption for the time being) closed with the Resurrection. We are dealing with the CENTRAL FIGURE in history. And it is not illogical to suggest that in a Person thus supernatural the Virgin Birth should be looked upon as a fitting prelude.

2. There is a rare and beautiful reserve shown by Matthew and Luke in speaking of this event, *lest* what is said might be misconstrued. For they had certain facts before them; on the one hand, Jesus' Davidic lineage was known, and on the other, His resurrection had already attested His Divinity to the satisfaction of the early disciples.

Their exquisite reticence, freshness and purity plead in favour of these narratives. There is an entire absence of morbid reflection and vulgar curiosity. If we would appreciate these features at their true value we should turn to the apocryphal gospels to see for ourselves what human imagination and invention can do. The startling fact, indeed, is that it was, ultimately, from these very apocryphal gospels that Muhammad got some of the details of the birth of Jesus that became incorporated in the Qur'ān (cp. Sūra xix., "Maryam"). These narratives quite clearly have been soiled and depraved by the coarse touch of later writers. "The one account is the reverent description of *fact*, the other the unclean imagination of *fiction*."

3. Finally, what is stressed by the evangelists, and what we are required to stress, is not the absence of a father, that is something negative, but the overshadowing of God's Holy Spirit, something very positive. And

because of this, it is for us to acknowledge, *and prove*, that with Jesus and through Jesus there has entered into the human current a new stream, or force, which has *not* been derived from humanity.

The Miracles of Jesus

This is an old subject of controversy and would not rightly come in for treatment here but for the fact that the attack is being made now in a new form. The line of argument is perhaps most clearly indicated in a small book, to which we have already referred, *Muhammad and Christ*, by Maulāna Muhammad 'Alī, President of the Ahmadīyya community, Lahore.

By an uncritical, not to say unfair, use of the gospel narratives the writer seeks to prove, for example, that physical healing could not have taken place in the instances mentioned, otherwise Christ would have had multitudes of believers. From the fact that there were apparently few declared disciples, though "all" and "many" are said to have been healed, the writer argues that the language used in these narratives is symbolical. The whole fault, he says, lies in Christ's too free use of symbolical language. One finds it difficult to understand how any but a prejudiced reader of the Gospels can draw such a conclusion, for in one of these same narratives of healing we find Christ Himself expressing astonishment that more did not believe. To the solitary grateful leper, and a Samaritan at that, He exclaimed, "Were not ten cleansed? but where are the nine? were there none found that returned to give glory to God, save this 'stranger'"? (Luke xvii. 11-19).

Here again we should see clearly and be prepared to state frankly that we do not need to defend Christianity, as such, by seeking the support of Christ's miracles (as was formerly done), nor do we depend on them for proof of His Divinity. The case for Christianity rests on other proofs than miracles, while the miracles themselves depend on the testimony we have to their actual occurrence. Each, if true, confirms the other: Christianity, the miracles, and the miracles, Christianity. Nevertheless, we can say without hesitation that the very character of Christianity makes miracles more credible. Certain general facts may be noted in this connection.

1. Even extreme critics in the West are inclined in our day to admit Christ's *works of healing*, including the expulsion of evil spirits, but not as "miracles." As for His other great works, science has so stressed the uniformity of law and has, until recently, so strongly objected to any interference with the normal order that we, in our turn, are obliged to demand that the evidence for these must be exceptionally strong before we can believe them.

2. These other "works," however, appear in a clearer light when we perceive that Nature is the expression of a Living Will, and that the very order we see in Nature betokens the wisdom of the Supreme Being on which all depends. Now even we human beings make our impact felt on Nature in a variety of ways—our present achievements would have staggered our forefathers—why then may not God, this Living Will, for higher ends, freely manipulate Nature which is after all but the plastic expression of His own Will?

3. Christ's miracles were not prodigies or mere "displays" of power, but witnesses to His claims, proofs of His deep and spontaneous compassion, and symbols of great spiritual realities. He never worked a miracle for private ends nor in order to convince sceptics. And while He estimated very highly the evidential value of His miracles for those who had in them the rudiments of faith, He was nevertheless perfectly aware that where there was no faith miracles had no educative value. They rather created an excitement and eagerness for merely physical benefit which distracted men's attention from His teaching.

4. Again, the evidence for Christ's miracles is very

strong. There is an intimate connection in the gospel narratives between the miraculous and the non-miraculous. You cannot cut out the one without doing violence to the whole story; e.g., many of His sayings presuppose His miracles.

Further, they bear the stamp of sobriety and dignity. Once more we are struck with the contrast afforded by the apocryphal gospels. There Jesus is portrayed as passionate, spiteful, and repulsive. If the miracles of the gospel did not occur how are we to account for the absence of such extravagances? Had the narrators no facts to go upon they would assuredly have blundered.

Nor does the people's credulity account for them. The facts as recorded point the other way: "We never saw it on this fashion" (Mark ii. 12); "Since the world began it was never heard that anyone opened the eyes of a man born blind" (John ix. 32). His enemies, who could not deny the facts, invented gross reasons in explanation of them.

Finally, we recollect that Jesus occupies a unique place in history—a new age was ushered in by Him—is it strange, then, if such things happened in His day?

Christ's Moral Character

Views concerning sin, propounded by Christians of past generations on the basis of narratives in Genesis concerning Eve, have been used not only by Western sceptics but by the Ahmadīyyas also, as arguments to prove that Jesus Himself did not escape the taint of sin. And in support of that assertion Ahmadīyya writers state that Jesus was given to drunkenness; that He insulted His mother and used vulgar abuse towards the Jews; that He showed impatience and lost His temper; that He was friendly with women of questionable character; that He was unstable under trial and lacked faith in God; that He transgressed many precepts of the Mosaic code; that He destroyed the lives of innocent animals; that

He hesitated to speak the truth when hard pressed; that He was a coward and afraid to face death, etc.

In this connection such writers are apt to speak of the doctrine of "original sin" as "the foundation of the Christian religion," and as "the very corner stone of Christianity." One wonders how many "foundations" the Muslim has been led to understand Christianity has. When shall we have the wisdom to make it unmistakably clear that "the Church's one foundation is Jesus Christ her Lord"?

We mention this doctrine here because Muslims have made use of it to deny the "sinlessness" of Jesus, a phrase that we ourselves are in the habit of employing. The phrase is an unfortunate one because it is negative. What we really believe of Him is something positive, something more nearly expressed when we speak of His perfect filial consciousness, involving perfect accomplishment of the Father's will.

What after all is it that we are anxious to maintain when we assert that Jesus was "sinless"? We owe it to ourselves no less than to Muslims that we should hold reasonable views on this subject. It can be shown that the two doctrines of "original sin" and "a substitutionary atonement" require a belief that Jesus was free from the liability to sin, i.e., that He was supernaturally sinless. This, in turn, requires us to believe that He was not only miraculously born but that He was miraculously conceived.

To the question "How did Jesus escape sinful taint?" those who hold the doctrine of the total depravity of the race reply, "Through His birth from a *virgin* He was immune." But in the minds of those who hold such a view of original sin there is surely a serious confusion between two very different things, viz., a *tendency* to sin and *actual* sin. One cannot inherit an *act*, nor can one be held guilty for what one has not done; that one is born with a tendency to sin is quite another matter.

Keeping before us this distinction we seem to be

under no necessity to demand *supernatural* immunity for Jesus. We have already seen that birth from one parent only does not give such immunity, and without irreverence we may say that if God could endow Jesus with " sinlessness " through one parent He could equally well have done so through two. It is not the absence of a husband that would render the mother of Jesus sinless. Unless, therefore, we are prepared to admit that this is so we are driven to hold the Roman Catholic view that Mary herself was *immaculate*. Nor can we stop there, but demand that her mother also must needs have been immaculate, and her maternal grandmother, and so through all generations back to an immaculate Eve. But just here the Muslim uses our own words against us and insists that the doctrine of the Fall must apply to Mary also, inasmuch as we Christians hold that sin came into the world through Eve.

Now in the synoptists we find no " doctrine " on this subject of Christ's moral character. They are not posing, nor are they critical, and yet it is the simple truth to say that we search their narratives in vain for anything in Jesus that we can call sin. They are not glorifying a " hero." Their story rings true; it is drawn from life. Their Jesus is neither weak nor sentimental, but a *man*, resolute, bold, determined, keen and eager in debate, terrible in wrath against wrong-doing and in denouncing hypocrites; yet, again, there is no *sin* in Him.

Nevertheless, honesty compels us to admit what the Ahmadīyyas have been eager to fasten upon, that there are incidents in these narratives which, while not attributing sinfulness, at first sight seem to exclude " sinlessness." Of these we shall refer here to three only.

1. Why was Jesus baptized? Matthew himself felt the difficulty (cp. Mark i. 4 and 9 with Matt. iii. 13-17); and the question inevitably arises, how could the Saviour of the World submit to a rite which amounted to a confession of sin?

But baptism was always something more, and in

Jesus' case something other, than that. It was the symbol of a fresh start, a new life, an act of public self-consecration marking the beginning of a new epoch. Even more than that; the outpouring of the Holy Spirit was the expected sign of the Messianic Age, and this was what Jesus experienced, as all the narratives declare (Mark i. 10; Matt. iii. 16; Luke iii. 22; John i. 32). There was in it for Him no confession of past sin, and no suggestion of purification.

2. What are we to make of Jesus' temptations? The main fact to be drawn from the synoptic writers is that Jesus was *really* tempted. What conclusion are we to draw from that if not this—there could have been no susceptibility to temptation unless there had been also the *possibility* of defeat?

We believe that Jesus' conflict was a real conflict. He had to repulse the temptations by exercising His strength. Nowhere is this more strikingly portrayed than in Gethsemane.

And if Jesus really was, as the writer to the Hebrews declares, "in all points tempted like as we are, yet without sin" (iv. 15), then clearly His "sinlessness" was not an inability to fall but an ability to resist and triumph.

Any other idea of His "sinlessness" would rob His character of all moral complexion. And the facts recorded of Him are against any other view. We see that He was spared no pang or obstacle. But the greatest fact of all is that He courageously surmounted all these. That is something that helps us who also wrestle, "for in that He Himself hath suffered being tempted, He is able to succour them that are tempted" (Heb. ii. 18).

3. Why did Jesus say, "None is good save one, even God?" (Mark x. 18; cp. Matt. xix. 17; Luke xviii. 19). Once again we see that Matthew is embarrassed.

Though the passage occasions difficulty it may be said without hesitation that there is no avowal of failure here, nor yet a denial of "sinlessness." On the face of it, the words imply that Jesus is gently declining the too-glib compliment of the ruler. But there is more than that. If we may presume to say so, Jesus here shows Himself to be conscious that He has still to battle against evil. The end is not yet. Surely His prayer-life throws some light on the matter. His works of healing alone made heavy demands not only upon His time and strength but upon His spirit, and He quite clearly "felt the need of constant prayer in order to keep Himself spiritually in tone for the acts of faith involved in His most striking cures" (A. G. Hogg, *Christ's Message of the Kingdom*, pp. 61-2, 133). This was something that could not be conceived of as existing in God. He is *perfect*, that is, goodness in perfection. Only after death was the last *possibility* of imperfection, sin, conquered in the holy life of Jesus. He was "made perfect through sufferings" (Heb. ii. 10), and the last suffering was the Cross.

Finally, we should notice that there is a total absence of a consciousness of moral guilt in the synoptic records. Jesus never prays for forgiveness, but He asks others to. He expresses no need for reconciliation. He has no seasons of self-abasement, born of a sense of transgression. This is something very impressive to the unprejudiced reader.

In Jesus this feature is an essential part of Him. It is not the effect of a pose. All others, the world's greatest heroes, are conscious of shortcomings. Even the "saint" has the sense of unworthiness, only more acutely. But in the case of Jesus His unbroken fellowship with God was maintained in the face of the most overwhelming temptation. *The perfect harmony was never marred.*

In a word, the Gospels record of Him no sin, because there was no sin to record. Jesus was "without sin" not supernaturally, but because He fought and won.

The Resurrection

We have already had occasion to refer to the attitude adopted by Mirzā Ghulām Ahmad of Qādiān towards the death of Christ. Maulāna Muhammad Ali in his book, *Muhammad and Christ*, shows himself to be the pupil of the Mirzā in this respect. But it is to be noted that he credits the Mirzā with having already accomplished the task which he bequeathed to his followers. Thus, "He has broken the cross . . . because he has shown from the gospels that the death of Christ did not take place on the cross, as has been wrongly supposed by Christians for nineteen centuries, but having escaped with wounds he died a natural death afterwards having lived to the age of 120 years, as a report expressly says." (He gives no authority for this. It seems necessary to state here that much use has been made by Muslims of a myth concocted by Nicolas Notovitch, a Russian traveller to Ladakh in 1887, who declared that he had found an ancient MS. in a Buddhist temple which stated that Jesus, in His youth, travelled to India. Max Müller, Prof. J. A. Douglas, of the Agra College, and Rev. Ahmad Shah, S.P.G., all proved the statement to be an impudent lie.)

He then concludes his book with the words, "It was 'through the blood of the cross' (Col. i. 20) that salvation was purchased; 'and if Christ be not risen then is our preaching vain'" (1 Cor. xv. 14). The writer then declares: "Christ never died on the cross, and he never rose from the dead; the preaching of the Christian missionary is, therefore, vain, and vain is also his faith. The Christian religion laid its foundation on the death of Christ on the cross and his subsequent rising; both these statements have been proved to be utterly wrong on the strength of the historical testimony afforded by the gospels themselves, and with the foundation the whole superstructure falls to the ground."

It is to be regretted that this writer, who speaks so readily of "the historical testimony," did not continue to quote Paul at 1 Cor. xv. Thus, "If Christ hath not been raised . . . ye are yet in your sins" (verse 17); and, "But now Christ hath been raised from the dead, the first fruits of them that sleep" (verse 20). Indeed,

Paul in the opening section of that same chapter gives the historical testimony concerning that event, and asserts no less than four times that "He appeared" both to individual disciples and on one occasion to 500 persons.

In his commentary on the Qur'ān on the passage, "Yet they (the Jews) slew him not, and they crucified him not," etc. (iv. 157), Maulāna Muhammad Ali incorporates a number of "reasons" from the writings of the Mirzā of Qādiān (asserting that they are drawn from the gospel narratives themselves) to show that Jesus did not die on the cross. He gives fourteen such "reasons." Two of these must suffice to indicate his inaccuracy when quoting, and the invalidity of his arguments.

"(12) Jesus Christ undertook a journey to Galilee (*sic*) with two of his disciples walking side by side with him, which shows that he was flying for refuge, for if his object had been to rise to heaven he would not have undertaken a journey to Galilee."

"(14) Jesus prayed the whole night before his arrest to be saved from the accursed death on the cross . . . it is the divine law that the prayers of a righteous man in distress and affliction are always accepted. He seems to have even received a promise from his Master to be saved, and it was to this promise that he referred when he cried out on the cross, 'My God, my God, why hast Thou forsaken me?'; Heb. v. 7, making the matter still more clear, for there it is plainly stated that the prayer of Jesus was accepted."

But the writer to the Hebrews has already (ii. 9) referred to, and constantly has in mind, the *death* of Christ. It is only reasonable to suppose, therefore, that the words at v. 7 have some other meaning than the one the Qādiānis insist they must have. And as a matter of fact when we turn to the gospel narratives we find that the supreme note of the "supplications" offered in Gethsemane "with strong crying and tears" and with sweat like "great drops of blood," was "*not my will*, but Thine be done" (Matt. xxvi. 39, 42, 44; Mark xiv. 36, 39;

Luke xxii. 42). We find, moreover, that *that* part of His prayer *was* answered, i.e., God's will *was* fulfilled; the other part of His prayer, "let this cup pass from me," though "heard" was *not* answered in that He "drank the cup," or, as the phrase of the writer to the Hebrews has it, He did "taste death for every man" (ii. 9).

In conclusion we may say that the historical evidence for the resurrection, as the leading scholars of the West are ready to admit, is very strong. We can only briefly indicate a few of the leading features.

1. There are the clear predictions of Jesus Himself recorded in the Gospels concerning both His death and resurrection.

2. The dramatic change in the disciples, at one time horrified and dejected by the shameful fate of God's Messiah, their Master, demands some adequate cause. It is written plainly for all to see that despair did *not* finally overcome them; that they learnt to interpret the cross not as God's sentence on Jesus, but as God's appointed means to Life and Victory; and that they, without delay, proclaimed both Jesus and the Resurrection boldly in the stronghold of His detractors, that is, in Jerusalem. There is but one adequate explanation, the one given by themselves; they were convinced that their Master had risen from the dead. Indeed, apart from such an unshaken confidence Christianity itself would have had, and could have had, no future.

3. The conversion of Paul, whose evidence in an epistle written only twenty-five years after the event has already been cited, likewise demands adequate explanation. How came it that this bitter opponent of the Christians, whose Pharisaic mind must at first have revolted against the very idea of a *crucified* claimant to the Messianic office—how came it that *he* became a convinced follower of the Nazarene? Paul himself supplies the answer; the Risen Christ had appeared to him also.

4. Together with the record of these appearances of

the Risen Christ to His disciples we have the very striking evidence of the empty tomb. The disciples simply could not have faced the authorities with any measure of confidence unless they had been quite sure that the grave was really empty.

Here, once again, we are obliged to recognise that we are dealing with no common incident, but with the most crucial event in human history. The words, the claims, the promises, the hopes held out by Jesus in His lifetime, required some vindication; and *God gave it* in raising Jesus from the dead; " He was raised for our justification," testifies Paul (Rom. iv. 25). We are required to account for Jesus Himself, for His triumphs in the lives of men all through the centuries; and we do so by believing that He is " the Living One," who once " was dead " and is " alive for evermore " (Rev. i. 18).

Chapter VI

A CANDID ENQUIRY INTO OUR METHODS

We are called to be "witnesses" of the redeeming love of God in Christ Jesus, and, as such, our concern should be to share with Muslims the benefits of the Gospel. Our task, however, is made unusually difficult by the attitude of mind described in the preceding chapters.

While others often hear the word gladly, Muslims frequently look upon preachers of the Gospel with suspicion and sometimes with contempt. Indifference to spiritual things is a feature to be met with among all peoples throughout the world, and when we find it, as we do, among Muslims, it occasions no surprise; but this determined and sometimes bitter opposition to the message of the Cross is both distressing and disconcerting.

One knows that there is that within the unregenerate heart of man that fights against the Message, and this will account for much of the opposition we encounter. But the question presses: Is there anything wrong with the way in which we present the Gospel to these people, or in the manner of our approach to them?

We are thus led to consider, first, our methods. Who of us is not tired of arid *controversy* with Muslims, in interviews, preaching and literature? And one is apt to become a little impatient at the reckless and often malicious statements of the modern rationalist who, while professing great regard for pure and undefiled religion, often pours scorn on the cherished beliefs and practices of millions of orthodox Muslims, and at the same time aims at bringing Christianity into discredit by going out of his way to speak disparagingly of Christ.

Nevertheless, here is our task—to preach the Gospel to these Muslims also. "Woe is me!" said Paul, "if I preach not the Gospel"; and we, with Paul, are in no doubt that this Gospel "is the power of God unto salvation to everyone that believeth"—to the Greek as well as to the Jew, to the Muslim as well as the Hindu. This being our confidence surely it ought to be possible to find some more effective way of approach to the hearts of Muslims. For we need to remind ourselves that, ultimately, it is "with the heart" that man believes.

In any consideration of our methods it is well to keep clearly before us our real objective. What is it that we have set out to achieve? In the light of that question it can hardly be denied that, heretofore, undue prominence has been given to certain features in the relations of Christians with Muslims. What are these?

I. There is, first, the important question of *controversy and controversial literature.* Not all Christian workers think alike about this method of approach. Some make it a rule to have nothing to do with controversy; others make as little use of it as possible; others, again, boldly employ this method both in preaching and writing, in order, as they say, to refute Muslim error.

Those who belong to this last group are apt to point to notable men of the past like Pfander, Imād-ud-dīn, Valpy French, Lefroy, Rouse, Tisdall. These, indeed, were men who did great things for the Kingdom of God. We cannot recall them without thanking God for them. Their labours have, in many ways, made our task easier.

Nevertheless, one would suggest that the task which these valiant men set themselves to do has, for the most part, been accomplished. They exposed the weaknesses of Islām and defects in the character of Muhammad, and also refuted Muslim error about the Bible and Christian doctrines. Consequently there is not the same urgent need in our day to go over the ground they covered.

This, in fact, was the view expressed long ago by one of that very number. That great controversialist Dr Imād-ud-dīn, writing in 1875 a report of the previous twenty-five years' work, said: "There is little use now in spending our time in preparing books for controversy with Islām. Why tread on the body of a fallen foe?" The intervening years have shown that that was not a correct diagnosis of the condition of the "foe," but our concern here is to point out that, whereas those words were written over fifty years ago, a quantity of the kind of literature which Imād-ud-dīn pronounced to be of little use has continued to appear at intervals since then, proving that the lesson he wished to teach to the succeeding generation had not been taken to heart. There is, indeed, still some literature to be found in our book depots, and some being distributed, which is written from the old standpoint.

Unfortunately, however, some of those champions of the Cross of Christ, while pursuing the method of controversy, accomplished more than they had intended. This can be illustrated in a variety of ways.

1. Because of the stress they laid on "reason" and "argument" there have been converts from Islām who have entered the Church rather as intellectual advocates of the superiority of Christianity over Islām, than as witnesses of the grace of God and as evidence of the power of His redeeming Love in Christ. In this way the Church in India has suffered a certain loss.

2. Similarly, as the result of controversy, there have been Muslims who, though defeated in argument, have not changed their faith but have become, if possible, more bitter in spirit. It was said that some Muslims in Egypt, who had read one of Dr Rouse's tracts, demanded the blood of the author!

Surely, here is a situation which should give us pause. Can that method be right whereby we win the argument but lose the man, and that a man for whom Christ died?

3. It is very obvious to those who have followed the

recent progress of the relations between Christians and Muslims that much of the bitterly anti-Christian literature (though not all of it) that has issued of late from the Muslim side, has been directly provoked by the anti-Muslim books and pamphlets of an earlier generation of Christian writers.

For years Christian writers have referred to this conflict as "The Muslim Controversy." Muslims are now retorting by speaking of it as "The Christian Controversy."

Is it not possible to approach the task in another mood and a different manner? Paul, writing to the Corinthians, said: "We are ambassadors on behalf of Christ *as though God were intreating by us*: we beseech you on behalf of Christ, be ye reconciled to God" (2 Cor. v. 20). Here is a conception of our obligation which will, if anything can, save us from degenerating into mere controversialists. It reminds us of something we are expected to do, which is far better and more urgent.

In this connection it is interesting to recall that a few years ago a group of Christian workers in Egypt agreed together to adopt certain guiding principles in respect of their literature for Muslims. These were:

1. To withdraw from circulation all that kind of controversial literature which, in the end, proves a hindrance or gives unnecessary offence to Muslims.
2. To use and produce only such literature as may inform and persuade them; that is to say, the kind that presents Christianity as a faith to live by.
3. To make no mention of Muhammad and the defects in his character.
4. To observe these rules while preaching.

II. There are, as we have already seen, certain traditional doctrines of the Church to which the Muslim takes strong exception. Quite obviously he does not understand them and so he takes every opportunity to denounce them. For instance, he hates to hear us speak of Christ as "the Son of God."

Now since things are so, surely it is worse than useless, it is wrong, to introduce such an irritant, without preliminary explanation and without necessity, into our ordinary preaching to an ignorant or prejudiced audience. What did our Lord mean when He said: "Give not that which is holy unto the dogs, neither cast your pearls before swine, lest haply they trample them under their feet and turn and rend you" (Matt. vii. 6)? He is not calling men "dogs" and "swine," but is pointing out the folly of persisting in speaking of the deep things of God to minds unprepared and unappreciative. And so here, in the case before us, we are only giving enemies of the Cross of Christ occasion to blaspheme.

All one need say just now is that we have far more important work to do on behalf of Christ than insist that prejudiced Muslims shall listen to or receive this or that "doctrine" about Him.

III. There remains to be considered the related question of the motives with which we approach Muslims, and our own personal character. Our motives should be above suspicion, and *we* should be free from reproach.

Writing from Dinapore, about 125 years ago, the saintly Henry Martyn said: "Above all things seriousness in argument with Muslims seems most desirable, for, without it, they laugh away the clearest proofs. Zeal for making converts they are used to, and generally attribute to a false motive; but a tender concern manifested for their souls is certainly new to them and seems to produce the same kind of seriousness in their minds." That is no less true to-day. What a grave responsibility, then, rests upon us. Our aim and object should always be, with God's help, to touch the heart of these people, to appeal to their conscience, and to lead them to a personal knowledge of Christ as Saviour.

Again, if we desire that Muslims should give us their respectful hearing we need to add to our earnestness of spirit, knowledge—knowledge of the more important elements in their faith and practice, and of the history of Islām. This is the more necessary so that we may avoid making blunders that disgust Muslims just as their misunderstandings and misrepresentations of Christian truth are apt to offend us.

Let us, also, assiduously cultivate the virtues of courtesy, humility and patience, in all our dealings with Muslims. True, these are not primarily Christian virtues and they can be met with elsewhere, but men have just reason to expect them in the "ambassadors" of Jesus Christ.

These qualities are greatly needed because there will come times when our temper will be tried severely. Bishop Lefroy is said to have been noted for his unfailing good-nature in his dealings with Muslims, and for his conviction that impartial fairness is the only possible attitude for the Christian towards them.

And yet there is nothing that counts for more in its influence upon Muslims than a holy life, lived among them and in their sight. We need to cultivate this not only that our own lives may commend the Gospel we preach, but also in order that we ourselves may be able to stand the strain on our faith and patience, on our sympathy and love.

Bulwer Lytton, in *The Last Days of Pompeii*, speaking of an importunate evangelist, says: "Those are formed to convert who are formed to endure." And Henry Martyn, recording his experiences in Shirāz, Persia, wrote: "The contempt and sneers of the learned Muslims are more difficult to bear than the stones which the boys sometimes throw at me."

But such a life of holiness presupposes a genuine religious experience in our own lives. To know God, to be conscious of His presence and power; to have talked with Him and to feel that He has spoken to us; to know Christ, and the sweetness of His friendship; to rejoice in personal salvation, and to experience the peace and joy of God in our hearts—these things are absolutely necessary for any really effective service among Muslims.

The man or woman who has not had such an experience, for whom these things are not real, for whom the redeeming and constraining love of Christ is not the one thing in life worth talking about, had better not engage in discussions with Muslims lest he be put to shame and suffer confusion of face.

Chapter VII

OUR SUPREME TASK

And now, in conclusion, and with the story of this great people still fresh in our minds, we would plead with all whom it may concern that they should make a more determined effort to cultivate ordinary friendship with Muslims.

We preach to them and teach them, we write books for them; we dispute with them, and criticise them and their beliefs and practices—all these activities have their place; but how comes it that we frequently withhold from them the most precious thing we have to give, our friendship?

The Christian religion, rightly interpreted, is the cultivation of a Great Friendship, the Friendship of Jesus Christ; and the positive indication that we have made that religion our own is to be seen in the way in which we seek to introduce that Friend of ours to others who at present live without Him.

If we should still need any stimulus to move us to do this for Muslims, then let us consider that they are, in solemn truth, the victims of an ancient blunder, a blunder that goes back to the days of Muhammad, the saddest result of which is this, that they see no beauty in the Crucified Christ that they should desire Him.

Or again, if we desire them to be more friendly, it is essential that we should show ourselves friendly. In this matter, whatever be the present state of affairs, it is for us, the followers of Christ, to take the initiative. Many reasons might be advanced in support of this, but is it not enough to remember all we owe to Him who loved us and gave Himself for us?

With this object in view—that of sharing the best we have with Muslims—let us consider some commendable and acceptable ways of approach.

1. Too often, one feels, Christians have been (if the figure may be pardoned) like those engaged in action with long-range guns: that is to say, we have not got into close touch with Muslims with a view to making their acquaintance.

It should be possible to draw up a list of Muslims on whom we intend to call, and to make it our business to visit them at intervals; not merely the well-to-do, but the poor and the uneducated. Few will resent it if on these occasions you show an interest in their affairs; in their children and their education; in their illnesses and marriages. Some there are who will ask your assistance in quite ordinary matters: in securing employment; in getting their children admitted into school or college; in interviewing on their behalf their landlord or the municipal commissioners. These demands take time, but they count for much. It is out of such little acts of simple, ungrudging kindness that the substantial bridges of understanding, sympathy and friendship are built.

And when Muslims call on you be at leisure to receive them. None should be made to feel that his visit is an unwelcome interruption. If so engaged at the time that protracted conversation is not possible, arrange some other day and time, and keep the appointment faithfully.

2. Muslims are very observant and quick to mark any indications of piety on the part of a Christian. That is all the more reason why one's home should be known to them as a place where prayer is wont to be made. No Muslim will be either surprised or offended if asked to wait until the "family prayers" are concluded. He would be amazed, indeed, were he to discover that you never have them.

Look upon it as a privilege if asked, as you may be in all seriousness, by a pious Muslim to pray to God for him, or her. An old man of sixty once made such a request of the present writer. He had read through the Gospels and had experienced a new concern and some doubt about the way, the truth, and the life. In earnest tones he pleaded, "Pray for me, pray to God for me; for I am an old man. I have not long to live, and all I want is to be sure of the way to God." The opportunity to do him this service came repeatedly some time afterwards, in the days of his last illness.

And this leads us to say that here is *work*, difficult work but of priceless value, that we can do for Muslims. When no progress seems to have been made; when hearts are hard, minds dull and wills perverse, we can take our burdens, *and theirs*, to God in prayer. If ever there was a task that demanded importunate prayer it is this one—the task of commending Christ, in patience and hope, to Muslims. Some one has truly said concerning it: "We shall make the most progress upon our knees."

3. It is good to seize every opportunity to lead the conversation from ordinary affairs to spiritual things. Most Muslims will appreciate and welcome the transition.

Travelling together in a railway compartment on one occasion were two Muslims and a Christian missionary. One of the Muslims, an elderly, well-to-do and zealous individual, sought to draw the missionary into an argument about the integrity of the Scriptures. The latter ventured to remark that little benefit would be derived by themselves, complete strangers, from such a discussion, and asked his fellow-traveller's permission to quote a passage from the Qur'ān about God's attitude to sinners, viz., "Is there any doubt about Allāh, Maker of Heaven and Earth? He calls you that He may pardon your offences . . ." (xiv. 10).

Proceeding, the missionary spoke of how men turn a

deaf ear to the call of God, continuing in their sins and rejecting His mercy; of how Jesus Christ has made unmistakably plain the attitude of God the Father—that there is sorrow in the heart of the Most High because men will not leave their sins and turn to Him. These simple words, spoken in utter friendliness, had a remarkable influence on the proud old man. His eyes filled with tears and for some time he could not speak; then turning to his travelling companion he said, "It's true; what the padre has said is true. We forget."

By lifting the conversation above the level of mere argument the Christian had been able to touch a soft place in the Muslim's heart. Be assured that something has already been achieved when at the close of a conversation of like nature your Muslim friend says, "It has been good to have had a talk like this."

4. We need to choose carefully the literature we use for Muslims, and distribute it with discrimination. It is a sound rule to make yourself acquainted beforehand with the contents of each tract and book that you are handling. A wise physician first makes a careful diagnosis of the patient's complaint and then decides which is the most suitable remedy at his command. Now, it must be admitted that there are "strong doses" in the available literature for Muslims, and some of it, if carelessly used, may produce not conversion but convulsion!

There has been a welcome change, in recent years, in the type of literature produced. Some of this shows an honest attempt to appreciate the Muslim's point of view, and to meet his difficulties, while at the same time avoiding any expression likely to exacerbate his feelings.

Nothing, of course, can take the place of the Scriptures, especially the New Testament. But since, as we have seen, many Muslims are, at first, prejudiced against the Scriptures, it should be our aim, through the use of this newer type of literature, to persuade Muslims to read the sources for themselves. Fortunately more of them are willing to read the Bible than ever before.

5. Don't neglect the extremely important work of following up. Concentrate on those upon which you have already made some impression. The door of their heart has opened a little to you; in God's name, press in! For this purpose give your main attention to a limited number of persons rather than dissipate your energies over many.

6. We have undertaken a task that demands of us our utmost and our best. We must, therefore, unite all our knowledge, all our skill, all our strategy, all our passion and persuasion, our prayers, our zeal and our love, for the one great purpose of presenting to these Muslims, Christ, the Friend of Sinners, the Crucified and Risen Saviour, the Living Master, the Way to God.

Unquestionably, in these days, *this* is the supreme task of every Christian preacher and worker among Muslims. And for this we must give ourselves.

The late Miss Lilias Trotter of Algiers, who spoke from long personal experience, once said that the lengths to which the real friend of a needy Muslim is sometimes called to go might be compared to the lashing of one's self, like a spar, to one wrestling with the waves of the sea. Indeed, a succession of missionaries to Muslims, following in the steps of Henry Martyn, have often felt that this arduous enterprise can only be carried on by those who are willing, if need be, to die in the pursuit of it.

7. Finally, as we bear in mind all that has been said, we are reminded of a more excellent way than any that has yet been mentioned. It is, emphatically, *the* method, and the only one which carries with it the assurance of success. It is set forth in those words of the Saviour, "I, if I be lifted up, will draw all men unto Myself." That promise covers Muslims.

It has often seemed to the present writer, as he has thought over the story of the past relations between

Christians and Muslims, that (to borrow again a figure from the field of battle) the Muslims have made their position exceedingly strong because they have dug themselves into trenches of long-standing prejudice. The Christian forces have repeatedly tried to "rush" their position by "frontal attacks," yet the success attending such efforts has been small. The Muslims have only dug themselves in deeper.

But in the strategy of war there is another and very effective method, that of drawing the enemy out of their position. Our Lord's words suggest something like that. It is the method whereby we make Him, not ourselves nor our arguments, the grand object of attention: "I, if I be lifted up, will draw all men unto Myself." Let us give ourselves more than ever to the study and use of this method.

But here it is necessary to stress the full significance of these words of Christ. Even the disciples were slow to grasp it. Whatever other legitimate meaning the words may have, they assuredly imply that we are to present Christ *as Crucified*. It is all the more important that we should remember this since to the Muslim, as to the Jew, the "cross" is a stumbling-block and foolishness, and he will do his utmost to remove it out of his way. In view of what we know to be the attitude of some of them, it is time that we determined, as did Paul regarding the Corinthians, not to know anything amongst them save Jesus Christ and Him Crucified.

While it is true that the Gospel is a message of Joy and of Goodwill to all men, it is none the less true—and this, also, is a stumbling-block to the Muslim—that it proclaims that the way to Victory is through the Cross; that its abounding Life comes through Death. Here, then, is our duty towards Muslims: "To placard before their very eyes Jesus Christ the Crucified" (Moffatt's translation, Gal. iii. 1).

And we believe—this is our confidence—that if we

faithfully perform our part, the Living Christ will draw these people to Himself by the power of His own inimitable love.

We may uplift Christ by our preaching and by our writing, but pre-eminently by our lives, if so be that we are Christlike in spirit. It is thus of the first importance that we should not fail in this respect.

Some one has described the task of commending the Gospel to Muslims in terms like these: it is an attempt to persuade the proudest man in the world to accept the thing he hates at the hands of the man he despises.

To this we would reply that pride is not the peculiar property of the Muslim; it is co-extensive with the human race. What the grace of God has done for the proudest Westerner it can do, and does, for the Muslim. The thing he hates is a thing he does not understand; he is the victim of misinterpretation and misrepresentation. Ours is the task to help him to see "the light of the knowledge of the glory of God in the face of Jesus Christ." Finally, where in the wide world is the Muslim who despises a really Christlike man or woman?

That question brings us face to face with our supreme need to cultivate the Spirit of the Master. Professor Henry Drummond, the man who urged that the earnest Christian should each day meditate on Paul's Ode to Love (1 Cor. xiii.), has a memorable passage in his booklet, *The Changed Life*, which is peculiarly applicable here:

"To become like Christ is the only thing in the world worth caring for, the thing before which every ambition of man is folly, and all lower achievement vain." He then goes on to develop the theme that "by looking" at Christ we are *changed.* We become like those whom we habitually admire, for this is the great law of influence.

"There are," he says, "some men and some women in whose company we are always at our best, while with them we cannot think mean thoughts or speak ungenerous words. . . . If, then, to live with men diluted to the millionth degree with the virtue of the Highest, can exalt and purify the nature, what bounds can be set to the influence of Christ"?

"I TRIUMPH STILL IF THOU ABIDE WITH ME!"

APPENDIX

NOTE I

ON TRANSLITERATION OF ISLAMIC TERMS

SINCE the ultimate purpose in the production of the present work is to have it translated into the vernaculars of India, the writer has not thought it necessary to employ an elaborate, nor even a generally recognised, method for the transliteration of such Arabic and Persian terms as it contains. As it happens, it has not been found possible to carry out even the simplified scheme originally intended.

With these explanations it should not be difficult for those conversant with Arabic and Persian (and we crave the indulgence of such) to determine the original form of these Islamic terms, with the help of such notes as are given below. And, further, because of the limitations inherent in transliteration, it is not to be expected that an exact idea of the pronunciation of these words and letters can be conveyed to the ordinary reader.

All Islamic terms used are printed in italics, and, on the occasion of their first appearance, are explained. Should the reader desire to ascertain the meaning of a term on its reappearance later on, he may refer to the Index, where the page containing the word with its meaning is quoted.

The elision of *alif* is indicated by an apostrophe ('), e.g., *rasūlu'llāh*.

th, kh, dh, gh are to be understood (in practically all cases) to represent, though lacking the customary underline, certain characteristic Arabic consonants.

No diacritical points appear under h, s, z, t, though these letters, when used to represent certain Arabic values, usually have them.

The Arabic letter *'ain* is represented by an *inverted* apostrophe (ʻ), e.g., *sharīʻat.*

The short vowels in the italicised terms are sounded approximately as follows :

a like u in Eng. pun. E.g., Panjāb (often written Punjāb).
e „ ê „ Fr. fête.
i „ i „ Eng. hit.
o „ o „ Eng. hole.
u „ u „ Eng. put.

The long vowels, represented by a short horizontal overline, ā, ī, ū, have approximately the sound of the vowels in the following words : f*a*ther, f*ee*t, sh*oo*t.

NOTE II

THE MUSLIM CALENDAR

The Muslim year has twelve lunar months, totalling 354 days. One hundred Muslim years correspond approximately to 97 solar years.

The year 1 A.H. began on July 16th, A.D. 622.
The year 1351 A.H. began on May 8th, A.D. 1932.

Anno Hijræ	Anno Domini
1	622
100	718
200	815
300	912
400	1009
500	1106
600	1203
700	1300
800	1397
900	1494
1000	1591
1100	1688
1200	1785
1300	1882

A GLOSSARY OF ISLAMIC TERMS

A. = Arabic. Gr. = Greek. P. = Persian. T. = Turkish.

'Abd	A.	a slave, bondsman; in particular "a slave *of Allāh*," as e.g., in the proper name, 'Abdullāh.
Ahādīth	A.	plur. of *hadīth*, a tradition.
Ahl-i-hadīth		the name of a sect in India akin to the Wahhābis.
Ahl-i-Qur'ān		a sect in India which places the greatest emphasis on the Qur'ān, founded in the Panjāb in 1902 by 'Abdullāh Chakrālawī.
Ahl-i-Kitāb		"The People of the Book"; Muhammad's name for the Jews and Christians, to whom a revelation was given by means of a *book*.
Ahmadiyya		the name of a modern Muslim sect in India; strictly speaking, applicable to the Lahore section that has broken away from the original party founded in 1889, at Qādiān, Panjāb, by Mirzā Ghulām Ahmad.
Anjuman	P.	a Muslim society or association for the promotion of the interests of the local community.
'Aqīqa	P.	a custom observed by Muslims after the birth of a child (in India, any time up to seven years of age or more), when the hair is shaved and goats and sheep are sacrificed; in some parts, two animals for a boy and one for a girl.
Āseb	P.	misfortune, calamity; especially such as is caused by the falling of the shadow of a *jinn* on one.
Ashāb	A.	plur. of *sāhib*, companion, master; especially the "Companions" of Muhammad.
'Asr	A.	time; afternoon. The afternoon prayer.
Āyat	P.	mark, sign; especially a sentence or verse of the Qur'ān (plur. *āyāt*).
Adhān	A.	the call to public prayer, usually chanted from a minaret of a mosque by the *mu'adhdhin*.
Banda	P.	slave, "humble servant"; creature, commonly used of man's relation to his Maker.
Bātini	P.	"esoteric," especially of doctrines having an "inner" or hidden meaning.
Bai'at	P.	allegiance, submission; initiation as a disciple of a "saint."
Bid'at	P.	"innovation" in religion; heresy.
Bihisht	P.	Heaven (Ar. *jannat*), the Muslim Paradise.
Bismillāh	A.	the Islamic invocation, "in the name of Allāh"; the full form is *Bismi'llāhi'r-rahmāni'r-rahim*, i.e., "In the name of Allāh, the Compassionate, the Merciful."
But	P.	idol, image; *but-parastī*, idol-worship, idolatry.
Dajjāl	A.	lit. "false"; used of religious impostors, especially of the *Anti-Christ* of Muslim tradition.
Dargāh	P.	portal; royal court; especially the shrine or tomb of a "saint," which is the object of pilgrimage and worship.
Dār-ul-harb	A.	"The Abode of War"; a term used by Muslims with reference to a country belonging to infidels, which has not been brought under Muslim rule.

Dār-ul-Islām	A.	"The Abode of Islām"; a country where the law of Islām is in force.
Darwesh	P.	lit. "one who goes from door to door"; a religious mendicant, also called a *faqir*.
Dhikr	A.	lit. "remembering," i.e., remembering Allāh. A religious ceremony practised by various orders of darweshes.
Dhimmi	A.	a non-Muslim subject of a Muslim government, who, because of the payment of the *jizya*, is guaranteed the security of his person and property in a Muslim country.
Dīn	A.	"religion"; (1) the religion of Islām; (2) more especially the practical duties of Islām.
Dozakh	P.	Hell; in Ar. *jahannam*.
Du'ā	A.	prayer. Simple prayer as contrasted with the liturgical, five times daily prayers (i.e., *salāt*, *namāz*).
Durūd	P.	benediction; praise or intercession offered to Allāh for Muhammad.
Fajr	A.	dawn. The prayer at day-break.
Fanā	A.	extinction, death. A Sūfī term for the final "absorption" of the personality of the mystic in Allāh.
Faqīr	A.	lit. "poor," in sense of "poor in spirit"; used commonly of mendicants and of members of a religious "order."
Farmān	P.	order, command, decree; a royal charter.
Farz	A.	that which is "obligatory"; used of rules and ordinances believed to have been established by the decree of Allāh.
Fātiha	A.	lit. "the opening one"; (1) the name of the first *Sūra* of the Qur'ān; (2) the words of which are used on various occasions as a prayer —the Muslim *Paternoster*.
Fatwā	A.	a legal decision in Islām based on the *sharī'at* given by a *Khalīfa*, *qāzī*, or *mufti*.
Fiqh	A.	the branch of Muslim learning which deals with the *sharī'at* (law).
Firdaus	P.	one region of heaven. The word from which is derived *Paradise*, in English.
Firishta	P.	an angel, messenger.
Furqān	A.	lit. "Distinguisher"; Al Furqān, another title for the Qur'ān (cp. Sūra xxv. 10).
Ghāzi	P.	one who fights against infidels in the cause of Islām; a hero.
Ghusl	A.	the "greater" ablution, or bathing of the whole body before prayer.
Gunāh	P.	fault, crime, *sin*.
Hadīth	A.	lit. a "narrative," or communication; the term used to indicate the authoritative collections of traditions, i.e., the records of what Muhammad did and said.
Hāfiz	A.	lit. "a guardian," "keeper"; one who has committed to memory the whole of the Qur'ān.
Hājī	A.	a person who has performed the *hajj* to Mecca; used also as an honorific title for such.
Hajj	A.	the annual pilgrimage to Mecca undertaken in the twelfth month, *Dhū'l-Hijja*.
Hajru'l-aswad	A.	"The Black Stone" in the Ka'ba at Mecca which the pilgrims kiss.
Halāl	A.	that which is permitted; lawful, right.
Haqīqat	P.	the final knowledge of things; the last stage to which the Sūfī attains in the "Mystic Way."
Harām	A.	that which is forbidden; unlawful, wrong.
Harīm	A.	a sacred place; the sacred enclosure at Mecca. Used in Turkey and other countries for the female apartments (harem) of a

Muslim household. (In India the word in common use is *zanāna*, P., a word meaning "women" and "women's apartments.")

Hijra	A.	lit. "migration." It has three common usages: (1) the dramatic departure of Muhammad from Mecca to Madīna; (2) the Muslim era; (3) the act of a Muslim leaving a country under infidel rule because of religious disabilities.
'Ibādat	P.	lit. "service." A term used for "worship"; the service of the *'abd* rendered as an act due to Allāh.
Iblis	A.	the Devil, who was expelled from Paradise for refusing to do homage to Adam (ii. 32).
'Īd	A.	festival.
'Īd-gāh		lit. "festival place." An enclosure outside a town or city where Muslims congregate for prayers at the time of the annual festivals, i.e., 'Īd-ul-Fitr (at the close of Ramdhān) and 'Īd-uz-Zuhā or Baqar 'Īd.
Ijmā'	A.	a term signifying the collective agreement of the learned Muslim doctors on points of law; the fourth "foundation of Islām."
Ijtihād	A.	lit. "exertion"; a logical deduction on a point of law reached by a single jurist (the opposite of *ijmā'*).
Ilhām	A.	Divine inspiration; revelation in the subjective sense (see *wahī*).
Imām	A.	a leader whose guidance or example is followed. Applied to (1) the prayer-leader in a mosque; (2) the Khalīfa of the Muslim people; (3) the propounder of a system of theology or law; (4) used by the Shī'as for the leaders of their sect.
Īmān	A.	faith; especially the six doctrines held by the Muslims.
Injīl		the Arabicised form of Gr. *euangelion*, Gospel; the Book of the Christians.
'Īsā		Jesus; the Arabicised form used in the Qur'ān (cp. *Mūsā*, Moses).
'Ishā	A.	nightfall. The prayer when night has closed in.
'Ishq	A.	love, passion; a term used by the mystics of Islām.
Islām	A.	lit. "submission," resignation to the will of Allāh; the name of the religion of the Muslims.
Isnād	A.	lit. "leaning upon"; the chain of authorities which precede and introduce the text of *hadīth*.
Jahannam	A.	Hell; the first of the seven divisions (Ar. form of Gr. *ge-enna*).
Jamā'at	P.	a congregation or collection of people.
Jāmi' masjid	A.	the congregational mosque; the large mosque of a city where Muslims are expected to congregate for the Friday prayers.
Janāza	P.	a bier with a corpse on it; a funeral.
Jannat	A.	the Muslim Paradise.
Jazīrat-ul-'Arab	A.	the island (peninsula) of Arabia. The territory claimed by Muslims exclusively for Islām.
Jihād	A.	an "effort," "striving"; particularly in the interests of Islām; a "holy war" waged by a Muslim ruler or group of Muslims against "infidels."
Jinn	A.	(Genii). A species of beings half-demon, half-human, who are thought to make themselves invisible at will.
Jizya	A.	the "poll-tax" levied by a Muslim state on non-Muslims only.
Juz	A.	one of the thirty sections into which the Qur'ān is divided, enabling the pious Muslim to read or recite the whole of the book in the month of Ramdhān. The Persian word *sipāra* has the same meaning.
Ka'ba	A.	lit. "cube"; the name of the central shrine at Mecca.

Kaffāra	P.	penance, expiation, atonement.
Kāfir	A.	infidel, impious; one who denies God.
Kāhin	A.	soothsayer, sorcerer.
Kalām	A.	Word; *Kalāmu'llāh*, "the Word of Allāh," a title for the Qur'ān (ii. 70).
Kalima	A.	lit. a word; especially the shortened form of the Muslim creed; "There is no god but Allāh; Muhammad is the apostle of Allāh."
Karāmat	P.	lit. "generosity"; used of the miracle performed by a *pīr* through the generosity of Allāh (plur. *karāmāt*).
Kashf	A.	"illumination"; a term used by the mystics of Islām.
Khalīfa	A.	a successor or vice-regent. The "Caliph" of Sunnī Islām.
Khairāt	A.	plur. "good works," charities; gifts of food, clothing, etc., not necessarily legal alms.
Khānaqāh	A.	a monastery of the *darwesh* orders.
Kharāj	A.	the land-tax, due to a Muslim government.
Khatā	A.	wrong action, fault, *sin*.
Khatīb	A.	a preacher. One who delivers the *khutba* in the mosque on Friday, while standing on the second step of the *mimbar*.
Khatna	A.	circumcision; an Islamic institution, though not enjoined in the Qur'ān or *Hadīth* (also called *sunnat*, P.).
Khilāfat	P.	the office of the Khalīfa (Caliph). The "Caliphate."
Khuda	P.	God. The term commonly used in Persian and Hindustāni (from *khud*, self).
Khutba	A.	lit. an address; the sermon delivered at the mosque on Fridays at the midday prayers.
Kufr	A.	unbelief, infidelity; especially *blasphemy*.
Khwāja	P.	lord, master; a gentleman, a title of honour or respect prefixed to a proper name.
Kitāb	A.	"book." Al-Kitāb, THE Book, the Qur'ān (cp. xliii. 1, 3).
Lailatu'l-qadr	A.	"The night of power." A special night in the month of Ramdhān (the precise date of which is unknown) in which the Qur'ān was sent down.
Madhhab	A.	lit. "rite," guidance; (1) properly the name of a juridical school, but (2) popularly used for "religion."
Magbrib	A.	the West; sunset. The prayer immediately after sunset.
Mahdi	A.	lit. "the directed or guided one." Muslims believe that a mighty one, Al Mahdī, will appear in the last days to lead them.
Makrūh	A.	"disliked"; refers to actions about which the unlawfulness is not quite certain, but they are undesirable.
Mansūkh	A.	"cancelled." A term used by Muslim theologians for a verse or sentence of the Qur'ān which has been cancelled or abrogated by a later one (see *nāsikh*).
Manzil	A.	a place for alighting, a day's journey; in particular, a "stage" in the mystic's journey. Also used to indicate a special division of the Qur'ān, of which there are seven in number, thus enabling the devout Muslim to read, or recite, the whole book in the course of a week.
Maqāmāt	A.	certain "stages" in the mystic way.
Ma'rifat	P.	"knowledge"; especially the *gnosis* of the Sūfī when in a state of ecstasy.
Marthiya	P.	a lamentation, dirge; especially one sung during the month of Muharram in commemoration of Hasan and Husain.

Masīh	A.	the Messiah, Jesus.
Masjid	A.	lit. "place of prostration," i.e., before Allāh. The Muslim "mosque" (French).
Matn	A.	the substance or "text" of *hadīth*.
Maulawī	A.	a learned man; a Muslim doctor of law (commonly spelt *maulvi*).
Maulāna	A.	a learned man of greater eminence than a *maulawi*.
Maulūd	A.	lit. "one who is born"; especially the celebration of the anniversary of Muhammad's birth (*maulūd sharīf*).
Mazār	A.	a tomb or shrine, especially of a saint. A place of visitation.
Mihrāb	A.	a high place; especially the niche in the back wall of a mosque which shows the direction of the *qibla*.
Mimbar	A.	the pulpit in a mosque, consisting of three or more steps.
Minār	A.	a tower; the *minaret* of a mosque.
Miswāk	A.	a tooth-*stick*, tooth-brush.
Mu'adhdhin	A.	one who chants the *adhān*, or call to prayer.
Muftī	P.	lit. "one who gives a legal decision" on Muslim canon law; a subordinate law officer who assists the *qāzi*.
Muhājir	A.	a refugee; a Muslim who abandons his country because of religious disabilities; plur. *muhājirīn*, e.g., the Muslims who left Mecca for Madīna in the early days of Islām.
Muharram	A.	lit. "that which is forbidden," hence anything sacred: (1) the name of the first month of the Muslim calendar; (2) the name of the festival observed chiefly by *Shi'as* in the early days of that month, in commemoration of the martyrdom of Husain at Karbala.
Mujaddid	A.	lit. "a renewer." The revivalist supposed to be sent by Allāh in every century for the renewal and propagation of the faith of Islām.
Mujtahid	A.	lit. "one who strives," or exerts his faculties to the utmost in formulating an opinion in Muslim law (see *ijtihād*).
Mulla	T.	(corr. of *maulā*, A.) a learned doctor of Muslim law; popularly used in India for the conservative type of Muslim priest.
Mu'min	A.	one who believes. A term generally used for Muslims in the Qur'ān and Muslim books (plur. *al-mu'minīn*, the true believers, i.e., Muslims).
Munāfiq	A.	hypocrite. A term especially applied to those who, in the time of Muhammad, professed faith in Islām but secretly were unbelievers (plur. *Munāfiqīn*).
Munājāt	A.	a "supplication"; a part of the Muslim liturgical prayers.
Murīd	A.	lit. "one who is desirous"; a disciple of a *pir* or *murshid* of a *darwesh* order.
Murshid	A.	lit. "one who guides aright"; the title of the spiritual director of a *darwesh* order. Also called a *pīr*.
Musalmān	P.	the Persian form of the word *Muslim*, a believer in Islām.
Mushrik	A.	lit. "one who joins," or ascribes associates to Allāh; a polytheist, idolater.
Muslim	A.	lit. "one who submits" to Allāh; a follower of the faith of Islām.
Mustahabb	A.	a "meritorious" act; which Muhammad sometimes performed and sometimes omitted.
Mut'a	A.	temporary marriage.
Mu'tazilī	A.	lit. "the separatists," i.e., from the orthodox body; a rationalistic sect of Muslims in the second century of Islām.
Nabī	A.	a prophet.

Nafl A. a voluntary act; a work of supererogation not demanded by the Quranic law or Muhammad's example.

Najāt A. escape, liberation, "salvation."

Namāz P. The term commonly used by Indian Muslims for the prescribed prayer (*salāt*, A.).

Nāsikh A. lit. "one that cancels." A term used by Muslim theologians for a verse or sentence of the Qur'ān which cancels or abrogates a previous one (see *mansūkh*).

Nadhr A. A vow; offering; a gift made to God, the State, or at a shrine.

Nikāh A. matrimony, marriage; the more honourable kind. (In Bengal, however, the term is used for temporary marriages.)

Nisāb A. property, or "stock," on which the legal alms, due from a Muslim, must be paid.

Paigbambar P. a prophet; one who brings *paigbām*, a message.

Parda P. a curtain, or veil; the term used for the system of seclusion of Muslim women in India (Purdah).

Pīr P. an old man, saint, spiritual guide. An alternative term used in India for a *murshid* of a *darwesh* order.

Pīri-murīdī the practice of making disciples by spiritual preceptors of *darwesh* orders.

Qāri A. a "reader." A term used for one who reads the Qur'ān correctly and is acquainted with the science of reading it (*'Ilmu't-Tajwid*).

Qāzī A. a judge who passes sentence in all cases of law: religious, moral, civil and criminal.

Qibla A. the direction to be faced by Muslims in prayer, viz., Mecca-wards; the Ka'ba (q.v.) is also called the *Qibla*.

Qismat A. lit. division, partition; portion, lot; fortune, destiny (KISMET).

Qiyāmat P. the Resurrection; the Last Day.

Qiyās A. lit. "reasoning by analogy." The third "foundation" for the formation of the *sharī'at*.

Qur'ān A. lit. "the reading" (or "reciting"). The name of the sacred book of the Muslims (KORAN).

Qurbān A. lit. "that whereby one draws near to God"; a sacrifice, victim.

Rā'i A. belief, opinion. A legal term signifying individual opinion.

Rak'at P. lit. "a bowing." A section of the Muslim prayers.

Ramdhān A. the ninth month of the Muslim calendar, during the thirty days of which a strict fast is kept from dawn till dusk.

Rasūl A. an "apostle" with a message which he is commanded to deliver.

Roza P. fasting (Ar. *saum*).

Rūh A. the soul, spirit, life.

Rukū' A. the act of bowing the body in prayer; genuflexion.

Sadaqa P. alms; offerings made at the time of the annual festival called 'Idu'l-Fitr, at the close of Ramdhān; or at any time.

Sahīh A. lit. "correct," "sound." A term applied to the six authoritative collections of the Traditions; others are said to be *hasan* (fair) and *za'īf* (weak).

Salāt A. the term used throughout the Muslim world for the prescribed prayers. In India the Persian word *namāz* is in common use.

Sālik A. lit. "traveller." A term used by Sūfīs to describe a disciple who has started on the mystic way.

Saum A. "fasting." In India the word commonly used is *roza*.

Sayyid A. lit. "lord," "chief"; any descendant of Muhammad. The term is often used in India to denote one of the four, and chief social divisions into which Indian Muslims are divided. These are Sayyid, Shaikh, Mughal, Pathān.

Shafā'at P. entreaty, "intercession." (See also *Sifārish*).

Shahādat P. "an act of witnessing"; a confession of faith; reciting the *kalima*.

Shahīd A. lit. "a witness"; one who dies in battle for the cause of Islām; a martyr.

Shaikh A. a senior; a man of authority, e.g., the head of a tribe, or religious order. The name of one of the social divisions among Indian Muslims.

Sharī'at P. the law of Islām both canon and civil, including that which is based on the Qur'ān and *Hadith*; but in India practically confined to canon law only.

Shī'a P. lit. "the followers" (of a person), or "party"; in particular, the followers of 'Alī.

Shirk A. "joining" or "associating" others with Allāh. Ascribing plurality to the Deity. A common term for polytheism and idolatry. The unpardonable sin in Islām.

Sifārish P. recommendation, introduction; "intercession."

Sirāt A. a bridge which all must cross in the Day of Judgment.

Sūfī A. (said to be derived from *sūf*, wool). A person who professes the mystic doctrines known as *tasawwuf*, Islamic mysticism.

Sunna A. lit. "a path," or manner of life; commonly applied to the Traditions which record the sayings and doings of Muhammad.

Sunnī A. lit. "one of the path"; in particular a follower of tradition. The term usually applied to the major sect of the Muslims.

Sūra A. lit. "a row" or series. A name used exclusively for the chapters of the Qur'ān.

Tābi'ūn A. "successors." People of the second generation after Muhammad who conversed with his Companions. (The traditions which they related are held to be of high authority.)

Tablīgh A. propaganda, particularly of the religious sort.

Tābūt A. (1) the ark of the Covenant (see Qur'ān ii. 249); (2) a coffin; (3) a representation of the bier used for the martyr Husain.

Tafsīr A. "explaining"; exposition, commentary (especially of the Qur'ān).

Tahajjud A. sleeplessness. A form of prayer repeated during the course of the night.

Tahrīf A. the term used by Muslim writers to express the corruption alleged to have been made in the Scriptures of the Jews and Christians.

Takbīr A. the term used by Muslims in referring to the ejaculation *Allāhu Akbar* ("God is great"), so commonly on the lips of Muslims.

Talāq A. divorcing (a woman); divorce.

Tanzīm A. lit. "ordering," arranging; a term of modern application used with reference to a movement for consolidating Islām.

Taqdīr A. "apportioning," decreeing. Divine decree, predestination, fate.

Taqīya A. lit. "guarding one's self." A Shī'a doctrine whereby one of this sect believes that, in order to avoid persecution, he is justified in concealing his sectarian views.

Taqlīd A. lit. "winding round"; a term used to signify blind and unreasoning compliance with the teaching of a religious leader.

Tarīqat P. lit. a road, path. The Sūfīs' term for their special form of the religious life; the Mystic Way.

Tasawwuf A. the term used to signify Islamic mysticism, or the doctrines and principles of the Sūfi.

Tasbih A. (1) the ejaculation *Subhān Allāh* (Holiness be to God!); (2) a rosary of 99 (or 33) beads for *telling* the "Beautiful Names" of Allāh.

Tauba A. repentance, penitence, recantation.

Tauhid A. the term used to express the "unity" of God, the fundamental doctrine of Islām.

Taurât A. the Pentateuch (Pers. *tauret*; Heb. *torāh*).

Ta'widh A. lit. "to flee for refuge." A charm or amulet worn by Muslims on the neck, arm, and other parts of the body.

Ta'ziya P. lit. "consolation." A representation or model of the tomb of Husain, which is carried in procession during Muharram.

'Ulamâ A. the learned doctors of Muslim Society (plur. of *'ālim*, "one who knows").

'Urs A. wedding festivities; a term that has come to be used commonly for the ceremonies observed at a shrine on the anniversary of the death of a "saint."

Ustād P. a master, teacher.

Usūl A. plur. of *asl*, root, origin; the plural is used technically for the "foundations" of Islām.

Wahi A. revelation, inspiration. A term used of the objective revelation of the Qur'ān (see *Ilhām*).

Wajd A. ecstasy. A Sūfi term indicating the state of divine illumination reached by the traveller on the mystic path.

Wājib A. "necessary" (but not "obligatory"); of religious "duties."

Wali A. one who is very near, i.e., to Allāh. A term used for saints or holy men (plur. *auliyā*).

Waqf A. lit. "standing." An endowment. Property which has been dedicated to charitable uses and the service of God.

Wasl A. "meeting," "union." The stage at which the "traveller" sees, as it were, the Divine One face to face. The stage before the last of all, *fanā*.

Wazīr A. minister of state, privy-counsellor (vizier).

Wazū A. the "lesser" ablutions before prayers.

Witr A. a form of prayer, in which an odd number of *rak'ats* are said, after the night prayer.

Zabūr A. the Psalms (of David).

Zakāt A. alms. The legal alms in Islām.

Zamzam A. the sacred well within the precincts of the mosque at Mecca. It is supposed by Muslims to be the identical spring from which Hagar and Ishmael drank in the wilderness.

Zanāna P. a term applied to the household of a Muslim, his wife or wives, and children, and the apartments which they occupy. (From the Persian *zan* (woman).

Ziyārat P. "visiting." A visit to the grave of Muhammad, or to the tomb of any Muslim "saint." In India, particularly in Kashmir, the term is used also to denote the place of visitation, i.e., the tomb itself.

Zuhd A. lit. "renunciation," of the world by the traveller on the mystic way. Asceticism.

Zuhr A. noon. The prayer immediately after midday.

INDEX

A

B